D1270743

# THE JOCKS

". . . a lively study of the less-than-heroic aspects of boxing, racing, basketball, baseball (including the franchises) and football . . . that shows up the hypocrisies of the sports moguls . . . Shecter amplifies stories many readers may have read in the newspapers during the past two decades . . . [he] knows much of the behind-the-scene dope on the various sports [and] is especially entertaining when he recounts his years of covering the Yankees."—*Publishers' Weekly*

"Mr. Shecter, for years a sports columnist for the *New York Post,* exhibits 'cynicism of the highest order' in this wicked, funny, and often startling exposé of the games played off the field and the scores that never got posted. And he's some paper tiger, lashing into the greed and corruption in a world where sportswriters are on payoff lists and almost everyone is in on some part of the point spread . . . [THE JOCKS] could well be the sleeper of the season."—*The Kirkus Review*

". . . Shecter has written . . . a good book. It is boldly informative, and there is no suspicion here that he has not told many truths when he writes of sports personalities, shocking as some of his tales may be."
—*The Washington Post*

# THE JOCKS

by Leonard Shecter

EDITOR OF "BALL FOUR"

WARNER

PAPERBACK LIBRARY
NEW YORK

Randall Library   UNC-W

# WARNER PAPERBACK LIBRARY EDITION

First Printing: *June, 1970*

Second Printing: *July, 1970*

Third Printing: *September, 1970*

Fourth Printing: *November, 1971*

Fifth Printing: *September, 1972*

Copyright © 1969 by Leonard Shecter
All rights reserved
Library of Congress Catalog Card Number: 70-81294

Small portions of this book first appeared,
in different form, in the *New York Times Magazine,
Life, Sports Illustrated,* and *Esquire.*

*For Ginny*

## ACKNOWLEDGMENT

To the people at the 42nd Street Branch and the Newspaper
Division of the New York Public Library for their patient assistance,
to Glenn Dulmage at the Time-Life sports library for his patient
indulgence, to Steve Gelman, Larry Merchant, Stan Isaacs and Jim
Jacobs for their patient reading, and to my editor, Bob Amussen,
for his patient nursing of this project from inception, through verbal
overkill, to conclusion, my thanks.

**This Warner Paperback Library Edition is published by
arrangement with The Bobbs-Merrill Co., Inc.**

Warner Paperback Library is a division of Warner Books, Inc., 315 Park
Avenue South, New York, N.Y. 10010.

GV583
.S5
1990

# CONTENTS

149623

## Introduction

THE MEN WERE IN THEIR LATE THIRTIES, EARLY FORTIES, fighting receding hairlines and paunches, and as they sat at the checkered tablecloth drinking coffee or sipping whiskey one of them remembered Pete Gray, an outfielder who had played for the St. Louis Browns during World War II. Pete Gray had one arm. He was a curiosity and people used to pack Yankee Stadium to see him, and seats in left field, where he played, were harder to get than good seats behind the plate. The men remembered going to the stadium as boys to see Pete Gray play and one of them recalled how swift and slick Gray was, catching the ball in the outfield, putting glove and ball under the stump of his left arm and, in one fluid motion, coming away with the ball in his bare hand so he could make the throw.

Another of the men said no, that wasn't the way it was at all. When Pete Gray caught the ball, he would flip it up into the air, secure his glove under his stump, reach out and catch the ball with his bare hand and then throw it.

The first man disagreed. He argued that he could still see in his mind's eye the exact legerdemain involved in Gray's putting the glove under his stump and coming out with the ball and the second man said hell, how could anybody do that and still do it quickly enough to make the throw, and the first man said well, that was the beauty of it, Pete Gray knew how. The second man said like hell he did, he flipped the ball into the air, that's what he did. They argued back and forth until an older man who was an acknowledged authority came over and he said yes, he remembered Pete Gray and how he used to catch the ball in his glove, flip it up into the air, put the glove under his stump, catch the ball in his bare hand and throw it. That stopped the argument, but now everybody started to kid the first man for remembering something that Pete

7

Gray never did and there was much laughter and it was very good.

This is what we want of sports, most of us, a remembrance of happy times and experience shared, warmth and kidding laughter, a marvelous sense of the importance of the unimportant.

And like the middle-aged men at the checkered tablecloth, we get it, sometimes. But around the simplicity which most of us want out of sports has grown a monster, a sprawling five-billion-dollar-a-year industry which pretends to cater to our love of games but instead has evolved into that one great American institution: big business. Winning, losing, playing the game, all count far less than counting the money. The result is cynicism of the highest order. There is no other business in this country which operates so cynically to make enormous profits on the one hand, while demanding to be favored as a public service on the other. Municipalities are badgered out of valuable property, coerced into building multimillion-dollar stadiums with public funds only to be deserted by carpet-bagging owners who have found a new town to strip-mine. Governments—local, state and national—are mulcted out of tax money by complicated write-off schemes that make Texas oil accountants look like choirboys. Newspapers are deceived into providing enormous amounts of advertising space at extraordinary rates—free. The population is brainwashed into believing that buying a ticket to a sporting event is a public service. Racetracks, animated roulette wheels, provide diversions which are illegal off their property, skim off huge profits and then demand to be treated as governmental tax-collecting agencies.

It is the custom in this country to view the sports industry with slack-jawed, gee-whiz admiration. We are all paper lions, the souls of athletes lying just below our short, stout exteriors. We idolize those who are proficient at sports as though they were a part of some saintly calling and we shower them with our love and gold. We fill the stadiums and buy warm beer and limp hot dogs. We watch the games on television, and when we shave we take it off, we take it all off. We smoke the cigarets and buy Detroit's monstrous automobiles. Our kids stuff their heads with the names of the backs of the Denver Broncos and the batting averages of Houston's utility infielders. They buy T-shirts with Mickey Mantle's name on them, and gloves and bats and balls must all be signed by some famous athlete or they are no good. We take functional illiterates with twangy accents and enshrine them as broadcasters because they once played a game for money. We make former athletes rich by paying them to speak to us or by buying the insurance or mutual funds they sell. We turn our colleges into farm systems for professional teams and then we buy tickets by the millions to finance this foolishly expensive and corrupting system. We do all of this and what do we get in return?

What we get, as opposed to what we think we get, is what this book is about. It's about the cynicism of American sports, the dump, the fix, the thrown game, the shaved points, the cross and double cross and the "I've got mine, bub." It's about the newspapers and the newspapermen who shill for sports. It's about television, the conscienceless and ruthless partner of sports. It's about the spoiled heroes of sports, shiny on the outside, decaying with meanness underneath. It's about the greedy professionals and posturing amateurs, the crooks, the thieves, the knaves and the fools.

These are not trivial things. Sports have a great and continuous impact on American life. Nowhere else in the world is such a large portion of the population so constantly engaged in sports and games. In 1967 there were more than 228 million paid admissions at major sports events. There were 67.8 million at racing events, 35.9 million at football, 34.7 million at baseball, 22 million at basketball. Not included in these figures, however, are the uncountable millions who attend little-league baseball and high-school basketball games around the country, play in golf tournaments on Sunday, bowl on Monday nights or watch sports on television. This is not mere preoccupation with sport. It verges on mania.

Moreover, we play our games, or watch them contested, with the same tenacious ferocity with which we fight a war

9

in Vietnam and with as little reason or sense. We are taught from the cradle that we have never lost a war and that winning is everything, tying is like kissing your sister and losing is nothing. We have long misplaced the purity of the notion that the importance of sports is in the competition, not in the result, and we all snigger at Grantland Rice's outdated doggerel about how to play the game. In our blind intensity about games, we have allowed ourselves to be put upon by gangs of two-bit swindlers, and we are marks for every hustler with a couple of jocks in tow. None of it has contributed to our civilization.

So this is, in a way, a sports book by a man who hates sports. On the other hand, I have spent a large piece of my life in the little world of sports and I have not come away untouched by the games or the men who play them. This book, then, is also about the men I've met and admired, some of them famous, some not. Somehow the people in sports I came to know best were the outsiders, the ones who made it only for a little while or never made it at all; the nice guys who finished last. They're the ones who didn't have the skills to make it big and turned out to be better people than they were athletes. They never got a lot of what sports people call "ink." I've given them some. What they gave me is worth a great deal more.

# 1 To Hell with the Newspapermen, You Can Buy Them with a Steak

WHEN THEY [NEWSPAPERMEN] DISCUSSED THEIR puissant craft at all, it was only to smack their chests proudly, boasting of their vast power in public matters, of their adamantine resistance to all the less tempting variety of bribes, and of the fact that a politician of enlightened self-interest, giving them important but inaccurate news confidently, could rely upon them to mangle it beyond recognition before publishing it....

A journalist still lingers in the twilight zone, along with the trained nurse, the embalmer, the rev. clergy and the great majority of engineers. He cannot sell his services directly to the consumer, only to entrepreneurs, and so these entrepreneurs have the power of veto over all his soaring fancies. . . . Above all, he is unable, as yet, to control admission to his craft. It is constantly recruited, on its lowest levels, from men who have little professional training or none at all, and some of these men master its chief mysteries very quickly. Thus even the most competent journalist faces at all times a severe competition, easily expanded at need, and cannot afford to be too saucy. . . . Most of the evils that continue to beset American journalism today, in truth, are not due to rascality of owners nor even to the Kiwanian bombast of business managers, but simply and solely to the stupidity, cowardice and Philistinism of working newspaper men. The majority of them, in almost every American city, are still ignoramuses, and proud of it. . . . The delicate thing called honor can never be a function of stupidity.

—H. L. MENCKEN, *Journalism in America,* 1919

For the usual reasons of self-esteem the news community clings to the conventional notion of a "free and independent press" arduously "digging out" information and purveying it to the public "without fear or favor" over the enraged shrieks of a monolithic government that wants to keep everything secret. In support of that myth, prizes are awarded every year to the diminishing handful of journalists, usually from small towns, who do happen to dig up new information, usually of no consequence. . . . If improvements are in order, the central requirement is that the press and TV find and promote more intelligent and better trained people. If there is a threat to the free press, it does not lie in outside influences by government or anybody else. On the contrary, the chief danger of a kept press lies in the intellectual poverty of the press itself. We need,

11

as Meredith once put it, "More brain, O Lord, more brain."

—JOSEPH KRAFT, *Profiles in Power:*
*A Washington Insight,* 1967

Each year at a gathering of newspapers editors and publishers in convention there is certain to be a major speech made about the public's right to know. This is indeed a right, although throughout the country and especially where it's all happening—Washington—considerably more money, brains, time and energy are successfully devoted to concealing rather than revealing. Unfortunately, newspapers are, practically without exception, geared less to letting the public know than to telling it things with which it is inexpensive to fill the space around the advertising. A leisurely journey with an agate line rule through most newspapers reveals an astonishing ratio of plain junk to what can fairly be described as news. Add up the space given to advice to the lovelorn, night-club columnists with juvenile values and talent at the typewriter to match, movie-gossip columnists, astrological blatherings, comic strips (especially including jingoistic garbage like "The Green Berets" and "Terry and the Pirates"), columns from Washington written by men who are afraid to say anything and wouldn't know how if they were not, semiliterate descriptions of debutante engagements, country-club social notes, and syndicated columns on dressmaking, stew-making, fortune-making, lovemaking and homemaking, and what's left for news space wouldn't be enough to wrap a fish dinner for six. Not that I am certain this a bad thing, since if a newspaper were to be really honest it would, on many days, not appear at all on the reasonable ground that there was no news today.

The days on which this is true can be counted by the number of stories which begin: "The mayor was still waiting today for . . ." or "The month-long shipping strike went into its thirty-second day today without . . ." There is even a name for these non-news stories. An anonymous editor invented it at a time when newspapers all over the country were exploiting the heart-attack death of actor

John Garfield in his paramour's apartment. It was deliciously speculated that he died in her, shall we say, arms? The headlines lasted for weeks and, presumably, sold newspapers. There were biographies of Garfield, his wife, his mistress, the life story of the janitor in the apartment building in which the tragedy occurred and the eyewitness story of a neighbor who had seen Garfield and the lady go for a walk in the park one day. At last, all avenues of further titillation seemed exhausted and at a sad and desultory what-are-we-going-to-say-about-Garfield-today editorial conference, one bright editor said, "I got it. Banner line. John Garfield Still Dead." To this day "John Garfield still dead" stories stuff the columns of our newspapers.

For this reason I had often thought that on my last day working for a newspaper I would conspire to run a blank page with a tiny agate line in the center reading: "No news today." It turned out that in the end I had neither the courage nor the opportunity. A colleague, however, left the New York *Post* in a blaze of in-group glory recently when he wrote a story the first letter of each paragraph of which spelled out "F-U-C-K Y-O-U." He was fired; groundlessly, I thought. Anyone who would puzzle out this cipher was, like the lady who was shocked to find "dirty" words in her dictionary, looking for trouble. I feel an authority on the subject because one Christmas Eve I wrote a story for the *Post* the first letters of each paragraph of which spelled out "M-E-R-R-Y C-H-R-I-S-T-M-A-S." Nobody noticed.

Indeed, it must be concluded that newspapers are *preoccupied* with "dirty" words. In a time when twelve-year-old children are viewing films which parade naked breasts and buttocks and tumultuous bedroom scenes, at a time when there is not a single taboo word on our stages and practically none in our movies (Edward Albee played "hump the hostess" in the nabes with *Who's Afraid of Virginia Woolf?*) at a time when *Playboy* has finally freed the female pubic area from folded drapery, at a time when complete nudity has become commonplace on stage, most of our newspapers are still holding "son of a bitch" to "SOB." Certain venturesome young editors have

13

recently liberated words like "bastard" from the taboo list, but by and large it's only through sheer stupidity that an occasional earthy expression slips into newsprint. A New York newspaper used the phrase "busheater" about a baseball player once only because neither the writer nor the editor knew what it meant.

Timidity reaches into the souls of editors and rots them. The mere mention of a libel suit, justified or not, throws a city room into trembling terror. City editors dump stories that in their view are "controversial" into the laps of lawyers. These lawyers, most of them, operate for obvious reasons with a handy slogan: If in doubt, throw it out. Recently *Ebony* magazine did a survey about the lack of Negro characters in cartoon strips which appear in newspapers. One top cartoonist put it this way: "If an editor gets one letter complaining about something, it carries more weight than 100 good ones. If one cartoon amuses 100,000 people but offends one, the editors make you change it." Timidity, the handmaiden of boredom, rules supreme.

In this American newspaper wasteland it seems altogether fitting that as much as 50 percent of editorial space —that is, counting Broadway three-dot press agentry, travel and restaurant columns written in advertising departments and similar rot as advertising rather than news space—is devoted to news of our sporting scene. We know, also, that this is often the most thoroughly read section of the paper even if largely by teenagers or those who have minds of approximately that vintage. Despite the space and readership, it has long been recognized in the newspaper industry that, since the sports section has little influence on our life and times, it matters little how it's put together. When one considers that there are, presumably, pains taken with the rest of the paper with results which are, unfortunately, not secret, one blanches to think of the imbecility which must be rampant in the sports sections.

It is astonishing how widely misunderstood this is. The list of men of good reputation who were once sportswriters is so long that an impression exists that sports

14

departments are crammed to the filing cabinets with bud-
ding James Restons, Paul Gallicos, Westbrook Peglers and
Damon Runyons. In fact, though, all this proves is that
there are two kinds of sportswriter—those with the good
sense and ability to go on to other things and those with
neither. There is a third group with good sense and ability
to match, but it is such a small one that it is statistically
insignificant and much of its energy is wasted trying to
trick timid editors into running bold prose.

To ensure the continuation of a system which sends
people with the most talent, ambition and imagination to
other fields, newspaper owners cleverly keep starting salaries desperately low. In lieu of reasonable remuneration,
they remind their employees from time to time that glory
is more beautiful and satisfying than gold. This means that
anybody who wants a writer, trained at some expense to
the newspaper, merely walks in and offers a small salary
increase. Magazines, television, public-relations outfits,
government bureaus and trade organizations discovered
this years ago and use newspapers much as baseball teams
use farm clubs. Naturally they take only the best men and
after each raid the level of talent at the newspaper de-
clines perceptibly.

Not that this is the only way to lose a good newspaperman. Each time there is a long strike (and newspaper
strikes arrive with great regularity, like plagues of locusts,
the result of careful planning, no doubt) top men drift
off into other fields. When the New York *Herald Tribune*
folded its tent after a glorious 131-year history, it gave
as one reason the fact that a 113-day strike had cost it
50 percent of its editorial staff. Another important way
to lose bright young men is to show them that newspapers
are edited by dolts. Nothing will send an intelligent young
reporter to an employment office more quickly than, for
one example, being sent to do a man-on-the-street interview, which is the last refuge of the dum-dum city editor.
"Smith, go out and find out what the man on the street
thinks of the earthquakes in Yokohama." If Smith has any
imagination, he spends a few pleasant hours in a local
watering place, returns to the office and invents a series

15

of amusing answers. "I still can't feel too sorry for Japs. Maybe we can send them a boatload of Band-Aids." The next time it happens, Smith might not get back to the office at all. "If anybody wants me," he'll tell the bartender, "tell them I've joined the Peace Corps."

Then there is the copy-editor ploy, or "There aren't enough clichés in this story, Sam." If a young sportswriter says that two teams play today, change it to "clash head on." Cross out "beat" and pencil in "defeat," change "base on balls" to "free ticket," "home run" to "round tripper," and if a man is puzzled, be sure he has a "furrowed brow." At all costs, ink the pact; preserve the reputation of sports journalism.

Finally we have the chickening-out method, which worked particularly well with a talented young man named Bill Roeder. He worked for the New York *World Telegram and Sun,* which died a dishonorable death in 1967. In 1959 young Roeder was, quite properly, the star of the *WT and S* sports department. He had been a schoolboy sportswriter, a baseball writer and now, being groomed for the column that would soon be vacated by an elderly Joe Williams, the Scripps-Howard sports columnist, he was doing a daily column that was being played as a feature. Roeder was intelligent, facile at the typewriter and wrote precise, taut English. He was an altogether unusual young man.

To set the scene for this little drama, it is necessary to describe the role of the New York Yankees in the local sports scene at the time. To the delight of playboy Dan Topping, the co-owner of the club (with Del Webb, the shrewd, hard-eyed construction millionaire), the Dodgers and the Giants had abandoned their franchises for California. This left the Yankees a monopoly of stadium and baseball in the largest city in America. During this period William A. Shea, for whom the Mets' new stadium in Queens was to be named, had just begun his campaign to bring another team to New York and to find a place for it to play. The Yankees were not exactly public-spirited about this quest. When there was talk of a New York team in a proposed new Continental League, the Yankees made abundantly clear it would not be welcome to play in Yankee Stadium. They liked to maintain that New York was better off just the way it was. What was good for the Yankees was good for everybody.

Possibly to show just how good, the Yankees announced one Friday in the spring that they were bringing big-time football back to New York, that they had talked Army into playing two of its games at Yankee Stadium the next season—Syracuse and Michigan. There were huzzahs all around, obeisances made to Topping, and the world was aglow with good fellowship.

Over the weekend Roeder did some quiet thinking. Then he made a few phone calls. Then he wrote a column for Monday's paper. The Yankees, he suggested, were setting up a smoke screen. Their major interest was not so much to bring big-time football into New York but to try to show everybody that there was no need for another stadium. Indeed, Roeder quoted an Army source as saying that the Yankees had been the *cause* of the demise of big-time college football in New York because they insisted upon charging such outrageous rentals for the stadium.

The rumbles began slowly. Roeder ran into Richard Starnes, then managing editor of the *WT and S,* in the corridor one morning and Starnes told him the Yankees were upset, but not to worry about it. Bob Stewart, the sports editor (later replaced and then fired in the merger, which preceded the demise of the *WT and S*), called Roeder to ask who his source was at Army. Now a reporter may not have to reveal his source before a Congressional committee, but when his boss asks, he has to tell. Roeder's man at Army was the knowledgeable Joe Cahill, public-relations chief, later PR director for the highly successful New York Jets. Roeder naturally assumed this information would stay locked forever in the archives of the imperishable *WT and S*. He was mistaken.

In a matter of days Topping was threatening a million-dollar law suit and a committee from the *WT and S* was calling on the suntanned owner of the Yankees. The committee consisted of Joe Williams, Dan Daniel, the elderly and widely respected Yankee writer, and Lee Wood, who was no less than the publisher of the newspaper, the number-one Scripps-Howard man at 125 Barclay Street. Right off, Topping demanded to know Roeder's source. Williams and Daniel had the good grace to attempt to look ignorant. "Joe Cahill," blurted the publisher, following one of the highest precepts of American journalism: When pressed, cave in.

Topping would not be placated by this information, however. He wanted Roeder's hide. He said he had proof, letters from colleges congratulating him on his reasonable rentals, that Roeder had libeled him. (Later on Roeder said he'd like to see the letters, and perhaps write a story about them, but his sports editor said no, better let it go. The web was tightening around the young writer.)

Now there were a lot of things Topping could have been told by the *WT and S*. The best would have been a suggestion to perform that famous and impossible physical act. Why this was not done is hard to say. What *is* known is that Topping travels in some pretty fancy circles, the same circles, say, as people who own newspapers. In any case, he must have known he was dealing from some sort of strength in the Roeder case.

The next thing Roeder knew, he had been summoned to Wood's office. Wood, now retired, was a newspaperman of the old tough school which taught that if you barked at everybody all the time, nobody would dare ask for a raise. The conversation, as Roeder recalls it, went like this:

WOOD: You sure got us into a lot of trouble. And don't you go trying to blame it on the desk.

ROEDER: It hadn't occurred to me. I'll stand by my story.

WOOD: We could have a million-dollar libel suit on our hands.

ROEDER: I think I can make the story stick. I think it's an accurate story.

WOOD: Well, we won't have to worry about it. Topping's not going to sue and I'm not going to fire you. I thought about it, but I'm not going to. Norton Mockridge [city editor] is willing to take you. I don't know why. I do

18

know you're not going to write sports on this paper anymore.

ROEDER: Look, I've been here 17 years and I've never been in any trouble before. I don't think I've done anything wrong this time, either, but even if I have, is this what you do because of one mistake in 17 years?

WOOD: I don't give a damn for your 17 years.

"After that I worked on the city side for a year," Roeder says. "I liked it. But the atmosphere wasn't healthy."

He did a good enough job on the city side to attract the attention of *Newsweek* magazine. He was offered a lot more money. He took it. He has been at *Newsweek* ever since and is now an associate editor.

There have been similar incidents on other newspapers around the country. A young man working for the Pittsburgh *Sun Telegraph* named George Kiseda mounted a campaign in 1957 which forced the Army football team to change its mind about playing on a segregated football field in New Orleans against Tulane. As a reward for his good work Kiseda had his stories published in the *Congressional Record* and Alan Nicholas, publisher of the Hearst newspaper, *ordered him to stop writing about segregation on the sports pages*. The *Sun Telegraph* is now defunct.

A man in Boston writes a story that offends Tom Yawkey, the largely unsuccessful but wealthy owner of the Red Sox. He no longer covers the team. A reporter in Chicago puts the rap on George (Papa) Halas, the tough old buzzard who owns and, until recently, coached the Chicago Bears, and the Chicago *American* shifts him to another assignment. Halas boasts that his best friend and golfing partner is managing editor of the Chicago *Tribune,* which owns the *American.*

In 1960 I made a survey of the three colleges in New York City—NYU, Manhattan and St. John's—which continued to play big-time basketball after the scandals of 1951. I found that a whopping 30 percent of the men who played varsity basketball for St. John's in that eight-season period had failed to obtain a college degree. This contrasted with less than half of that percentage of dropouts at NYU and an even lower figure at Manhattan. The implication was clear that while NYU and Manhattan appeared to have learned something from the scandals (CCNY and LIU quit big-time basketball altogether). St. John's was asking for trouble by hiring basketball players who obviously were not students. It was a legitimate point and a good story that had been difficult to research. But it was never printed. The executive editor of the *Post,* Paul Sann, killed it. He said he didn't want to hurt Joe Lapchick, then the basketball coach at St. John's, because Lapchick was his friend.

Then we have the story of William Barry Furlong, who is now a free-lance writer. He was doing a sports column for the Chicago *Daily News.* He describes it this way: "It was a text column three times a week and a letters column three times a week. The letters column was as important as the text: it gave the readers and the sports fans—who were experts all—a chance to sound off and to exchange with me a few pointed remarks. (Most of the time they were better than I was—which made for a lot of ebullience all around.) It was a swinging column—it inspired a blessed mixture of rage and laughter." A column like that was bound to offend the sports powers of the city. It did. To this day Furlong isn't sure who applied the pressure—although he has some good ideas—but the next thing he knew, he was called in and told that he was no longer a sports columnist and no longer in the sports department. He was now a general-assignment reporter for the city desk. No column. No more money. Just a transfer.

Furlong told them what they could do with their job. And another good sportswriter bit the dust.

The reason more reporters don't get into hassles with sports organizations and their own newspapers, the reason more of them aren't fired is that it takes an uncommon man to buck the system. By and large, the people who work in sports departments are so droolingly grateful for the opportunity to make their living as nonpaying fans at sporting events that they devote much of their energy to stepping on no toes. This leads to an easily discernible genre of sportswriting, the kind we get in most of the

20

sports sections around the country—consistently bland and hero worshipful presented in a pedestrian, cliché-ridden writing style. Some occasional invective can still be found, but this is usually reserved for threats to the establishment —new sporting enterprises, or creative, boat-rocking ideas. When Bill Veeck, baseball iconoclast who wrote *Veeck, as in Wreck* and, as owner of the St. Louis Browns, sent Eddie Gaedel, the midget, up to the plate in a ball game, first proposed interleague play he was hooted down on almost every sports page. Now the American League is actively seeking games with the National League during the regular season and it is considered civilized to be for it. I do not believe, however, that there is any possibility that the cynics who suggest that every sportswriter in America is on the payroll of our sports magnates are in any way correct. But there was a time when this was at least partly true (it wasn't called the "golden age of sports" for nothing) and the tales told about that era are both legion and hilarious.

In those days, sportswriters, especially boxing writers, had style in their typewriters and larceny in their hearts. When a newspaperman encountered Tex Rickard, the flamboyant fight promoter—one could go to a fight six nights a week most weeks during the era—he would be sure to examine the breast pocket of his coat. Usually he would find a hundred-dollar bill in it. Mike Jacobs, who came after Rickard, had trouble getting a set of dentures that would not clack in his mouth like the sound of a crap game, but he reduced payoffs to newspapermen to a science. After every big fight Mike would call a press conference, during the course of which he would nod, one at a time, to the newspapermen and they would follow him out into the hall, where he would reach into one of his many vest pockets and pull out a bill neatly folded into a small square. The fee ranged from 50 dollars to as much as 200 dollars, depending on how well the fight did and how much circulation the reporter's paper had. Legend has it that Mike was infallible in his judgments but that once he paid a 50-dollar man from the 200-dollar pocket and, when he realized his error, demanded a refund. He got it.

Reporters, in those olden, golden days, thought nothing of going into partnership with promoters. (Most recently several sports-department men made themselves rich by buying trotting-track stock at bargain levels while their contemporaries were writing that the hayseed trotting sport would never make it in sophisticated New York.) Damon Runyon is said to have sold out his piece of the 20th Century Sporting Club (later absorbed by Madison Square Garden) to Jacobs for a large pot of money. Many writers owned pieces of boxers. And in the oldest hustle of all, reporters used to run a "milk fund benefit" fight card for themselves every year. The kiddies got very little milk out of it. In addition, fight managers felt it necessary to pay off boxing writers. That's because clippings were important to them. With enough clippings they could go on the circuit around the country and their boys would fight as often as twice a week. It was also the golden age of cauliflower ears and punch-drunk fighters.

At the time, this kind of bribery was easy to handle. Jacobs, for example, ran his ticket office out of his pants pocket. He dealt in large volumes of cash and no one ever heard of the Bureau of Internal Revenue.

A former assistant district attorney in New York once told me that the DA's files contain a list of names, dates and payments made to sports reporters and columnists on every newspaper in the city and some outside it by the Madison Square Garden Boxing Department. This list would now be about ten years old. I have no reason to doubt that it exists and that possibly payments are still being made to old-line reporters. In fairness, it should be noted that it's possible for there to be lists of payoffs and no payoffs. Murray Goodman, once a newspaperman and now the last of an old and venerated line of grubby, cigar-smoking, ash-flecked publicists who buy newspapermen drinks, puts it this way: "I been on hundreds of payoff lists and I never got a quarter. Those lists are larceny."

What he means is that a publicist could make out a list of payoffs, take the money from his client and pocket it.

Or his client might want a list so he could knock it off his income tax. This is not so far-fetched. On January 20, 1966, a man named Lew Burston, since deceased, was charged by U.S. Attorney Andrew J. Maloney with setting up an arrangement to bribe a revenue agent. Burston worked for the Madison Square Garden Boxing Department as "international representative." This meant, as near as I could tell, that when Dick Tiger, the Biafran boxer, came to this country, Burston held his hand. Burston does not cut a very impressive figure and the only dealings I ever had with him were getting him to keep his mouth shut while I interviewed Tiger. Yet Maloney charged in court that Burston was trying to *cover up kickbacks* made to sportswriters. I would guess he might have been trying to cover up something else altogether. A picture of sad little Lew Burston handing out money to sportswriters simply refuses to register in my mind.

No matter what has gone before, I question the necessity for bribing a sportswriter. George Weiss, recently retired president of the New York Mets, once put it this way: "To hell with the newspapermen. You can buy them with a steak." This might be overstatement. Sports reporters who like their jobs so much have a tendency to *want* to please the management of the sporting organizations. They easily become what are called "house men." The man who covers a baseball team year after year spends a good deal more time with the management of the ball club than with his own editors; indeed, with his own wife. He becomes, if he is interested enough in his job to want to keep it, more involved with the fortunes of the team than that of his newspaper.

The obligations of a house man are subtle. It was the duty of Yankee house men, for example, to defend the trade which brought Roger Maris to the club from Kansas City as fair and equitable to both parties. In fact, it was a form of acquiescent larceny. The Yankees had been using the Kansas City Athletics as a farm club for years. They had some sort of arrangement at the top. Yet it was important to the Yankees that they be considered only good traders, not corporate manipulators. The house men were willing to write it because they *believed* it. The New York and San Francisco Giant house men did such a good job for Horace Stoneham, the convivial let's-all-have-another-drink owner of the club, that he emerged in history as the greatest handler of merchandise since R. H. Macy. Even the perspicacious Veeck swallowed this propaganda. He devotes an entire chapter in his book, *The Hustler's Handbook,* to the brilliant machinations of Stoneham. Yet in 1966, when it started to become apparent that the Giants were not only not going to win the pennant, but were being victimized by the very talent Stoneham had traded away, people started checking around. Matty Alou, Manny Mota and Orlando Cepeda, all traded by the Giants, were burning up the league for other teams. Felipe Alou, Stu Miller, Bob Shaw and Mike McCormick, also dropped by Stoneham, had gone on to do wonderful things for other clubs. More important, the Giants had very little to show for giving up these men. One thing Stoneham can depend on, though: the house men will continue to shower him with roses. They are a dependable lot.

Another illustration of the power of the house man comes in boxing, where the fighter who is not on the inside with the promoter "can't fight a lick." I heard an old-line boxing writer deliver this line about Jose Torres just before he won the light-heavyweight title. Torres not only could fight, he was, when he was younger, possibly the most promising middleweight of his decade. Because his manager, Cus D'Amato, a man born a thousand years too late, a man who should have been able to wear armor, carry a lance and rescue fair maidens from dragons, would not deal with Madison Square Garden, Torres was labeled by the house men as a man who couldn't fight. The fact was that D'Amato wouldn't let him. Without arguing whether D'Amato was justified or merely paranoid, he at least *thought* he was fighting the good fight against Madison Square Garden monopolists. He deserved a better break in the press.

House men can, in addition, be expected to support highly debatable decisions that "in" boxers seem to win all the time in the Garden. If an out-of-town boxer comes in to fight one managed, say, by the ubiquitous Gil Clancy, who manages the man who won both the welterweight and middleweight titles, Emile Griffith, and seems to be in the corner of whatever fighter of note climbs into the Garden ring, he knows he must win by a large margin or a knockout in order to win the fight. This is not to cast aspersions on the honesty of boxing officials, who are appointed by the state. It just seems to work out that way. As long as there are enough newspapermen who don't complain it will stay that way.

Madison Square Garden also trusts its house men to avoid calling a stinker a stinker. A really dull boxing match can ruin the next three dates if it's written about as a substitute for sleeping pills. Harry Markson, who runs the Garden Boxing Department from a certain Olympian height—he listened to Mozart but never Frankie Carbo—has been known to call a sports editor and suggest that this young non-house man type who covered last night's fight and was so amusingly cynical about the tempo of the main-bout waltz might be so jaded he'd be better off covering baseball in future. Why doesn't the sports editor tell Markson to take a flying leap out of the loge? Because he isn't so damn secure himself. Maybe Markson is right. Maybe the kid *is* too cynical. Besides, he probably knows Markson longer than he knows the kid. Markson cultivates sports editors as diligently as he does his considerable vocabulary. And a pass list *does* exert a certain charm in a lot of places.

My own strange confrontation with Markson came early in 1968, when, as the first boxing program in the new Garden, a fight between Joe Frazier and Buster Mathis had been arranged. The Garden had even managed to convince Boxing Commissioner Ed Dooley to sanction the fight as being for the heavyweight championship of the world. Only four other states agreed. The rest believed that Jimmy Ellis, who had won a series of tournament bouts set up by the American Broadcasting Company after Muhammad Ali was stripped of his title, was the champion. My own feeling was that the Frazier-Mathis fight was a logical match but that neither was worthy of being

25

called champion and that the Commission had prostituted itself with its sanction.

By this time I was a sports commentator for Westinghouse Broadcasting (WINS in New York) and outlined my position on the air, rather scathingly I admit, several times. Of course, I planned to cover the fight for Westinghouse, but when I called for a working-press ticket, I was told that none was available. However, since I was able to purchase a 75-dollar ticket (which Westinghouse paid for), I was more bemused than angry. And I guess I really felt that I had called too late to receive a working-press ticket.

It turned out that I was naïve. Markson had deliberately withheld the press credential. The promotion was exceedingly important to him personally and everytime he heard me on the air objecting to calling the fight a championship, he felt that I was advising people not to buy tickets to his fight. Businessmen often develop highly selective hearing. The worst thing about it, of course, is that few newspapers, especially outside of New York, would pay 75-dollars for a ticket if a promoter elected to bar a newspaperman from his promotion. The worst naïveté of all is to think that men like Markson have no power.

It is a curious thing that the house-man syndrome is encouraged by many newspapers. They like to brag that their man with the beloved baseball (or football or hockey) team is on the "inside." Indeed he is. So far inside that he would have his fingernails extracted before he would write anything about the ball club which would, in the eyes of its management, be damaging. This attitude is encouraged by the owners of ball clubs, but another paradox is that even from a selfish view it is a mistake. They would do well to weigh carefully the theory of Bill Veeck, who says that it is not the house man who helps the club but the perky, interesting, controversial writer who is willing to swat club management over the head with a rolled up newspaper from time to time. Because this kind of writer is interesting, he's read. Because he's controversial, he's reacted to. Veeck sees quite clearly that this leads to heightened interest not only in the newspaper but in

26

the ball club. Other owners either can't or won't. I often suspect they care more about their own egos than their enterprises.

Because the wedding of sports departments and sporting organizations has been so thoroughly consummated, I am amused by a debate which flares up from time to time about the morality of a baseball team's paying the expenses of a newspaper reporter's traveling with the club. Most newspapers will no longer accept expenses for their men on the shaky ground that a newspaperman can be corrupted by a ball club's picking up the tab for his transportation, meals and lodging. "Whose wine I drink, his song I sing" is a seasoned enough theory. Except in this case it does not apply. It makes no difference to a reporter which large corporate entity—the New York *Times* or the New York Yankees (a subsidiary, of course, of the Columbia Broadcasting System)—pays his expenses. If his gratitude is what's demanded, a list of the live bars in each town he must visit would accomplish more. A reporter who will let his small opinions be swayed by the corporation on the other end of his air-travel credit card will respond infinitely more readily to the direct and palpable burden put upon him each day by the personnel of the team. The pressure is to be nice, to write a pleasant story that will get no one angry. A ball player who doesn't approve of a story a sportswriter has written might well accost him in the clubhouse the next day, call him several choice and colorfully vile names and offer to punch him out of his mind the next time it happens. Of course, the reporter deserves to be reprimanded. He has probably written that Joe "No Hands," the shortstop, "should have fielded the ball more cleanly."

It is, as one might suspect, a less than pleasant experience to be offered a punch in the nose by a burly young athlete at, in the immortal words of Peter de Vries, the pique of his career. I know because it has happened to me several times. My most memorable brouhaha was staged by Roger (Red Ass) Maris the year after he hit 61 home runs. A little background is necessary.

Maris had come up to the Yankees in 1960, having

27

been obtained for Don Larsen, an elderly right-hander. Marvelous Marv Throneberry, who was to gain immortality as the personification of the ineptitude of the amazing New York Mets, a used-up Hank Bauer, and Norm Siebern, a pretty good first-baseman who was ruined as a left-fielder in a single game in Yankee Stadium when fly balls dropped around him like apples in an orchard. The Yankees also got Joe DeMaestri, a utility infielder who helped, and Kent Hadley, a first-baseman who released all the grouch in manager Casey Stengel by ducking away from a sharply hit ball. Maris arrived at the Yankees with a somewhat seedy but well-earned reputation as a pisser and a moaner, in baseball parlance, a complainer, a griper. Something terrible was always happening to poor Roger. "Everytime I'm going good I get hurt," is one of the lower-keyed ways he'd put it. The first time you sympathize. The second time you cluck your tongue. The third time you tell him, "Yeah, Rog, things are tough all over." He would complain bitterly of a hangnail, accuse the wind and weather of conspiring against him and, when he did have a good day, accept compliments with poor grace. "I'll be lousy again tomorrow."

The first thing Maris did when he reported to the Yankees was hold out for more money. Then he had the audacity to hit 39 home runs, drive in 112 and beat Mickey Mantle out for Most Valuable Player. None of this sat particularly well with the Yankees.

As a result, Maris was an outsider, a Yankee and yet not a Yankee. He was uncomfortable and lonely, just as he had predicted he would be when he was traded by Kansas City. Other players threw parties when that happened. Maris expressed serious regret. "It means leaving the friends I made on this club," Maris said. "You may not realize it, but it takes a long time for a player to be accepted after he goes to a new team." Especially if he's Roger Maris and he wears a red ass.

Maris was so far out the house men wouldn't have much to do with him. Left with so little choice, he became friendly with the out, or non-house-men reporters, me among them. I rather liked Maris. What I liked best

28

about him, I suppose, was his accessibility, nothing to sneer at in a man who played on the same club as Mickey Mantle, whom I called "the taciturn Oklahoman" for three years. What I liked next best about Maris was the characteristic which would hurt him so much, professionally and emotionally, later on. I mean his pissing and moaning. It was so chronic, it was amusing. I made it my business each day to stop and ask Roger Maris how he was faring. It was like asking a hypochondriac how he feels. He invariably responded with a string of complaints and then seemed reassured by a pat on the shoulder and an airy, "Oh, things will work out for you."

When Maris began hitting a lot of home runs in 1961, I was asked by an editor at MacFadden Publications if I would start writing a paperback book about the life and hard times of Roger Maris—"Home Run Hero," as they were to put it with so much juvenile zest on the book's jacket—for very little money. I accepted on the basis that a little money is better than none and that I liked Roger Maris. Thereafter I spent a great deal of time with him. I found that after about an hour of interview his attention would wander, even when he was talking about himself. So I spent about 40 separate hours with him over the next several months. He was friendly and amenable, talked with great freedom, revealed himself a lot more than he probably intended.

But once it became apparent that he might break Babe Ruth's record of 60 home runs, he was besieged, bedeviled, bugged, blinded by flash bulbs and put upon in a manner only television reporters—the American *paparazzi*—could conceive. I thought that by and large he responded rather well. Given his limitations, intellectually and as a man, he did his best. Even at the end, when he was losing what little cool he had, he never became the monster he could have. At one point during that hectic time, I wrote 30 Roger Maris stories in a row, day after day. I tried to be supportive. I said what I have said here, that he was a young man behaving well under the most difficult circumstances. I felt sorry for him and somehow close to him. Well, he hit his 61 home runs that year—in over

154 games, however—and I wrote my book and he survived.

During that winter Maris emerged with a new—shiny, surly—image. Of course, he hadn't really changed very much. It was only that now he was in the spotlight and, when he pissed and moaned, there was always somebody there listening. Sixty-one home runs didn't change Maris. They changed everybody else. Very soon poor Roger, without understanding what was happening, was nailed to the wall. A man from United Press International got on his nerves and Maris threatened to punch him. Maris' red ass hit every paper in the country. Another wire-service idiot caught him signing a baseball for a little boy—facetiously—with an X. As the story spread, the little boy became blind, crippled by polio and a victim of tuberculosis, multiple sclerosis and cancer. It was not a good scene.

I spent the spring with the new Mets and did not pick up the Yankees until the All-Star break. By that time Maris was accumulating enemies at a far faster rate than he had hit home runs the year before. Bedeviled by a low batting average and a high strike-out record, annoyed and hurt at the reviling attention he was getting from fans who resented him as a rival to Super-Mickey Mantle for their affections, stunned by the negative reaction of a fickle nation which had taken him to its heart the year before, Maris was responding the only way he knew how, with anger. A doubleheader in Yankee Stadium against the White Sox on July 30 seemed to bring Maris' strained relations with the fans ("animals" he was calling them by this time) to a head.

A couple of golf balls which had been thrown out into right field by the fans were thrown back into the stands by Maris. "I'm through trying to win friends and influence people," Maris explained after the game. Fortunately, the golf balls didn't hit anybody.

The fans responded by waving handkerchiefs and throwing more debris onto the field. It reached the point where the umpires had to escort Maris into the outfield each inning. And they weren't particularly sympathetic to Maris.

30

"He antagonizes them," Ed Runge, one of the umpires, told reporters after the game. "This thing has been growing all week. He waves his hat at them and one day last week he gave them the fingers."

"Ah," said Joe Paparello, another umpire, "he's only human. It's hard to take."

"Maybe so," Runge said. "But for that kind of money I'd take a lot."

The story I wrote in the *Post* about the incident included all of this vital information and went on to say, in a bantering tone, that Maris didn't understand the fans' reaction, that his lack of understanding was causing them to react even more and quoted him as saying, "Let me put it this way. I don't give a damn."

It was an accurate and, I thought, relatively innocent story. The next time I saw Maris was two days later in the visitors' clubhouse in Washington. Actually he saw me first. Clad debonairly in his underwear, he charged at me. "You fucking, ripping, mustached cocksucker!" he shouted, probably because I wear a mustache.

All I could think to do, instead of quite properly indulging in what I call Leo Durocher, or fuck-you-too, repartee, was mumble, "Look, Rog, isn't that the way it happened?"

"That's got nothing the fuck to do with it," Maris said. And, on reflection, he was exactly right. The last thing a ball player cares about are the precepts by which a newspaperman is supposed to live. We settled the problem by never talking again. This makes a large point about professional athletes. They may not all have Maris' gift for phrasing, but they will react pretty much the same way to any story they decide is negative. Nor does it matter what has gone before. The only thing a ball player wants to know is what you have done for him lately.

Sometimes he even wants to know what you can do for him retroactively. After Casey Stengel was fired by the Yankees (this turned out to be, by the way, the beginning of the end of the Yankee dynasty), John Blanchard, a catcher, took the opportunity to put the blast on the old man. "He's a goddamn louse," Blanchard said, or some-

31

thing equally kind, "and you can put that in the paper." So I did. Just like that. The next day a man of the cloth berated Blanchard for using bad language when he should be an example to the youth of America. Naturally Blanchard blamed me for the uncomfortable position he found himself in.

"You shouldn't have put it in the paper," he said.

"But John, you said to put it in the paper."

"What the fuck does that matter?"

As a final example, we have Bill Stafford, also of the Yankees. Stafford had a couple of fair 14-9 years with the club and thereafter, in the way of big-league ball clubs, hung on for much longer than he was able to pitch. This was in Kansas City on July 15, 1963, and Stafford had come in to pitch in relief and had filled the bases and walked the winning run across. In a routine check I noticed he had been knocked out a lot lately and decided the story of the day should be Stafford's telling about the troubles he'd seen, a legitimate if routine story idea. I approached him in the locker room the way one is supposed to approach a loser, with commiseration. "Damn, it's going tough," or some such bit of solicitude. Stafford turned his beady eyes and tiny IQ full on me and said, "I don't want to talk about it." I could have let it pass, but it didn't seem to me to be quite fair. Why should a ball player have the right to decide when he will talk to a newspaperman? Why didn't he say, "I don't want to talk about it," when he was winning and sportswriters were quoting by the yard his opinions about pitching? So I told him no, that wouldn't do, that he had talked as a winner and it was now his turn to talk as a loser. It happens to almost everybody. It's one of the beautiful things about the game of baseball. Stafford wasn't seeing much beauty, however. "Get away from me or I'll punch you in the mouth," he said. I do not enjoy being threatened with a punch. None, by the way, has ever been thrown at me, although Hank Bauer once delivered a "friendly" punch in the arm that left my best typewriter hand paralyzed for two days. A sportswriter-player fight is bound to be unequal as Earl Lawson, of the Cincinnati

32

*Post and Times-Star* who has been in several, will attest; the player is usually young, large and strong, the writer small, pudgy and weak. But when one talks of the subtle pressures that are on sportswriters to write things which aren't likely to arouse the ire of ball players, the subtlety of a punch in the nose must be prudently considered.

The pressure to have a ball player like you or, in the case of some, like Mickey Mantle, merely to have him say good morning, is a lot more direct and important than the pressure of what address one puts on his expense account. It can get achingly lonely covering a club every day if nobody says good morning.

The reporter who has the fortitude to be uninfluenced by this kind of pressure will not consider whose wine he drinks; the reporter with no fortitude at all will worry only about having *somebody's* wine to drink. He's not so much selling his song as trading it for his ass.

The aftermath of the Dodgers and Giants moving out of New York proves this point rather neatly. At that point only the *Post, Journal American, Daily Mirror* (the latter two both Hearst-owned) and the Long Island and New Jersey newspapers of S.I. Newhouse, a scourge of American journalism who runs his many newspapers as though they were five-and-dime *schlock* stores in underprivileged neighborhoods, were still accepting expenses from the baseball clubs their reporters were traveling with. (It's nice to note that Newhouse gets pretty much what he pays for. One day not long ago his top editor at one of his little New Jersey newspapers decided that the best story of the day for the screaming page-one headline was: "Wood Ibis Faces Extinction.") For many years it was an accepted practice for all newspapers to allow ball clubs to pay expenses. The premise was uncomplicated. The ball clubs wanted daily reporting of their activities. If they had to buy this space, it would cost them millions. They were delighted to pay the expenses of a reporter—about 10,000 dollars a year per man including transportation, meals and spring training—in return for coverage. I have often wondered why other entertainment organizations did not insist upon equal space. Certainly a play preparing for Broadway would, in ten weeks, provide many more interesting stories about its cast and the adventures of same than would ten weeks of baseball spring training. No newspaper has thought of this, I suppose, because Broadway is a frankly commercial enterprise, while baseball clubs have cloaked themselves in civic righteousness. A baseball club, the public has been brainwashed into thinking, is like a city's army going out to do battle with the mercenaries of other cities for the honor and glory of its citizenry. It thus becomes all but a court-martial offense *not* to buy a ticket to the daily enactment of a battle. This is a pretty good thing the boys have going for them and one would think they would be delighted to pick up some minor expense tabs in return for such ardent spreading of their gospel. Yet at the precise point at which New York was left with only one baseball team the Yankee monopolists decided they would no longer pay expenses. They carefully planted rumors of their decision, permitting the newspapers to take what they thought was the only face-saving action open to them. "You can't fire us," they said, "we quit. We have decided that we will no longer expose ourselves to the moral trauma of permitting the baseball club to pay the expenses of our baseball writer."

What was the result? None. The sportswriters didn't change. When the New York *Times* insisted, long before, upon paying its own way, it did not stop one of the most distinguished members of its staff from earning the marvelous reputation as the most patiently formidable lurker behind hotel-lobby potted palms in both leagues. The purpose of this lurk is to step out in front of the road secretary when he is on his way to breakfast or dinner. If you look hungry enough, the secretary invites you to join him and he pays. The gentleman from the *Times* wore a hungry look all his life.

So the new policy was meaningless as far as the writer was concerned. The house men remained house men. If there were any changes at all, it was in the economy of the house man. He now made more money, liked his job better as a result and was firmer than ever in his resolve to keep it at all costs. What gave him more money was the meal-expense arrangement. Where a ball club would deduct from its meal money (recently this has been 15 dollars a day) any meals provided on airplanes, the reporter could now put in for all his meals with his newspaper and still eat the free ones. Also, with the club not paying expenses for the reporters, road secretaries and publicity men felt freer to entertain them. Hence more free meals. If anything the reporter now owed more allegiance to the ball club than ever. I do not think, however, that the ball club planned things that way. In their own way club officials are as dense as people who run newspapers. They just wanted to save expenses.

The Sportswriter is not young anymore and he worries about what will happen to him if he loses his job or if his newspaper folds. He likes to feel like part of the organization he covers and hopes that, when the job opens, somebody will ask him to be publicity man or road secretary. But he will not be hurt if someone else gets it. Players like the Sportwriter, and club management likes him because he never hurts anybody. The people at his newspaper, if they have any opinion at all—usually they don't—say he must be good because everybody likes him. More likely the managing editor does not read the Sportswriter's stuff because it bores him. But fortunately for the Sportswriter, he doesn't know it can be done better.

Chances are the Sportswriter likes to travel. On the road he has a wide group of acquaintances who entertain him in return for inside stories about baseball players, free tickets to ball games and autographed baseballs. When the Sportswriter was young, he tried to have a pretty girl in each city with whom he was reasonably certain he could spend the night in bed. Now the girls aren't so young or pretty anymore and sometimes he pays the transportation for one of them to travel with him to several cities. He tells his wife he spends the money on booze.

The Sportswriter turns in clean, uncomplicated copy because, by and large, he has nothing to say. He is typing rather than writing, filling space rather than reporting. He is inclined to credit hitting streaks to borrowed bats, slumps to off-the-field drinking and girl chasing, although he suspects that if this were the case, most baseball players would be in slumps all the time. He likes to think his technical knowledge of the game is without peer and it might be, because baseball is a simple game, but the fact is that the Sportswriter doesn't watch many baseball games. In the press box he is usually occupied by trivia, girl watching or writing a piece for the *Sporting News.* (The *Sporting News* is a trade publication of inestimable value to perusers of minor-league box scores and college journalism instructors who need examples of how not to write sports.)

Because the Sportswriter indentifies with the organization he covers, he is a rooter. He gets angry at players who don't do well and those on other teams who are successful against his team. There is this story told about the Sportswriter. Once he watched an opposition outfielder have a particularly brilliant day in the field against his team. The fielder scooted to his right and caught a ball that looked like a triple, then he went to his left and took away a double, then to the fence. jumped up and pulled a home run out of the seats. Finally the star player of the Sportswriter's team hit a ball that landed 20 rows deep into the right-field seats. The Sportswriter glared out at the outfielder for a moment and then said, "Let's see the son of a bitch catch that one."

When his team loses. the Sportswriter always has somebody to blame. When a player is traded, he will berate him as a shirker and a slacker In his heart the Sportswriter believes he should get a World Series share because it was on his advice that the manager so successfully switched the shortstop and second baseman. The Sportswriter despises the manager as a fool. believes he could handle the team better, but is unfailingly polite and pleasant. until the manager is fired. Then the Sportswriter tells the world what was the matter with the manager all the time. Club management enjoys this immensely.

The Sportswriter feels threatened by young sports-

36

writers coming along on other papers. He wishes he worked in a city where there was only one newspaper. He wages war against young sportswriters until he molds them in his own image. He warns ball players not to talk to them. He himself is unfriendly. After two weeks on the road, unless the young reporter is made of old baseball shoes, he is talking to himself. Now the Sportswriter knows he is ripe for the look-kid-whaddaya-want-to-rock-the-boat-for ploy. When the kid understands what's expected of him, the Sportswriter proves his friendship by getting the kid laid.

The Sportswriter knows that players do not read most sports stories, but that they will be sent a deluge of clippings of any unfavorable story written about them. So he is very careful about what he writes. He enjoys being in the company of famous ball players and will waylay them into long hotel-lobby conversations. He will also be very resentful of the former ball player turned sportswriter who actually runs around with ball players. There are many things the Sportswriter doesn't understand about this type, but he is jealous, nevertheless.

In his own way the young ex-player is just as hung up as the Sportswriter. Hanging around with major leaguers makes him feel like a major leaguer, and nothing pleases him more than to be walking with ball players and to be asked for his autograph. He will share his best phone numbers with the surliest and grossest of hillbillies if the guy is on the roster of a big-league ball club. His editors will be impressed by the friends he has made among players, but his copy will be extraordinarily innocuous because he can't afford to offend any of his friends in the slightest degree. The Sportswriter has nothing to fear from him, but he will complain to the ball club management anyway and see if he can't break up the friendships by warning that the writer is leading young ball players astray.

The Sportswriter despises his sports editor (although he will act as his lackey, given the opportunity), hates the penuriousness of his newspaper and steals as much as he is able on his expense account. But when he is asked his occupation he squares his shoulders and says, "Journalist."

Are there any ambitious, intelligent young men who resist the path of the Sportswriter and yet remain in the sportswriting business? There are, but not many. Unpleasant things happen to the resisters. They find themselves knuckling under in order to make things easier; first they are harried, then restless and unsatisfied. My very first important experience in the sports department of the *Post* nearly drove me out of the business and if I had been more secure, it would have. Of course, if I had been more secure, the whole thing wouldn't have happened. I still squirm when I recall the incident and I question whether I can be objective writing about it, but I shall try.

I suppose my major problem, when I first began to cover a baseball team, was that I was more interested in being a newspaperman than a sportswriter. There is a distinction. I did not approach sports with the proper awe. I thought I could cover a club the way one covers police headquarters. It was a foolish notion. It compounded my problems.

The year was 1958 and I had recently begun to cover the Yankees on a regular basis. I ran into all the usual problems and some, I understand now, which were of my own making. Still, the Yankees didn't help much. The first treatment I got was the silent one. I found Mickey Mantle taciturn, Yogi Berra a mumbler, Billy Martin suspicious, Frank Crosetti an enigma, Casey Stengel totally charming and equally frightening, the other reporters cold and distant. I wanted to be a newspaperman, but I wanted to be *liked*, too. I found I was willing to go to some lengths to arrange it.

I attempted to form alliances with other reporters by bribing them with little tidbits of information. I leaned over backwards to be nice to ball players and was rewarded by arrogance. I accepted the arrogance and even began to feel it was my due. I never got angry. Once Whitey Ford and Mantle came at me wild-eyed and threatening and demanded I stop taking notes in a public restaurant where the team had stopped and where they were kidding with some very young girls. The kidding was innocent and I knew it, but they didn't know I knew it and didn't trust me, besides. (Possibly they had more to hide than I knew about.) What they also didn't know was that, if the talk was not innocent, they were safe. I had established a set of ground rules for myself which I followed as closely as I could. The rules said that what a ball player did off the field was not my business because I was not a gossip columnist. As long as he didn't get into trouble with the police or fined by his ball club, he was on his own. But anything around the clubhouse, hotel, airplane, train which was not of a *personal*—translate that to "financial and sexual"—nature, was open to being printed in my newspaper. If I heard one player berating another in the clubhouse about a baseball matter, I would print it. Was I eavesdropping? Probably. I considered that part of my job.

This time, though, my ground rules took a terrible beating. The Yankees had clinched the pennant in customary early fashion. (Once they stopped clinching pennants they all got a lot easier to live with, by the way. There's nothing like adversity for bringing out the human qualities, even in a baseball player.) Place of the clinching was Kansas City and the schedule called for catching a train for Detroit right after the game. In anticipation of the great event, their ninth pennant in the last ten years, the Yankees had stocked a club car with assorted liquid goodies. As the great train roared through the quiet night of middle America, the Yankees gurgled down these refreshing fluids. The results were varied. As Joe E. Lewis has remarked, some people they don't charge enough for whiskey—it should be five dollars a shot and two to a customer. One such customer was Rinold George Duren, Jr., a nearsighted pitcher with an extraordinary fast ball. He had had the fast ball for many years, having started out with it in 1949 with a team in Wausau, Wisconsin, but he was just completing his first full year in the major leagues, having only recently learned to control it. He's had a good year, pitching in relief, appearing in 44 games and compiling an earned run average of 2.01. His contribution to the club was important, but this affected neither his *joie de vivre* nor his inability to handle firewater.

In a burst of boozy brilliance, what Casey Stengel called getting "whiskey slick," Duren playfully mashed a cigar into the finely chiseled features of Ralph Houk, who was then a coach. Houk had the cigar between his teeth and was preparing to light it, anticipating the taste of the first delicious puff, when the well-oiled Duren slipped up to him, reached out with the palm of his hand and leaned on the end of the cigar until it spread like jelly over Houk's granite face. This had to be a fairly funny sight, except that Houk, who has been known to exhibit a small amount of bellicosity when he has had a drink, or when he has not, for that matter, didn't think so. Houk, who was to go on to become manager, general manager and then manager again, runs his ball clubs with an iron fist. He believes in the theory of being gentle when you instruct a mule—only first rap him on the head with a two-by-four to make sure you have his attention He commands respect from his players because they are afraid not to respect him. Now Duren knew all about Houk's reputation, and how he was a tough captain in the Rangers during the war, and how he was promoted to major on discharge. No matter what Duren had been drinking, he could not have taken it into his head to fight the burly ex-captain (his sycophantic buddies call him "Major"). Duren was only being playful. Since Houk does not have much of a sense of humor, however, he swatted Duren the way one would a troublesome fly, with the back of his hand. Purely by mischance, Houk was wearing one of those large, hard, diamond-encrusted World Series rings. It opened a cut on the side of Duren's eye you could have driven a martini onion into. This enabled Duren to wander through the train complaining tearfully that this was no way to treat a nice fellow who had done so much for the ball club.

It was this last scene that I observed. I didn't know at

first whether Duren had obtained his lovely eye by wandering into a closed door or a previously occupied upper berth, but inquiry soon disclosed the truth. What should I do? The best bet was to get off at the next stop and phone in the story. All right, but what about the code? Was I obliged to report a friendly little purple eye to my newspaper? I sought the advice of one of the veteran sportwriters on the train. "I know what I'm going to do," the man said. "Nothing. Absolutely nothing."

I was so impressed by his logic that I decided to do the same. My conscience pricked me only slightly and this was soon assuaged by the approval that was forthcoming as soon as my decision became known. I felt I might have sacrificed a point of honor, but I had gained the confidence and affection of my confreres and the ball club. I was, of course, quite wrong.

Two days later, while the Yankees were waiting around the lobby of the Statler in Detroit for a bus to take them to the ball park, the talk was about the clumsy detective who had tried to follow some of the players around the night before. This was not too unusual. George Weiss, then Yankee general manager, liked to have dirty ammunition available at contract signing time. He was also prone to cheapness, so he got himself a lousy detective. The gumshoe had trailed only the chocolate-soda drinkers while the others had shaken him off as easily as they would a bore at a bar. He followed Bobby Richardson to an ice-cream parlor, Tony Kubek to the YMCA and watched him engage in a hot game of ping-pong, and Elston Howard to a secret pizza joint around the corner from the hotel. This dick was so inept he soon had the ball players following *him*. He had difficulty understanding why he was so noticeable since he was dressed inconspicuously in a setting-sun purple suit and white sneakers.

Pretty funny, I stood there thinking. Yeah, yeah. When did it happen? Last evening. Did anybody send stories about it back to their papers? Yeah, sure; it was so funny. Well, how come nobody told me about it? The guy was so obvious we thought everybody knew. Lousy reason. Lousy feeling. I was just as much an outsider as before

41

I had decided to forget about Duren's eye. The way things really work is this: if you are not an outsider, you're *protected*. Something happens, you get a phone call even if you happen to be in a bordello in an obscure part of town. Understand, I thought I *needed* protection and I was in my room all evening. I found out in later years that almost everybody on the beat is so basically lazy, involved with the club, stupid or incompetent that *they* needed protection from *me*. Unaware of this yet, I felt I needed a friendly shoulder to cry on. So I called my sports editor on the telephone. His name was Ike Gellis.

I told him I was nervous about the way things were going around the ball club. I told him about the detective and he laughed and said, yeah, he thought he had seen something about it in one of the other papers but he didn't think it was very important. Then I told him about Duren and Houk, and he said, "Wait a minute," and my goose was cooked. In my confusion I had mislaid Gellis' problem, which is the problem of most sports editors around the country. When I talked with him I wasn't talking with a sports editor, I was talking to a middleman. That is, he was one of the many unfortunates who worked for an executive editor, in this case my old friend, Paul Sann, who was interested in sports and sensationalism. So Gellis did not make any decisions. He merely provided the information which Sann used to make them. Looking back, a sort of view from the peak of humiliation, I realize what a dangerous combination that is. Sports are too dull to be sensationalized; any attempt to squeeze them in that direction ends in, at best, untruth, at worst, disaster.

What happened thereafter is a minor blot on the history of American journalism. It was Sann's decision to make a big splash, a big noise in the little world of sports. I was instructed to get on the telephone with a rewriteman, and in his expert hands the simple tale grew and flowered. Had I called the story in from a station platform in Indiana the night of the event, it would have been received by a bored night sports editor and probably turned into an amusing box. Like "It wasn't only champagne that

42

flowed in the Yankee victory party aboard their train last night. There was a small amount of blood mixed in." Two days later it came out "a bitter, bloody brawl." Alliterative, but untrue.

When I saw the follow-up stories the next day, I demanded that my byline be removed. I was told sure, I had that right. But if the byline was off, I would be quoted in the body of the story. The hell with that. I knew newspapers too well. Remember this, friends. Unless you have a particular ax to grind, unless you have a prepared statement, don't let yourself get quoted by a newspaper. It never comes out the way you intended.

The story, plastered over page one of the *Post,* spread over the country in great, wide ripples. It was as though a boulder had been dropped into a quiet lake. As it spread, it took on new dimensions, new distortions. More people were involved in the "brawl." A foolish lot of noise the Yankees had made when they came into the Kansas City railroad station became a riot. Casey Stengel's philosophical understanding of his men becoming "whiskey slick" became a foot-stomping reprimand. It was American journalism at its worst and at bottom I knew it was all my fault. All I could think about was a high dive into shallow water.

In saying that the story had been "delayed," the newspaper gave an extremely lame explanation. Of course, there was no good one. On the other hand, it wasn't the story it was made out to be, either. If it had never been printed, the world would not have been a worse place to live. With the advantage of years I say the best thing the paper could have done was call me in, read me the riot act about hesitating to call in what might have been a good story and let it go at that. If anybody was really enraged I could have been fired, I suppose. But for the sake of a two-day wonder, to lie, distort and put itself and its reporter in such an embarrassing position is sheer stupidity.

I submitted my resignation. I don't kid myself about that. I felt as though I had been regurgitated and I should have sped away, trailing my stink behind me.

43

But I needed the job and I knew that if I left at that point I would probably never work for a newspaper again. I confess I still wanted to. My resignation was not accepted; that is, my severance pay was refused and I could use that as an excuse for staying on.

About a month later, when everybody had calmed down, I got into a conversation with Gellis about the affair. "What would you have done if you were me?" I asked him.

"I've thought about it," he said. "I'd have given it a pass."

He meant that I should never have called him from Detroit. It was the best advice a newspaper ever gave me. But it led to a disturbing question. What I had to ask then was, "Why didn't *you?*" I didn't ask because I knew the answer. If he was the reporter and kept his mouth shut, he was protecting himself. Once he, as middleman, knew about the incident, the only person he had to protect was me. Why bother?

Around the Yankees the reaction to the whole thing was automatic. Most of the ball players stopped talking to me. I remember having the perfect book to take along with me on the next train trip with them. It was Jerome Wiedman's *The Enemy Camp*. I don't think any of the players got the point. I do think that, if it were not for one man, I would not have been able either to do my job or to stand the gaff. That man was Casey Stengel. How he behaved in that time of high indignation will be told in a later chapter on the man I love.

There is a story told around the *Post,* probably apocryphal, that Dorothy Schiff, who owns the paper, once said to a politician at a cocktail party that she was thinking of eliminating the sports section. "My dear lady," the politician is supposed to have said, "the sports section is the only reason I read your paper." And thus 25 jobs were snatched from the brink. The reason this story makes the rounds is the widespread understanding that very little attention is paid to sports departments by people who own newspapers. Except for those few who own racing stables and thus are interested in their man at the track, most publishers care only enough about the sports department to cut its budget from time to time. This indifference and penny-pinching leads to sports departments being crammed with sports buffs, not newspapermen. They *play* at being newspapermen, however, and the results are often ludicrous. There are few things, for example, more embarrassing than the sports scoop that doesn't come off.

I have enough of the juvenile newspaperman in me to believe there *is* such a thing as a scoop. While my admiration for him is not unreserved, I believe that Drew Pearson, for one, has come up with many real scoops, stories which, were it not for him, would never have come to light. I point particularly to his investigations of Senator Thomas J. Dodd of Connecticut, which showed serious misuse of campaign funds, led to a Senate censure and to one of the most amusing bits of Senate men's room graffiti ever recorded: "Dodd is dead." Pearson gets credit for an exposé not only of Dodd but, by coincidence, of American journalism. That's because all the time he was writing about the activities of the U.S. Senator his columns were being run in hundreds of papers around the country. Yet in all of them his column was treated as though it were about some dog show, often buried under a stock head designed to attract no attention. There are two ways to handle that kind of story. Either you believe it isn't true and you don't print the column, or you decide it is true and it requires large headlines. It is vastly amusing to students of the newspaper scene that newspapers chose neither course.

Anyway, that's what a scoop is all about. What a scoop is not is a prediction of things to come, especially if these things never come about. Walter Winchell was a great scoop man of this kind in his heyday, that is, when people were still paying attention to him. Over a period of several months he would make predictions on every side of a question. The U.S. is thinking of raising interest rates. It will not raise interest rates. It will raise interest rates. Informed sources in Washington say that interest rates are on the way down. Then, no matter which way the

Treasury acts, you read it in Winchell first. This scheme works with births, marriages, divorces and love affairs. It also works with the hiring and firing of baseball managers, football coaches, the trading of players, the selling of franchises and the expansion of leagues. This has not escaped the attention of sportswriters, especially those who work for wire services. A particularly avid practitioner of this art was Joe Reichler, who worked for the Associated Press. Reichler fired Casey Stengel for ten years in a row and was right once. (The year Stengel *was* fired the Associated Press flash said he had "resigned.") Reichler might have been right one more time if he had lived long enough, but the old man confounded him by breaking a hip and retiring. I'm not sure why Reichler insisted upon firing Stengel so often except that I suspect he didn't like him. If so, the feeling was mutual, and Stengel was the man who said, "I've been around so long I like almost everybody."

Reichler made hundreds, if not thousands, of trades on the wires of the Associated Press that were never made elsewhere. His specialty, though, was hiring and firing managers. In the space of a couple of winters he told the world that the Los Angeles Dodgers would fire Walter Alston, that Alston would become manager of the Cincinnati Reds, that Casey Stengel would leave the Mets and become manager of the Dodgers, that the Yankees would refuse to fire Yogi Berra after he had managed the club for only a single season, that Leo Durocher was about to become manager of the St. Louis Cardinals, that Charley Fox would take over as manager of the San Francisco Giants and that Mayo Smith was about to move in as manager of the Chicago White Sox. Not one of those things ever happened.

Just for that Reichler was hired to do public relations for the Commissioner of Baseball, General William D. Eckert, who will forevermore be a legend of the game because, when his appointment was announced, Larry Fox, a sports reporter, clapped himself on the head and said, "My God, they've named the unknown soldier." After two years of Eckert's bumbling, however, he was fired.

There are limits, apparently, to the sufferance-of-fools quotient even of baseball moguls.

It was with long, somewhat irritated amusement at wire-service scoop histrionics that a trio of reporters—Larry Merchant, then with the Philadelphia *News*, Stan Isaacs of *Newsday*, on Long Island, and I—were moved to construct a fake. This was at the Yankee-Pirate World Series in Pittsburgh in 1960. We were sitting around a table in the ballroom of the Hilton Hotel, surrounded by Beat 'Em Bucs signs and partaking of a buffet provided by the Pittsburgh club. The buffet is a World Series and All-Star tradition, the home club providing an eating and drinking room for the assembled newspaper, radio, TV and advertising men, club officials and assorted freeloaders. Those who can afford it usually eat elsewhere because the food is seldom better than ordinary. Most newspapermen eat there, though, and bill their offices for meals. This is equitable, because they will probably spend their meal allowance on foolish things, like clothing for their kids. It also gives them the opportunity to say after a ten-hour double-header, "The pay is small, but you can't beat the hours."

The Merchant-Isaacs-Shecter conversation went about like this:

"Let's invent a good trade and spread it around."

"Maybe we can get Reichler to put it on the wire."

"Only way to do that is to seem to be hiding it from him."

"But it has to be a good trade, something with a ring to it."

Several possibilities were discussed and discarded. Finally:

"I got it. Johnny Antonelli from the Giants to the Yankees."

"Sure, the Yankees need a lefthander. But Reichler's made that one a couple of times."

"Yes, but for Yogi Berra? They're desperate for a catcher."

"Oh boy, Yogi Berra."

"But he might quit rather than leave New York."

"Nah, he wouldn't. But let's do it up brown. Johnny

47

Antonelli to the Yankees for Yogi Berra, who will become player-manager of the Giants."

"You think anybody would go for that?"

"It's so dumb it's delicious."

"Has a definite ring to it."

"OK, men, spread the word. Remember, out of the side of your mouth."

At that point the idea of Yogi Berra's becoming a manager was considered ludicrous. That the Yankees later did indeed appoint him manager only proves that life follows art and how foolish the clichés of sport are. Then the only thing Berra did to get fired after one year was win a pennant. By that time, apparently, Dan Topping had come to believe in the cliché.

Alas, we could not con Reichler into putting the Berra-Antonelli story on the wire. But in any large gathering of newspapermen it is not difficult to spread rumors which will be accepted as fact. We got the story into at least 15 papers around the country.

The sad truth is that newspapers are often more eager to print fiction than fact. And not only in sports departments. A rewriteman on a New York newspaper tells the story of the child who ate a sugar cube soaked in LSD. The kid hallucinated and wound up in the hospital. Newspapers all over used this incident to point out the dangers of LSD, which, incidentally, they know nothing about. On the second day, the rewriteman checked the hospital to find out the condition of the LSD kid. "Good," said the girl at the hospital. He told his city editor. "Well," the man said, "let's keep her on the critical list another day." And the headline read: "LSD Baby Still Critical." Probably of the newspaper business.

A Boston reporter tells of a series on gambling he wrote. He carefully left out any figures on dollars bet on the ground that they were impossible to compile with any accuracy. He was instructed to write an insert, including the figures. He did so, but pointed out in a qualifying sentence that the numbers were altogether unreliable. When the article appeared, not only had the qualifying

48

sentence been excised, but the headline had been written on the figures.

Another reporter tells of the time he was sent to New England to investigate a murder that, according to a morning tabloid, might have been caused by jealousy in a wife-swapping set. He checked carefully, found the murder a generally interesting one, but was certain that there was no wife-swapping involved. He called his city editor and told him what he had found out. There was an ominous silence. Then the city editor said, "Whaddaya mean, no wife-swapping?" When he wrote the story, there was wife-swapping in it.

I have had a similar experience. At an exhibition game between the Yankees and the Mets at Yankee Stadium on June 20, 1963, there was a burst of exuberance from the fans after the game. That is, they jumped out onto the field and tried to steal baseball caps, home plate, a few box seats and maybe the left-field foul pole. All in good fun, of course. The Stadium and New York cops grabbed the boisterous and beered-up lads, being careful to do nothing that would register as police brutality, at least not where it would show, and pointed them in the general direction of home. This was enough for the *Daily News*, a tabloid with an undeserved reputation for maintaining high journalistic if not moral standards, to leap into print with a black headline that declared unashamedly that there was a "RIOT!" at Yankee Stadium.

I had no idea what the *News* was up to. I merely did the routine reporting job. I checked the police to find out if there had been any arrests. They said no. (The *News* said six.) I wrote a blithe little piece saying that boys will be vandals at Yankee-Met games, quoted the police as saying there had been no arrests, and went home to bed. In the morning the *Post* had a large, exciting story about a riot at Yankee Stadium. It said six people had been arrested. How did this happen? Easy. The brains on the desk liked the story which wasn't true better than the one which was. It was another case of "Whaddaya mean, no wife-swapping?" Reporters seem to be kidding

49

when they say, "Never let the facts interfere with a good story." They aren't.

And now we need a footnote to the story of the Berra-Antonelli nontrade. It illustrates further how American journalism functions. This is about the newsman, as he likes to be called, who fell for the false rumor. A guy who was in on the fix noticed the newsman writing the breathtaking details of the rumor and, conscience-stricken, tapped him on the shoulder and said, "Don't send that. There's no truth to it. A few guys made it up and spread it as a rumor." Mr. Newsman tore the sheet out of his typewriter and went on to tell the world other truths. A day later, however, he did write the story and it appeared in his paper as a hot probability. "Now why the hell would you want to do that?" the conspirator asked him. "You knew it wasn't true."

"Well, it was like this," Mr. Newsman said. "I'd heard the story was a phony, but I ran into Frank Gibbons (late of the late Cleveland *News*) and he told me about the deal. I said nah, it's a phony, but Gibby said the hell it was. He said he's just had lunch with Horace Stoneham owner of the Giants and was told the deal was on for sure. It had kind of a ring to it."

The second Sonny Liston-Muhammad Ali (nee Cassius Marcellus Clay) fight provides another vivid and hilarious example of this kind of newspaper nonsense. This fight was a gypsy. It had been tossed out of nearly every major American city and finally, at virtually the last moment, it was banned in Boston. Committed to a date for theater television (which provides the largest share of fight purses these days), the promoters frantically settled on Lewiston, Maine, as a site for the fight. Fight headquarters and Liston's training camp were established at the picturesque and crumbling Poland Spring Inn. This hotel, home of Poland Spring Water and once a baroque spa for the wealthy, has now been converted to use by the poverty program. The fight was its last fling.

The Poland Spring Inn was some ten miles outside of Lewiston, which means it was in the exact geographical center of nowhere. This led to even more incest than

50

usual among the many reporters milling about on the scene. And one of the incestuous stories was that Clay was in danger of assassination by (1) the same Muslims who had killed Malcolm X, because Clay was thinking of becoming a Malcolm X type of defector or (2) Malcolm X supporters who wanted revenge on the Muslims for killing their leader. Since there was not a shred of evidence of either of these two possibilities, they received great currency.

Now it happens at heavyweight championship fights that promoters bring well-known fighters and fight people to the event and pay expenses in return for their acting as shills. Joe Louis says Liston can't lose. Barney Ross picks Clay. Once, by the way, Joe Louis picked one fighter for the promoters and a different one in the ghostwritten articles he was doing for a newspaper syndicate. He needed the money. It's a harmless pastime and nobody cares much about it, least of all lazy boxing writers who get easy stories out of it.

One of the people who was invited to the Lewiston fight was Jose Torres, who had recently turned light heavyweight. Torres also writes a column for a Spanish-language newspaper and the fiction was that he was in Portland as a correspondent. On this evening he ran into Harold Conrad, the man who does publicity for heavyweight title fights, in the dining room of the hotel. "Hey, Torres," Conrad said, by way of making conversation, "if you're up here as a correspondent, I got to seat you in the working press, don't I?"

Torres, an alert, bright man who boasts Norman Mailer as a close friend, pretended shock. "Not me," he said. "With those Muslims coming up here to kill Clay, I don't want to be in the line of fire." This was a joke and meant as such. But it was overheard by Jimmy Cannon, the eminent sports historian, and taken quite seriously.

"Dammit, Conrad," he said. "I told you. Even Torres knows it's going to happen." He appeared to be most agitated.

Conrad thought fast. It is his job to get the fight into newspapers, not only in Lewiston, but all over the country.

51

Newspaper stories stimulate ticket buying for theater television. He knew instinctively that the best thing that could happen would be a hot story which said that Clay might be assassinated in the ring. The memory of Jack Ruby rubbing out Lee Harvey Oswald right on the tube was still fresh in everybody's mind. Since a lot of people saw it only on re-run, this might be their first chance to see an assassination live. Although he had no precedent, Conrad imagined that tickets to an assassination ought to go like—well, tickets to an assassination.

And he knew there was only one way to be sure the story was printed. He grasped Cannon by the arm, looked sincere and said, "Jimmy, please. Do me a favor. Don't print that story." This was a master stroke. He knew the story wasn't true. He had given sound advice. He was in the clear. He was also certain that Cannon would pay no attention to him whatever.

The next day the story broke on page one of every Hearst paper in the country. By Jimmy Cannon. Exclusive. Other newspapers felt obliged to pick it up. Not because it was true, but because it was *there*. The scurrilous British press, which covers heavyweight championship fights in force, came up with its own scoops. These in turn were picked up by the wire services and sent back to this country. One New York columnist said to Conrad: "Give me some stuff on the Muslims. I know the story isn't true, but I got to protect myself."

"It couldn't have been better," Conrad says, chuckling. "I hit page one of every paper in America with a fight story. Two days running."

Now the police started believing the stuff they were reading in the papers. Two New York detectives, who wanted to see the fight, were dispatched to Maine. The Lewiston police asked Conrad if he thought they ought to search the people coming into the fight for weapons. Conrad, who has a long, sad face, made it longer and sadder. "It's up to you, Chief," he said. "You got to do what you think is right." Conrad then leaked the story that the police would be searching for weapons. More headlines.

What the police really wanted to do was search only Negroes. But they realized this would look very bad. At the same time, if they frisked every person coming into the arena, it would take hours, and heaven only knows what they would do if anybody objected. So they hit on a plan. *They searched only women's purses.* It was the perfect lunacy to go with a series of idiot assumptions. A man could have walked into the place with a machine gun strapped to his back, but the police were searching only purses. They found a lot of lipsticks.

There were, of course, no incidents in the arena, except for the fight, which was rather an incident itself, a one-round, one-punch knockout of Liston. No one pulled any guns, no one tried to kill anybody. But in the end even Cannon was satisfied. "The cops did a hell of a job guarding this place," he told Conrad. "I even saw two of them up in the rafters over the ring." The two men in the rafters over the ring were photographers from the Associated Press and *Sports Illustrated.*

There is a subtle pecking order in the business of sportswriting. At the top is the columnist, who has risen there for one of three reasons:

1. He is the best writer, or was, since there are now three young men in the department who can write better. They will, of course, become bored with waiting for him to die and move on to better things.

2. He knew somebody. Nepotism lives in the newspaper business.

3. He is a bum that nobody had the guts to fire. So he was made a sports columnist on the ground that this is the least important job in the paper and that chances are nobody will know just how bad a writer he is. Not only that, he had discovered a way to get lots of mail; he puts the knock on dogs, rips fishermen and writes things like "Mickey Mantle is a bum" and "Who said Stan Musial is a nice guy?"

Next in line is the baseball writer. Baseball writing used to be the full-dress suit of newspaper jobs, a position for gentlemen. A typical day on the road involved arising

53

at 7:30, breakfasting at some length and heading for the golf links. Lunch was after the ninth hole and one arrived at the ball park at 2:45, 15 minutes before the game, to pay one's respects to the manager. The game itself, usually less than two hours long, was over before five. In those days a man wasn't a baseball writer, he was a critic. He reviewed each game as though it were a theatrical performance. After the game, he opened his typewriter, wrote his little review and was ready for cocktails, dinner and other diversions.

The life of a baseball writer these days is far different; the work is harder, the diversion slimmer, the hours impossible. Whether one works for an afternoon or evening newspaper, night games, expansion and coast-to-coast tight jet-plane scheduling have conspired to reduce the comfortable little world of the baseball writer to a psychedelic nightmare. Baseball players complain that the havoc wrought on them by the schedule is shortening their careers. And they are young and fit rather than fat and fortyish.

The morning-paper man's life is crammed full of:

1. Early-edition stories. These are written before night games and give the customers a baseball story in the editions before the game starts. Often they are much better stories than the late-edition game stories but they are thrown out of the paper just the same because that is the way it has always been done. Newspapers represent one of the most plodding bodies of conservatism in America and sports departments are more conservative than the rest of the paper.

2. Bunk leads. Just what it says it is, bunk. "The Montreal Expos clashed head on here today with the San Diego Padres in the most meaningless game of the season." It is as valuable as all newspaper stories which arrive before the event.

3. Running stories. "The Yankees jumped away to a quick two-run lead in the first inning when Joe Pepitone powered a home run into the potted palm on the porch of the house across the street from the ball park. Joe has

hit 16 home runs this season, but this was his first into a palm, potted or sober."

4. Closing bars. The only advantage a morning-newspaper man has over an afternoon man is that he is finished writing sooner. This gives him time to put down enough whiskey before the bars close to anesthetize himself. The afternoon man usually isn't finished until the bars have closed. He can drink himself to sleep in his room but this makes him feel like an alcoholic, which sometimes he is.

The evening-paper man's life is crammed full of:

1. Wasting time. Since he doesn't have to write early-edition stories, his days are empty. He always has a book with him that he's been meaning to read for years, a paperback abridged *War and Peace,* but never gets to it.

2. Post-game locker rooms. The afternoon man does his work after the game. He must go to the clubhouse (old-timers call this "jock-strap sniffing") and elicit clever quotes from dull men. The theory, and it's valid enough, is that there is no use writing about the ball game because everybody has found out what happened on television or in the morning paper. In fact, the recounting of the events of a baseball game in print is so dull as to be stupefying. So it is necessary to write of other things, the dietary habits, for example, of the hero of the game. "Joe Verb, who hit the home run that gave the Cardinals a firm grip on sixth place last night, likes to eat his words. 'I particularly enjoy poly-syllables with pigeon sauce,' he commented while toweling the sweat off his tail. The more words Joe Verb eats, the better he hits. After the game, St. Louis management presented him, as a token of their affection, with the latest edition of the *Oxford Universal Dictionary.* In no time flat, Joe had eaten his way all the way through betulaceous [belonging to the *Betulaceae,* a family of trees and shrubs]. 'Delicious,' commented Joe Verb, burping an apostrophe."

3. Looking for after-hours bars. By the time the P.M. man is through with his stories, he has no place to go. If he has real class, he goes back to his hotel room and cries himself to sleep.

55

One thing A.M. and P.M. men have in common covering baseball is dyspepsia, the result of mealtime problems. For night games, and most of them are, the conscientious reporter shows up at the ball park by 6 P.M. This gives him a chance to find out what lies the manager has been telling lately, which pitchers are soaking their aching arms in the whirlpool and other such earth-shaking developments. It is obviously not possible for a gentleman to eat dinner before going to the park. Gentlemen do not dine at five. So he eats at the ball park in a press room provided by management. The food runs the gamut from poor to terrible. Some managements provide with a relatively lavish hand. Charles O. Finley of Kansas City and Oakland, however, is said to count the oatmeal cookies, which make up the best dish served in his press room. Bill DeWitt, until recently owner of the Cincinnati Reds, was a knockwurst clocker who complained loudly at any rise in food consumption. The shrewd Walter O'Malley in Los Angeles has found the ideal way to keep the eating within reason in his press room. He provides a room too small, with too few tables and chairs to handle the crowd, and a set of the surliest waiters this side of the Iron Curtain.

After the game in most cities there is no place to eat except some ham-and-egg joint. If there was a single thing that pushed me into retirement from covering baseball on a regular basis, it was the vision of never having to eat again in the Minute Chef in Cleveland. One returns from a two-week trip poorer—the meal money having gone not so much for food as in barrooms ("Can I buy you a drink, honey?")—with an excess of stomach acidity and a badly functioning liver. It is a chastening experience and one not calculated to keep intelligent writers in the business. Newspapers, have, for some years now, found it increasingly difficult to replace departing baseball writers. "I'd rather cover pro football," sports editors are told.

Writing about professional football used to be a step down from baseball writing, but it is coming up fast and in the minds of many is a better deal all around. That's because it is not only easier to cover pro football (with only one game a week, there is a lot of time left for golf, eating, drinking and girl watching), but because of the rising popularity of the game. This surge in interest has led to some jolly paradoxes. For many years sports editors were content to put their weakest men on pro football. Men do not change as rapidly as fashions, however, so editors suddenly found themselves with out-of-fashion writers covering an in-fashion sport. Professional football people liked this fine. Men who have been pushed around in their newspaper offices find it particularly easy to identify with teams they are covering. Newspapermen actually cheer in professional-football press boxes. It is a sobering experience to hear grown, presumably sophisticated men violating the code sportswriters get with their first press card—do not root in the press box, except for the game to be over quickly. (Another phenomenon here. There is always a great deal of tearful hand-wringing from sportswriters about how long it takes to play a baseball game these days. Aside from them, the TV people and players, no one else complains. Fans believe they get a better deal for their money from a three-hour ball game than from one that lasts only two. Proof is that in close games they root for a tie and extra innings and that more than twice as many fans show up for a doubleheader as would for a single game.)

It is a mark of the emotional maturity of pro-football reporters that they pound their desks and shout in excitement when a man on their team catches a long pass. And it sets them up for all manner of inconveniences. Papa Halas, for example, had a rule that reporters could not enter the portion of the clubhouse in which his players dressed. This does not mean he prohibited his large charges from talking to reporters. It's just that the newspapermen who cheered his team to victory, rah, rah, had to cool their heels in an antechamber until the players, fully dressed, came dashing out on their way to see their wives and girl friends, who, football custom decrees, they have been separated from since Friday. Since this is Sunday and some urgency exists, the reporter usually has just about enough time to say, "Hello. Have a good time." If the defensive lineman, reeking of Vitalis and perhaps some blood, happened to stop off to explain how he managed to behead the opposition quarterback, it is guaranteed that the middle linebacker, who claimed credit for half the kill, will have slipped by in the confusion (it's hard to tell football players apart if they aren't wearing numbers), thus eliminating the possibility of proving dissension on the defensive team over who killed the quarterback.

This can be an enveloping question as the week goes by. Of course, no one will be sure of anything until the films are checked. I am often amused at the people who discuss the activities of interior linemen with such deep knowledge in barrooms after football games when (1) they were probably drunk by the second quarter and (2) no one knows what the interior linemen were up to until the films are studied for two days—in slow motion. ("How was the honeymoon?" says the coach to his returning assistant coach. "Don't know," assistant answers. "Haven't seen the films yet.") In the meantime, men like Halas have effectively deprived the newspapers of their *right to know*. Why do they put up with it?

Several reasons. One is that newspaper management doesn't know what's going on and probably doesn't care. The reporter accepts the limitations put on him because he is so grateful to be around altogether. One old reporter I know actually cried when he was relieved of his football assignment. (The move was made on the ground that a younger man would do a better job. But for the benefit of gerontologists, the young man didn't do any better than the old one. Lack of skill is no respector of age.) Another problem is that the small-boy-with-gaping-mouth approach is *de rigueur* even among supposedly hardheaded editors. If there is any conflict these editors will count the reporter wrong, the golden heroes correct. The most secure reporter will hesitate to bring down the wrath of both a football team and his own top management by rocking a boat. A reporter who works for the Chicago *Daily News* got under the skin of the general manager of a ball club by reporting front-office and on-the-field bumbling and was removed from the job when the general manager complained. The grounds? The reporter was "flaunting" his mistress. How's that for a newspaper abdicating its right to know?

Then there is the recent example of the sports reporter who was throttled to near unconsciousness by a furious Ralph Houk over a mild story which he took to be a knock The reporter never reported the incident in his newspaper or to his sports editor on the ground that he didn't want anybody to know he was not getting along with the Yankee manager. And he didn't want anybody to know because he was afraid he would be taken off the ball club

Finally there is the real possibility that the newspaper needs the team more than the team needs the newspaper. The Shector Theory of Cycles in Sports has it that, when a sport is on the up wave of its cycle, it doesn't need help, not from newspapers anyway. If there were to be a surge in interest in cockroach racing, it could be declared illegal and fattening and it would still thrive in back rooms all over America. On the other hand, there has never been a sport or fad—roller derby, Friday night TV fights, the hula hoop, the stock market—which hasn't had a down cycle. The best time to kick a good man is when he's down. Newspapers, had they been run by people intelligent enough to plan ahead, could have set ground rules when times were difficult. Relations with the upstart American Football League have been distinctly easier for the press than they were with the older NFL. Now that there has been a merger of the two leagues, however, and Joe Namath has won a Super Bowl, I suspect the people in the AFL, especially the most successful ones, will pick up the worst habits of the other league. Public-relations-conscious Pete Rozelle, Commissioner of the merged leagues, has had to warn several coaches that they cannot bar accredited reporters from their dressing rooms, but coaches often do it anyway. Besides, there is more than one way to make a man's job difficult. It is the way of the sporting world; the indecent drives out the decent; the stupid, the intelligent.

There are some exceptions to this unhappy rule. There will, fortunately, always be some few men too intrinsically decent to get some sort of scrotal kick out of knocking about some elderly sportswriter who has been drinking too much free whiskey for too many years. These men will always be aware that football is a game, a business sure, but unimportant in the scheme of American life. Football, they will understand, is an entertainment, no more. Such a man is Sonny Werblin, who made his first fortune building the Music Corporation of America, the theatrical agency. It was not an accident of time or ball park, as some would have it, that Werblin bought the New York Jets from Harry Wismer, the storied radio announcer (who greeted everybody he saw with a hearty "Congratulations!" on the ground that if he didn't know why, they probably did), and moved them to Shea Stadium that he brought not only the Giants, but the entire NFL to its knees. It took him only four years to effect a merger and, when it came, he could howl that the terms were not so good as he thought they should be. What this proves is that everybody else must have been doing something wrong. But then Werblin didn't have a thorough grounding in the sports business. He even believed in *paying* for advertising. In the end, though, Werblin had to sell his interest in the Jets and he no longer owned them when they won their first championship. Pity.

The Giants, on the other hand, are a clammy organization which has a tendency to hire rude publicity men. The club seems willing to become sort of a fatherly patron to one man from each newspaper (providing his stories are sufficiently innocuous) while adopting an insipid columnist or two along the way. At bottom, though, Giant management has the kind of suspicion of newspapermen that bookmakers have of police. No doubt Wellington Mara, who runs the team now, comes by this feeling naturally, since Tim Mara, who bought the franchise for 500 dollars in 1925, was a well-known and highly respected turf accountant.

The Giants even have a house man of the cloth around, an earnest Father Dudley, to give his blessings before each game. This raises only a tiny question. If God is on the Giants' side, should the Bears demand a handicap?

After the columnists and baseball and football writers, the sports-department hierarchy gets a little blurred. It is rather clear at the bottom, however, where one finds the people who cover dog racing, harness racing and, for the most part, horse racing. If these are sports, Attila the Hun was a humanitarian. Proof can be neatly and simply obtained by removing the pari-mutuel machines and counting the people who would come to watch the beautiful horses run around. A cross-country foot race in the rain would draw more. Racing may be the sport of kings, but there aren't many kings around anymore.

Still, sports sections give an enormous amount of space to racing. Possibly there is some sort of public service in printing pages of agate entries and results. I do not believe, however, that it is the function of the newspaper to provide this service. Moreover, I suspect it's a service that few people desire. Even the casual bettor will seek more specialized information from the *Racing Form* and various scratch sheets. I would, if I were running a newspaper— the only thing that has separated me from this long-standing ambition has been about 50 million dollars- -provide the only information bettors really want in newspapers— selections. Even at that, I would feel I was practicing a particularly vicious form of pandering which, like the worst kind of pimp, takes the money and does not deliver the goods. For racing selections are frauds. The best handicapper will, in his good years, come out even. In an ordinary year he will lose a lot. In a bad year he will have to hock his wife and kids.

It is, I believe, both immoral and unnecessary for newspapers to run all this racing agate. The New York *Daily Mirror,* which died famous for the volume of its agate selections, entries and results (and also for its remarkable ability to sell 800,000 papers a day while attracting no advertising), is an excellent case in point. It is, however, a characteristic of the American press to refuse to learn from mistakes or Lucky Bucks. Indeed, one of the first official acts of most new managing editors is to increase the space given to racing. This has the usual effects upon circulation—none at all. Horseplayers may buy newspapers, but I'm not sure they're people. And if they are people, advertisers know they are people without money. That's what killed the *Mirror;* that and merit. No newspaper ever had such good reason to die or was missed less.

As for those who make their living writing about horse racing, they are, by and large, a lost lot. Hang around a racetrack every day and you soon become a victim of the system. The system is the ten-percent bite put on each bet by the city, state and track. Put a dollar through the windows ten times and it doesn't just come out as a mere shadow of its former self; it has totally disappeared. Nor does the machine have the decency to burp.

Racetracks make it convenient for reporters to lose their money. They put betting machines in the press boxes. They have been known to give reporters revolving credit of as much as 1,000 dollars so he'll have something to gamble with or take home to buy milk, whichever he counts as more important. Everything is easy at the track —gambling, eating, drinking, snacking—everything but the reporting. Horse owners and trainers are largely a reticent and suspicious lot. Jockeys and harness drivers are distant, avoid controversy and, one suspects, truth, at all costs. No one is willing to discuss the central fact of his business—the betting. It's like a politician's refusing to talk about votes. But how can a jockey tell a newspaperman that the owner of a horse didn't want to push it so that later on, when it won, it would pay a good price?

At the trotting tracks it is the custom of reporters to interview the winning driver of the feature race on an open phone, with everybody but God plugged in. You're going to get a lot of nothing but platitude that way. But everybody settles for that because the drivers' quarters are so far away from the press box it takes an intrepid reporter indeed (and a young one) to make the trek. It's much easier to stay in the press box and let some publicity flack fill you in.

I do not, by the way, include among the faults of racing writers their inability to come up with accounts of fixed races. This is something the district attorney has problems with and he has the power of subpoena. The laws of libel being what they are, it is difficult for a reporter even to hint that he saw something he didn't think was kosher. If the fans rip out a couple of tote boards in anger, however, he may indicate that *they* thought something wasn't on the level.

Still, the people who run the racetracks try to make things so comfortable for the writers that they won't go looking for trouble. It is hard to stumble upon a good story in the press box. The racing beat is, as a result, both delicious and impossible. Largely hedonistic men who know their careers are behind them, or used-up old gentlemen with no place to go in the business abound in the newspaper division of the racetrack money factories. Consequently the copy that emerges is so inconsequential that no one reads it. And this is just fine with the people who write it.

Why do newspapers carry these articles? I suspect that it's tradition at work again. Also there are some particularly high-powered press agents at work here. Roosevelt Raceway on Long Island had, for example, in Joey Goldstein, as gifted a young press agent as there was in this country. (He resigned recently to set up his own public-relations firm.) And good press agents know how to lean on sports editors. Some of this leaning is subtle, some about as subtle as one of George Weiss' steak dinners. Racetracks have elaborate means of entertaining newspapermen—as the trotting scandal of 1959 during which huge Florida hotel bills paid by the tracks for reporters became public, revealed. Make the sports editor or his assistant a regular patron of this entertainment— cocktails, dinner, good conversation, even a junket to Europe from time to time—and he must of necessity think it's an important scene. If it's important, he will see that it's covered. There is, in fact, nothing to cover and no one is more aware of this than track publicity men. Yet papers all over the country regularly assign men to write daily stories about the goings-on at the racetracks. One might with more profit cover a floating crap game.

When there is something to cover, one must wonder about the kind of coverage that's provided. When Brooklyn District Attorney Aaron Koota announced a grand-jury investigation of possible fixing of races at New York's harness tracks, there were many stories written which criticized Koota as a publicity-grabbing wretch. Seldom have so few been defended by so many. The tracks were even able to buy full-page advertisements quoting critics of the DA.

"Get the guilty parties and stop making a production out of it." *Newsday* (L.I.) August 30, 1966.

"[Call your witnesses] before the Grand Jury without the three-ring circus and the publicity. . . . *Then* hold your press conference and let the world know about it. Such an approach would only hurt the guilty—not the innocent, too." *Newsday,* August 31, 1966.

"[Why is it that in harness racing] it seems the way to do it is to smear everyone in the business and make political capital of a thread of evidence?" Long Island *Press,* September 4, 1966.

"Koota was quick to emphasize that the summoning of these drivers was no reflection on them and in no way implicated them." New York *Post,* August 29, 1966.

Koota was unquestionably overzealous in some of his announcements to the press, but this is a familiar phenomenon of the American press. It even happens during murder investigations; witness the Supreme Court reversal of the conviction of Sam Shepard of the killing of his wife in Cleveland in 1954. What *is* unusual is the sight of newspapers berating a DA for giving out information to them. The concern for the judicial process is so notably absent in so many newspapers that one must be suspicious of it in this case.

Between the writer of professional football and the racing writer there comes a motley assortment of golf writers, college-sports writers, track and field writers, boxing writers, bowling writers, automobile writers, etc. The etc. men cover things like hockey, tennis, college rowing, and fishing. These are young fellows on the way up, old fellows on the way down, or wild specialists, trapped at great expense by a publisher who happens to have an interest in the field (hunting and fishing, say). Here again, though, there is little care given to the copy these writers get into the newspaper. The automobile writer, for example, can have a high old time riding around in cars that have been loaned to him, free of cost, by auto companies. And he can enjoy junkets to watch auto races all over the world. But he has to be careful never to knock cars of companies which advertise in his newspaper. That's why the book which changed the automobile business, Ralph Nader's *Dangerous at Any Speed,* was not written by a newspaperman.

How far, actually, should this right-to-know premise go? What is a newspaper *entitled* to know? A fair answer, it seems to me would be this: From the public or quasi-public official, say the president of a utility, *everything.* From everybody else, *nothing.* Anybody who doesn't need the media—and politicians, entertainers, ball players and certain entrepreneurs do—is advised to keep silent. Distortion, inaccuracy and sheer stupidity stand between the newspaper reader and fact. I am not sure I disagree with a confrere who believes that *nobody* should talk for publication unless he is paid, cash in advance. This is not so outrageous as it sounds at first. Magazines have realized the rectitude of this position for years. "How I Lived Through a Walk in Central Park at Midnight," by Primo Carnera as told to Thomas Hoving is paid for in fees to both Carnera and Hoving. *Life* signed up the astronauts for an astronomical amount of money. The Associated Press once found it necessary to buy the story of a miner trapped in a shaft where he saw God and other things. There is, among magazines, an informal agreement not to pay subjects unless they are involved in what are called "signers" or first-person articles. What the magazines do about that is cheat. If they want the article badly enough, they will pay.

Well, then, shouldn't the athlete expect to get paid for talking to a newspapper reporter? Obviously some think so. I count it as one of my most amusing experiences in the little world of sports that a used-up old baseball player once asked me for money in return for the privilege of chatting with him on the steps of a dugout in, of all places, Osaka, Japan.

I was in Japan covering the Olympics in 1964 (partly at my own expense, which is the way a lot of newspapers operate), when the *Saturday Evening Post* cabled to ask me for an article on Japanese baseball. I flew up to Osaka from Tokyo for brief talks with Gordon Windhorn, who had been a spear carrier for the Yankees for a while, and Daryl Spencer, who had a mediocre career with the Giants. Windhorn was glad to see a visitor from the U.S. We spent the afternoon in his home, chatting about old times and about his experience in Japanese baseball. Then I went to the ball park to meet Spencer. The park was alien. The infield had no grass. The manager spoke Japanese and wore an inscrutable look and sandals. And the first thing Spencer said to me was, "How much are you paying me?" I admired his courage, but I had to tell him I was prepared to pay what he was worth, nothing. This established a quite satisfactory relationship.

The thinking may seem somewhat twisted, but there is logic to it: I believe that justice demands that while a coal miner, lost in a mine shaft, might well demand payment for his story, the ball player must not. It should be clear that the ball player is, after all, only one figure in a large entertainment business. By cooperating with the press, he is helping to perpetuate interest in the medium in which he makes his living. No press, no interest, no baseball, no twenty-two-year-old shit-kicker making 35 grand a year at an animal occupation which requires less talent in many ways than it takes for a girl to remove her clothes in a burlesque show. In many respects the girl is a more interesting person and more worthy of the extraordinary space the shit-kicker gets. Like a quickie interview with Virginia Bell, 44-inch-bust burlesque queen. "It's a big deal to have a big bust today, but when I was young it wasn't that big a deal and I had a lot of embarrassment. I wore a coat all the time, even in summer. . . . When I'm through with this business, I'm going to have an operation. I'm going to make them smaller." Few baseball players have ever said anything that touching.

Not that I found it particularly generous of Miss Bell to be this open about her feelings. She, like the ball player, is in an entertainment industry. When she talks about herself, she is helping herself and her industry.

Obviously the relationship between newspapers and sporting teams is somewhat peculiar. In their own way newspapers support these teams. If it were not for the newspapers in New York and a gallant band of semi-unemployed baseball reporters, there is serious doubt whether the New York Mets would have been born. Make no mistake, this makes the Mets and the newspapers *partners*. In that case the newspapers are not just entitled to know, they are entitled to *participate*.

Therefore I don't think there should ever be any closed clubhouse meetings. Nor should newspapers be prohibited from stationing men in the dugout to record for posterity and today's pointy-heads the glamorous and dirty insults ball players hurl at each other. When professional sports stand themselves far away from the press, one must suspect they are doing something immoral or illegal.

Why should sporting teams insist upon operating as though they were nations? A secret revealed about a sporting team will not cause the dropping of a hydrogen bomb. These teams are, in a way, property of the people who pay to see them perform. And they are bedfellows of newspapers in that they are in the same business—entertainment.

It's a partnership, but it's not equal. Newspapers give sporting teams millions of dollars' worth of free space. In return they get the back of the hand. The *least* the team can do is pay the traveling expenses of the men who cover. *Esquire* magazine will permit a Hollywood company to pay transportation and expenses for a writer doing a story about a movie being made in Madrid. This has not corrupted the magazine. Movie companies are sophisticated enough to be grateful for *any* publicity. In fact, they often arrange fancy junkets for newspaper, magazine and television people, fly them to the Congo, wine and dine them on the finest antelope silver bullets can shoot, and ask only that an occasional story be sent back home. It doesn't have to be a favorable story. Even one about how tough antelope meat is. Just spell the name of the movie right.

If movie companies understand this, why don't ball clubs? The answer can only be that newspapers insist upon being pushed around. One has only to observe a slack-jawed newspaper executive being led around by his "man" at the ball park, two young sons trailing behind carrying baseballs and pens, a look of foolish delight on his face, to understand that the mesmerizing influence of hero worshiping has penetrated the highest echelons of the business. Some of these executives would pay their own money for the privilege of traveling with a ball club. No wonder they think it's fair that the newspaper should pay for its own men. Indeed, if there is an argument and the sportsman grows abusive, the newspaper executive is delighted. Being told off by a sporting celebrity is like being insulted by Toots Shor. There is a prestige value to it.

In the best of all worlds the newspapers would approach sports the way it does any other news story. It should be possible, I believe, to cover a baseball team only once in a while rather than every day. Obviously a lot of games are not worth any expensive newspaper space. If baseball teams want everyday coverage, let them buy the space and hire their own men to write it. They wouldn't think of allowing an objective reporter to broadcast their games. They hire their own. We might then be treated to twin stories on some days, one by the baseball team's flack, the other by a reporter who, the day before, might have covered a bus drivers' strike. Good reporters can cover anything, certainly a baseball game. There need be no sportswriting division as such. At best it dulls a man's brain to be around nothing but sports. At worst it corrupts him.

I think any specialization in the newspaper business is wrong. The man sentenced to hang around police headquarters all his life begins to think like a cop. The man who covers city hall every day becomes so interested in his card game he will not, in the immortal words of Eliza

68

Doolittle, move his bloomin' arse. Some of the best reporters in the country move to different assignments almost every day. They might stay with one story for a while, but when it's finished, they go on to a new subject. This helps make a good reporter better, because it keeps his level of interest high.

This simple logic appears to be beyond the ability of sports editors to comprehend. When faced with crisis, they head blindly on some old well-worn path, like lemmings to the sea. As an example, take the case of the discovery of professional football. When pro football was a sort of stepchild of the sports section, it could not break into the paper until the season started and then, usually, it was back-of-the-section stuff until the World Series was over. An interest in the game grew and managing editors suddenly became aware that there was a pro game out there some place, sports editors went headlong in the opposite direction. Now they couldn't print enough about the pros. They began assigning men to the training camps in July. That's like putting five men on a politician who hopes to be nominated to run for mayor on the Republican ticket in a city which hasn't elected anything but Democrats for 65 years. Nothing happens in football training camps except some shoulder separations. To pay a newspaperman a salary to cover that nonsense while the ancient and honorable art of muckraking, possibly the highest function of a good newspaper, is left to dry up and die from indifference, is to be dishonest to whatever traditions the business has. Less football coverage and more muckraking and our newspapers might start looking a little less like *Playbill* and a lot more like newspapers.

I am not suggesting that we eliminate sports sections altogether. Interest in sports in this country runs too deeply for that. Besides, it is possible for a well-written sports story to brighten a day. I am proposing, however, a re-examination of the way information about sports is presented. "This is the kind of shit they want" was the favorite expression of a sportswriter I knew and he said it every time he closed his typewriter after giving his day's work a 30-minute brush-off. It's the kind of shit they get, but I'm not sure at all it's what they want. Even if the public does, by some quirk of ignorance, insist upon bad sports journalism, that is no reason it has to be provided. Newspapers have the right to be tastemakers. Let television pursue mediocrity; newspapers should want to lead toward excellence. Instead newspapers are catch-penny stragglers, dancing to any off-key tune that comes along.

At bottom, sportswriting need be no different than any other good newspaper writing. At its best, it could be much better. What it needs to be is entertaining, incisive, informative, revealing and intelligent enough to appeal to an adult brain. Instead, what we get, mostly, are stories and columns written by lazy men who are typing, not writing; filling space with clichés and inconsequential blatherings that are often illiterate to boot. We get statistical claptrap that is almost a parody of itself. We get pointless rambling. We get men who are helpless with the language, who could not, if they were ever to be assaulted by a thought, express it clearly.

We also get a disturbing conservatism that acts as a force against colorful people in the sports business and against good sportswriting. When Cassius Clay first came along, innocent of the Muslim religion for which he had been so sharply condemned, he was talkative, funny, bright, indifferent to the American queasiness about braggadocio, a charming, handsome outgoing, ambitious young man. He was fun to be with, amusing to write about and wrote poems—silly doggerel, really—that had some startling rhymes. He was immediately condemned in the press as a "big mouth," "wise guy," "know-it-all" and braggart. It was also said about him that he could not fight. A lot of well-known sportswriters have been forced to change that opinion, but now they all say they knew it all the time.

Other interesting sports figures have been similarly attacked. The imaginative Bill Veeck, who made it an adventure for people to come to his ball park, was condemned as a show-biz show-off who didn't care about "The Game." Frank Lane, who kept the pot boiling with interesting trades during the years in which the Yankees were

70

making the American League a stupefyingly dull place, was attacked as a compulsive, psychotic trader; also, of course, a show-off. When Casey Stengel was not a winning manager in his youth (about fifty) in Boston, he was hit by an automobile and had a leg mashed up. A sportswriter wrote that it was the best thing that ever happened to the Boston Braves. At the same time secretive, sly George Weiss, who kept himself aloof from the press and the public, while he drove the American League to the brink of ruin, was praised everywhere as a genius. The bright, the colorful, the new are always attacked by the oldline sportswriters. Change threatens them. Noisy personalities make them work too hard.

The old-line sports reporter likes to say that the way to handle a story is just to tell what happened. Since he is largely incapable of understanding subtleties, much less convey them, he deals in a kind of simpleminded world of numbers, full of blacks and whites, rights and wrongs, winners and losers. Yet there is very little that a newspaper can tell about a sporting event that is not general knowledge by the time the paper hits the street. Who hit the home run, who scored the winning touchdown is fairly dull stuff anyway, of major interest only to the man who did it and, perhaps, his wife. What is of greater moment is the man behind the touchdown. What emotions, what conflcts, if any, were involved? How did the play develop? Was it, as so many things are in sport, an accident? Luck, Branch Rickey was fond of saying, is the residue of design. More likely it's the residue of putting the ball in motion. Was this the situation? Was there a feeling of triumph, of vengeance, of letdown? Had anybody made any important mistakes? And, most important of all, did anything funny happen? Is there an amusing way to tell the story? This is the only way for a newspaper to beat television. That's because TV is so financially involved with sporting events it has decided it cannot afford to reveal the stupid, seamy or ludicrous things about the game. It hides the warts, Newspapers should not.

There are days when a routine ball game is played with all the enthusiasm of a yawn. If a city-desk reporter were

71

involved, he could call in and say no story, nothing happened. A sports reporter should be able to do the same. No news today. Why clutter up valuable newsprint with accounts of meaningless, dull events? If one asks, one is told, "That's the way we've always done it." Year after year, in fact, sports, sports editors will search back issues before a big event to see "how we did last year."

This kind of foolishness is not confined to newspapers, by the way. During the Tokyo Olympics I tried for a month to find out why no bus was being provided for newspapermen who wanted to cover the marathon, a 26-mile race that had begun to attract a lot of attention in 1964 when Abebe Bikila, the barefoot Ethiopian, won it. This time there was an American, Buddy Edelen, who was given a slight chance. No American had won this race for 60 years. So a lot of press people wanted to follow the race as it wound through the streets of Tokyo. For a month we were met with stony stares and "So sorry, do not understand." On the day before the race I finally pried out the reason there would be no bus. There had been no bus in Rome in 1960. Damn scrutable, these Japanese.

So are most sportswriters. They are transparently interested in keeping things smooth and quiet and uninteresting, Worse, they are dewy-eyed *fans* of the people they write about. There is a look certain of them get on their faces when they are talking to famous athletes—Mickey Mantle, Sandy Koufax, Joe Namath, Arnold Palmer. It's a smile of mindless joy, something like the look a little boy gets on his face when confronted by a can of paint and clean hands. I have seen intelligent young men, even good sportswriters, get this look. It confounded my theory that it was a look of sheer idiocy, but I believe that a man who wears that soft look will never get the hard story. Nor does he have a desire to do so. I suspect when he's wearing that look he is incapable even of thinking clearly. Strange things happen as a result.

I use as example here my adventures with Dodger pitcher Don Drysdale. When the Dodgers and Giants left New York it became the policy of some New York papers

72

to cover them when they came to Philadelphia. (That's because Philadelphia is the cheapest place to reach from New York, except for Hoboken.) It was in Philadelphia one day that, chatting with Drysdale, I asked how he was getting along with the pitching coach and manager. He let loose a tirade of complaints that made rather juicy reading the next day. At this distance what he said is unimportant. The point is that Drysdale was waiting to explode at the right question. The Los Angeles reporters were angry with me and angry at Drysdale because the story broke in New York rather than in Los Angeles. They should have been angry only at themselves for not probing in the right area. The wide-eyed ones with the hero worshipping expression seldom do. And there are a lot of them around.

Another trap of the wide-eyed is the printing of sappy quotes. Just because a sports hero says something, it doesn't mean it is interesting enough to appear in a newspaper. Yet the most inane conversations are printed because the reporter thinks they *must* be important. Arthur Daley is a Pulitzer Prize winning sports columnist for the New York *Times*. A conversation he printed in his column was picked up by the *New Yorker* under the heading: Great Moments in Sport. This is what Daley had written:

"During spring training one year Joe Garagiola was up to his old trick of giving the needle to his one-time St. Louis Cardinal teammate, Stan Musial.

" 'Sometimes I feel sorry for you, Stan,' said Joe, his voice gushing with pseudo sympathy. 'Throughout your career you missed the supreme thrill that us ordinary ballplayers would get every day. It was looking at the lineup card to see if our names were on it. You never had that thrill because you never had to look. You knew you'd be somewhere in the batting order.'

" 'But I still had to check to see where,' said Stan, laughing at him. Musial has always enjoyed joshing with the amusing Garagiola."

We may leave that as our text on sports conversations that need never have been reported.

There are two ways to sum up my feelings about how

sports should be handled by newspapers. The first is to take a broad view of large reforms that need to be made but won't because they are so sweeping as to paralyze the synapses of the newspaper brain. Under this heading I submit:

1. No sportswriters, only reporters. It would be nice for a lad who's been at police headquarters for a month to cover a football game. Just as every sports reporter should know how to handle a city-desk assignment, every city reporter should be able to write well enough to cover a sports event.

2. Change the amount of coverage. It is not necessary to cover every baseball game, every hockey game, every basketball game. If an editor is nervous, he can send a man to every event with instructions to write a story only if there is a *good one*. Or to write one in any event and leave it to his own judgment to spindle stories that are not worth running in the newspaper. Obviously, too, a game between Minnesota and Oakland may well be more interesting than one between the home team and the White Sox. Sports are a national scene. Home teams count less than good competitions. So if a newspaper would attempt to forget its penury and send reporters to out-of-town events that looked as though they might be of unusual interest, sports sections would become far less parochial. If the editor guessed wrong, at worst the correspondent could wire back: "No news today."

3. Rotate columnists. If a man is good enough to write a good sports column, he is good enough to do a column on other subjects. This will broaden his outlook. If it turns out he's not good enough to write politics, which is, after all, our national game, then he's not good enough to write sports. And wouldn't a Washington columnist be less inclined to be pontifical after a month covering the Cubs? Besides, it's not a good idea to make a man cover sports every day of his life. It rots the edges of his soul.

4. Establish a training program. Beware of the kid who comes to the sports department with a great love of sports and games. He may have an amazing store of knowledge of obscure facts, including things like Mickey

Mantle's wife's maiden name, but he will louse up your sports pages with worshipful statistics if you give him the chance. Take on the lad who wants to be a newspaperman. This is bad enough. Teach him to cover a baseball game as he would a fire or a political convention. Sometimes they amount to the same thing.

5. If the newspaper is indeed a marginal one financially, as so many are, let the sports organizations pay expenses and use the money saved to elevate salaries. Sporting people have surrounded themselves with all the accouterments of importance—flacks, off-the-record press conferences, the whole *spiel*. But it is sheer sophistry. A baseball team is not a U. S. Senator. It is no different than a movie company or a manufacturer of widgets. If they want publicity, make them pay for it, buy space, pay the expenses of reporters who travel with them. And while we're at it, let's try assigning a reporter to rehearsals of new shows coming to Broadway. It might prove a great deal more worthwhile than spring training with the Kansas City Athletics.

6. Have a realistic pay scale. This is getting to the very guts of the newspaper business. Good men can't be hired for a hundred dollars a week or kept with a top of two hundred and fifty. At a press-association meeting in Chicago in mid-1966, R. W. Haverfield, placement director of the University of Missouri School of Journalism, said that figures he compiled showed that most young men going into industry out of college could expect to start at 150 dollars per week. A typical newspaper job, he noted, started at 100 dollars. And a youngster at the meeting noted he had been paid 110 dollars a week for greasing trucks before going to college. He said: "After four years in school, I feel I have a raise coming." On the other hand, Frank B. Gilbreth, assistant publisher of the Charleston *News and Courier,* has written that newspaper pay scales are fine. The only thing lacking, he said, was the prestige of a public-relations job, meaning expense accounts, golf-club memberships and a company car. Did that mean he proposed providing his reporters with those accouterments? Nah. His idea was to give them a private office and a secretary.

At this point in time I well know that these reforms cannot be made. But is there any method for improving the kind of material being churned out by our newspapers? The answer is an unqualified maybe. If I ran a sports department, there are some things I would and probably could do given even the present rigidities. It must be understood that large changes cannot be made because of the system which newspapers have permitted to evolve. They have some irrevocable commitments. Because of bad judgment, foolishness and lack of attention to what is supposed to be their job, newspaper executives have permitted a proliferation of elderly men in their shops who have neither the desire nor the ability to do creative work. This is especially true in sports departments. What is more, these people are, and quite rightly, under the protection of their union, the American Newspaper Guild. This union has many faults, but the union did not hire these men. That was done by the little hatchets of cement-headed executives. These poor old employees grew up in the newspaper business, had families, grew old. One does not discard them the way a baseball club discards a thirty-four-old man after paying him too much money for 12 years. These men didn't make enough money. Many ruined their livers drinking free whiskey. They have nowhere to go. If their skills as newspapermen are minimal, their talents in other directions are nonexistent. We have to live with them, even if they are to be full-time pensioners. This is the price newspapers must pay for grievous errors of the past. With those imposed limitations kept in mind, this then is my second list of reforms. the possible ones.

1. Engage a literate sports editor. Even if this sounds like obvious advice, it isn't. There have been many men who for years ran sports sections around the country who were functional illiterates, men who couldn't construct an English sentence, much less understand the nuances of good writing. This is the result again of indifference in the top levels of management.

2. Let the sports editor run the sports section. Many managing editors believe they can run the sports depart-

ment in their spare time better than the sports editor can do it full time. When they are right, it is time to change sports editors. It is practice in many newspapers to permit the sports editor to become a sort of errand boy for the managing editor. That's because the ME's son has just reached the age of seven and developed a whole string of theories about sports, sports sections and the men in the sports department. The result is that the section is being run by a hot little seven-year-old mind. Many of them read just that way.

3. Allow the sports editor to do the scouting for help as well as the hiring. In many newspapers, when a vacancy occurs, a relative of the city editor fills it, or the first idiot to walk in the door looking for a job. It's not difficult to scout. If the editor can read, he need only to subscribe to newspapers, especially the growing suburban newspapers, around the country, keeping his eye on the bylines which are doing the interesting work. It is not difficult to recognize talent.

4. Give the young people who start out as copyboys a chance to move up, but don't lose your head about it. If they can't do the job, tell them so. Let them seek other fields. Of course, one must be damned certain that the man who's making these vital decisions about lives and careers knows what he's about.

5. Rotate assignments. Nobody, not the best writer, not the worst, should be bogged down covering only one or two sports or organizations. Identification with one team is bad for the newspaper and bad for the reporter. A good sportswriter should be able to cover all sports and a fire as well.

6. Rotate inside assignments. A sour copy editor can reduce to flatness in six quick strokes of his fat pencil the livest, brightest copy ever written. If the copy editor must, for six months of the year, suffer the agonies of creation himself, he will treat other people's copy with respect. Conversely, even the best of writers will be renewed by a taste of the drudgery of desk work.

7. Give young people a crack at writing columns. Columnists aren't born, they are made. Each man on the

staff should be good enough to write a column once a week. If he isn't, the column will show it quickly. A good column by a staff man keeps the regular columnist on his toes.

8. Broaden coverage. Not only the sports that have press agents are good sports. It might be a good idea to send a grown man to a high-school track once in a while so he could write about the sights, sounds, smells and the parents on the sidelines.

9. Help stamp out the telephone-book of journalism. This school holds that the best thing a newspaper can do is print names. Then the names will run out and buy the paper. Thus we have lists of club-tournament golf scores, little-league box scores and the like. The telephone book may be widely distributed, but it's read very selectively. So are newspapers. And people do not read lists of names unless they are composed of crash victims.

10. Sports are people. What happened in the game is not enough to grab the reader's attention. I am not certain that sports, as has been suggested, is ordinary people under extraordinary stress. But I do know that the only thing everybody has in common is interest in other people. Even in events of relative importance—a World Series game or a heavyweight championship fight—the participants need to be reported about more than the action. Television shows the action. Movies show the action. Newspapers must show the people.

11. Finally, and probably the most important, sports are games. Children play them in the street. By all means take them less seriously than I have in this chapter.

There are, I am certain everyone knows, important exceptions to all the broad condemnations I have made in this chapter. There *are* sports entrepreneurs who understand what their proper relationship with newspapers should be. There *are* athletes who are intelligent enough to understand what the press means to them. There *are* good newspapers (alas, not many). There *are* many excellent, dedicated newspapermen who do suprisingly good jobs under most difficult circumstances. There *are*

78

good sportswriters. Those who do understand, those who are intelligent about the press and sports, those who are capable, dedicated, accomplished, know I do not direct my ire at them. On the other hand, those who take offense at what I say are probably right to do so.

## 2 The Tube Triumphant

TELEVISION HAS TWO THINGS. IT HAS MONEY. IT ALSO has the ability to bring to the spectator a close, intimate view of sports that he could not attain even if he actually attended the field of contest. The first gives life. The second contains seeds of destruction. Television is like some gentle, mindless robot carrying sports tenderly in its arms to the top of the mountain and then over the cliff.

So where it is possible to discuss the relationship between sports and newspapers in this country, it is not possible to discuss the relationship between sports and television. Because they have become so inextricably entwined that sports *are* television and television *is* sports. As poorly as newspapers do their job there remains at least a thin line of journalistic separation between the newspaper and the sporting event. There is none between television and sports. Television *buys* sports. Television *supports* sports. It moves in with its money and supports sports in a style to which they had to become accustomed and then, like a bought lady, sports become so used to luxurious living they cannot extricate themselves. So, slowly at first, but inevitably, television tells sports what to do. It *is* sports and it runs them the way it does most other things, more flamboyantly than honestly.

The buying process, once subtle, the way it was with boxing, has become straightforward. That is, there are a lot of zeroes following the dollar sign. Important money. There is no doubt, for example, that the American Foot-

79

ball League would have died were it not for the money that the National Broadcasting Company poured into it.

Here's how that worked. The AFL was organized in 1959 to go into competition with the established National Football League. The NFL, having chewed up and swallowed a couple of previous efforts at competition—notably something called the All-America Conference, the remaining evidence of which are the Baltimore, San Francisco and Cleveland franchises—was unconcerned. Certainly the five-year television contract which the AFL signed with the American Broadcasting Company for 1,785,000 dollars a year, or just over 200,000 dollars for each of the eight teams, was not imposing. In modern sports economics this is barely better than nothing, especially since the AFL was going to have to compete for talent coming out of college with the wealthy NFL.

Of course, the AFL had some important money backing it. Lamar Hunt, owner of the Kansas City club, and Bud Adams, owner of the Houston club, are not the kind of men who have to ask what anything costs. And in 1963, when Sonny Werblin took over the New York Jets (then the Titans) from the inspired bumbling of ex-sportscaster Harry Wismer, it was apparent that the AFL was settling down for a long war. It was a war it nevertheless could not win without serious money help from television. This did not appear to be forthcoming. ABC, plagued by financial problems, did not seem willing to pay an enormous amount of money for what was a relatively inferior football product.

In the meantime, the NFL contract with CBS was expiring and NBC began to cast envious glances at the NFL ratings. Even more important than the ratings was the prestige involved. "The image of a network," says Roone Arledge, vice-president in charge of sports for ABC, "is built on news and sports." It also doesn't hurt Sunday evenings ratings to have something on Sunday afternoon that almost everybody watches. So NBC decided it wanted the NFL. That was fine with Pete Rozelle, the NFL commissioner. He let all the networks bid.

Arledge, a round, redheaded man with piercing dark

eyes he can't hide behind thick eyeglasses, treasures the memory of that 1964 bid meeting. "The intrigue that was going on," Arledge recalls with a grin, "you wouldn't believe. There was a thing in there [the bid specifications] that we picked up, also CBS, that made us think we could do doubleheaders. We checked and Pete Rozelle said yes, we could. NBC hadn't seen this. So we had the bidding, which was like a confrontation of heads of state. Outside there were all sorts of reporters, lights and cameras. Pete shuffled the envelopes with the bids and as luck would have it, he opened NBC's first. Their bid was 21 and a half million [for two years]. That was more than twice what it had been before. They were absolutely confident that was a closeout bid, that nobody could come close. Then Pete read ours and we were 26 and a half million. We had them beaten by five million dollars. Then CBS took it with over 28."

Poor NBC. The network not only had egg on its face, it was like a girl who had just broken up with her boy friend, wondering what to do with its Sunday afternoons. Also like a girl, it started shopping around for a new boy friend. The AFL was available.

The people at NBC may be avaricious, and they may have been dumb about reading Rozelle's specifications, but they are shrewd businessmen for all of that. They knew that merely paying the AFL what it was worth in order to broadcast its games would not do the trick. What the AFL needed was enough money to go out and do battle for future stars with the NFL. To that end NBC decided to give—subsidize might be a better word—each club to the tune of a million a year for the next five years. The package cost some 38,000,000 dollars and it not only helped make a lot of youths just out of college wealthy (Joe Namath's 400,000 dollars is one example), it changed the course of professional football history. "We couldn't have competed without television," said Joe Foss, then Commissioner of the AFL.

The AFL competed so well that in 1966 it was able to effect a merger with the NFL. Not only was this a recognition of years of effort, it immediately cut down the expenses of *all* pro football teams. With a common draft of college players nobody was able to walk out of college into a million dollars. It may not have been nice for the young players, but it was delicious to the owners. Now, instead of giving away all that nice TV money, they could keep it. Not only that, there was more and more of it. For its last contract with the NFL, CBS shelled out 41.6 million dollars for two years. A survey by *Broadcasting* magazine not long ago showed that the TV industry paid 13.9 million dollars for the rights to televise college and professional football in 1963. By 1968 this figure had grown to 54.7 million dollars.

But a funny thing has been happening. Now that football—the collegiate variety, too—has become so dependent on television (Art Modell, owner of the Cleveland Browns: "Without television I'd be out of business"), it has been finding certain strings attached. As the price of broadcasting football went up, a way had to be found to recover this enormous boodle. The way was simple. More television.

"If you spend that much money," says Arledge, one of the leading exponents of spending large amounts of money on sporting events, to the extent of driving up the price of the Cotton Bowl from 200,000 dollars to 450,000 dollars and tossing in a gratuitous 500,000 dollars to make sure he'd get the rights to the Mexican Olympics, "you're selling to get your skin back. If you can't sell ads for 40,000 dollars a minute, you say well, if we put on twice as many games we might find people who will spend 20,000 dollars a minute. Ultimately we're going to bore America to death with football as we did with Westerns."

Everybody understands this. Just as everybody understands that the population explosion will one day kill us all. But nobody is willing to do anything about it, least of all Arledge.

It's strange, because the NFL had long prided itself on the way it handled television. Under Commissioner Bert Bell, NFL football bloomed because he insisted that no team broadcast its home games. That mean if you wanted to see a football game on the day there was one in your city, you had to buy a ticket. Eventually it came to pass that in many cities you couldn't buy a ticket even if you wanted to. But this is no longer the case in many places. And you can see at least two games, often four on TV every Sunday. In New York City, where once a football fan could see only seven Giant road games on the tube, it was possible during the 1966 season to see 45 professional games. And that figure does not include preseason, postseason and championship games. By 1968 this figure had grown to 65. Counting college and post-season games, this made an astonishing, home-wrecking total of 95 games available on the tube. This is saturation unto boredom.

I will therefore predict that the popularity of professional football has topped out. (It happened with college football some years back.) I predict that pro football is in a down cycle and at the bottom of it television will be a dropout, the way it was with boxing and the roller derby. Not that I think that pro football is going the way of the hula hoop. Nor do I know what it needs to do in order to go into a new rising cycle, although I suspect that pay TV may one day be important in this area. In any case, I believe that pro football has provided television with another victim.

In the end it will be television that deserts football. The handwriting is on the wall. Not long ago Edward M. Stern, vice-president of Foote, Cone and Belding, a Chicago advertising agency, pointed out that "pro football ad costs are surprisingly inefficient on a cost per thousand basis."

That's the way the boys think. They don't talk of the grandeur of sport, of the thrill of competition, of playing the game. They talk of the cost of getting the message to a thousand videots. It's not only their business, it's their way of life. It explains our television wasteland. Stern exhibited a cost per thousand (CPM) chart.

|  | CPM OVERALL | CPM MEN |
|---|---|---|
| NFL | 7.75 | 8.00 |

| AFL | 7.45 | 8.35 |
| Popular night entertainment show | 3.50 | 5.00 |

The message is clear. It's cheaper to sponsor *I Love Lucy*. The law of diminishing returns is setting in. And once the addition of more football games stops working, once the advertisers are satisfied that *The Beverly Hillbillies* will do the job better than football, forget it. The networks will drop pro football quicker than you can say, "That Was the Week That Was," prestige or no prestige. When that happens, it will be up to the game to find its own way. Television will provide no help.

But as long as television has control, it demands even more. And as it becomes evident that television might be losing interest, people who own sporting enterprises will lean more and more to giving television further perquisites. It is ever thus. Once, when a crew from ABC wanted to film the young men who dive off high cliffs into damp handkerchiefs in Acapulco, the divers union, or whatever it was, demanded 100,000 dollars. They were turned down. After lengthy negotiation, they accepted 30 dollars.

Television has made it abundantly clear how it would behave in sports if it had the power to dictate terms. It took a hand in the apparently futile struggles of soccer to make it as a big-time sport in this country and the first thing the boys found out was that soccer has no times out. What follows is a not altogether imaginary conversation in the conference room of a television network:

"For crissakes, Manny. How the hell did you get us into a bind like this? We got a lot of money invested. What are we gonna do, paste the commercials on the backs of the players?

"That's a terrific idea, boss. I wonder why I never thought of it. You're a genius."

"Shut up, Manny."

"Yessir."

"Seymour. Tell me, Seymour. What have you been doing about this thing to earn your 65,000 dollars a year?"

"I been thinking, sir."

"That's nice. Considering how much you get per thought. What have you been thinking?"

"That soccer doesn't have absolutely no times out. When a player is injured and has to be treated on the field, there's a time out."

"How many injuries are there in a game, Seymour?"

"Well, the sad fact is that soccer players are a rather rugged lot. Sometimes there's an injury. Sometimes two. Sometimes none."

"Great. We can sell time on an if basis. General Motors will love us for that."

"Er, boss. Maybe we can arrange to hurt a player every seven and a half minutes. I mean send someone in to trip him. Maybe kick him a couple of times where it won't show. I mean off camera, of course."

"Shut up, Manny."

"Yessir."

"Actually that's not a bad idea, you know. Of course, it's not necessary to actually injure a player. All we have to do is have him act as though he's injured."

"Now you've got it, Seymour. Great. Hermione, get me whatisname, the president of that soccer league, on the telephone."

"You think he'll cooperate?"

"Don't worry about it, Seymour. That's *my* department. He'll cooperate."

If all that sounds rather far-fetched, it's only because it's true. Soccer referee Peter Rhodes confessed just such chicanery to reporters in May of 1967. He said that during the game he was asked to wear an electronic beeper on his shoulder. When a TV executive beeped the beeper, Rhodes signaled an injury. A one-minute commercial here, please.

There was such a flap about this episode that CBS, the network in question (which denies all), announced that in future the *action* of the game would be interrupted for commercials. As a result it is now possible for a TV viewer to miss the only goal scored in a 1-0 soccer game.

Says Arledge: "If you move the starting time of a

football game, or if you ask a college team to play this week instead of that week, I don't think anything has been tampered with. A lot of promoters think that if they make any change to accommodate television they are prostituting themselves. The same people will say that we won't play on this day because we won't draw well against that carnival in town. They think that if you arrange for a game to end at seven o'clock instead of six so that millions and millions of people can see it, you are doing something morally wrong. Yet no one thinks it's morally wrong for baseball to play night games so that people can see them after work.

The fervor and ardor of this kind of statement is impressive. But the innocence of television is not persuasive. Arledge's sweet reason collapses in the face of a bit of history. Commenting about the U.S. Open at Baltusrol in 1967 (TV by ABC), Jack Nicklaus, the eminent golfer, said: "We were all bothered by the late starting time both Saturday and Sunday. It was bad for the players, the gallery, the press and the image of golf—to say nothing of the havoc a brief rain delay would have caused. The only thing it accommodated was television, and I don't think television should rule golf."

It was television which demanded a four-o'clock starting time for baseball's 1967 All-Star game in Anaheim, California, so the Eastern markets could be reached in prime time. The late-afternoon sun made it so difficult for the batters to see, the best hitters in baseball managed to score only three runs in fifteen innings.

It was television that prohibited red-dogging—close pursuit of the passer—in an NFL All-Star game in order to keep the game wide open and, in the opinion of television, more interesting.

It was television which, at a swimming meet, blithely restaged the beginning of a 500-yard free-style event because the cameras had missed the real thing. Viewers were, of course, not told of the fakery.

And it was television which once induced a golfer to lose a TV match in the interests of theatricalism.

Says Bill Russell, player-coach of the Boston Celtics:

"If you don't watch those TV people they will devour you. First they ask you to call time-outs so they can get in their commercials. Then they tell you *when* to call them. Then they want to get into the locker room at half time. Then more and more and more. If you don't put on the brakes they'll tell you when to play."

Television told Russell's Celtics and the New York Knicks to play the first game of their 1969 Eastern Division playoff on Sunday afternoon. Then it put cameras all over the court until Russell had to complain loudly that his players couldn't see the 24-second clock. And afterwards, when Russell was still complaining to the press about the encroachments of the cameras, a TV man came into the dressing room and handed Russell an envelope which he made sure the reporters knew contained Russell's fee for appearing on the tube.

(There was a parenthetical moral nicety involved in this particular TV caper. New Yorkers had been told when they bought tickets to the game that home games would not be televised locally. Since the game was a sellout, ABC, the network involved, prevailed upon the Garden to allow it to televise to this rich market anyway. Public service and all that. There were a lot of howls from ticket holders, though, people who had paid up to ten dollars to see a game they could have seen at home for nothing. Not only that, there were thousands of empty seats because speculators, who expected to make their sales at the last minute, were stuck. There was even a howl from the Garden. Ned Irish, vice-president, complained that ABC had promised not to advertise that it *would* televise in New York and had gone back on its word.)

The fact is that it's the nature of television to take more and more control. It was in all seriousness, for example, that the president of ABC, Thomas Moore, suggested not long ago that baseball play its games only on weekends, that it cut its schedule from 162 to 60 games, that it play seven innings instead of nine and that the traditional three strikes and four balls be reduced to two and three. Tradition means nothing to television. It is too young to have a tradition, except one of greed.

Of course, there *is* a problem between baseball and television. It is that baseball, unlike other sports, does not lend itself to being squashed down to 21 inches or an expensive television time slot. It is a leisurely game, meant to be played on sunny afternoons before people who have no place else to go, nothing else to do. It is a game to watch while reading a newspaper. So although the astute Buzzy Bavasi, long vice-president of the Los Angeles Dodgers (and now president of his own club in San Diego) has said, "The Dodgers only televise nine games a season. We don't believe in giving away a product we want to sell. We had that in Brooklyn—and that is part of the reason we are now in Los Angeles." Baseball is, in fact, an incomplete game on the tube. One can still see much more at a ball field than on the screen. It is why television has tried to put microphones on the plate umpire (and had to remove them as soon as some real language was spoken), installed cameras in the dugout (and took them out when newspapers demanded equal representation), and microphones on managers in spring games. (Another ploy which didn't work. Once Bob Scheffing, then manager of the Detroit Tigers, in an effort to be helpful to television, went out to talk to his pitcher, Jim Bunning. When he got there he couldn't think of anything to say. So he said, "I want you to get this man out, Jim." Bunning nearly fell off the mound laughing.)

If it is beyond the power of television to make baseball more interesting, the TV boys would, if the occasion demanded, destroy it altogether. That it has not so far done so is a testimony to the endurance of baseball as an American sport. This does not mean that television will ever stop leaning. It is the nature of the beast.

Television even dictated the unconscionable move the Braves made from Milwaukee to Atlanta. There were other reasons for the carpetbaggers who own the Braves to move them out of the city which had supported them so well—they could have, indeed, if they were as financially pressed as they contended, sold out at a good price to local interests—but television was the main one. Atlanta, simply, was a much better television market than Milwaukee. In Milwaukee the Braves were hemmed in by the Chicago White Sox and the Cubs to the southeast and the new Minnesota Twins to the northeast. Atlanta wasn't hemmed in by anything but Coca-Cola. The bags were packed for two years before the Braves finally got out.

The power of television could be seen, too, in the sudden explosive expansion of the National Hockey League from six to twelve teams. Promoters of the six new clubs might have hesitated to take what was basically minor-league hockey and sell it as major league. But television was perfectly willing, and with the money in their hot little fists, the promoters were happy to go along.

One of the more amusing things about television is that while lusting after the money on the one hand, it speaks piously of having the highest motives on the other. Again Roone Arledge is an example. "I think it's absolutely wrong for a network to become involved in promoting sports events," he says.

Well, fine. He's right. But television goes along doing it anyway. There would have been no roller derby without television. The silly spectacle of wrestling could not survive without it. Soccer, which is not an American sport, was being played by elderly Hungarians on back lots on Sunday afternoons until the TV boys got the idea they could make some money out of it. So for a while we had a so-called major league, whose players could not compete with the worst European and South American teams. TV is not concerned with the beauty of the game or the reporting of events; it is, like sport itself, concerned with money. For TV to promote sports is rather like a reporter setting fires, but if TV must promote its own sports in order to fill dead air, it will do it happily and with no pangs of conscience.

I discuss at some length in Chapter 10 what television did to boxing. It is not yet through. In its latest caper ABC underwrote a heavyweight title elimination to find a successor to Muhammad Ali. If TV were to remain as objective in this area as it pretends to be, ABC would have to spend this time fighting the obscene injustice done to Muhammad Ali when he was prevented from earning a living while his case—as objector to the draft—was still in the courts. But when ABC saw a way to make a buck, it waved goodbye to justice. Justice doesn't pay.

The tournament was not a bad one, which is to say none of the fighters was very good and thus they were evenly matched. In the end Jimmy Ellis, fittingly enough the sparring partner of Muhammad Ali, won it. Everybody made a lot of money, including ABC. Says Arledge: "It's wrong, but I think networks will always be involved in promoting sports events."

There's another area in which TV people assume an eyes-rolled-up-into-the-head innocence. This matter of approaching sports as news. Networks lump sports and news together in the books and use the money they make from sports to pay some of the enormous cost of their news program. (Arledge say that sports at ABC generates 20 percent of all the network's business. A CBS spokesman says that nine percent would be more like it there— "And that means an awful lot of money"—and an NBC man said he thought nine percent was "rather high.") Like newspapers, they pretend as much objectivity in their coverage of sports events as they do in any news event. Like newspapers, too, they are sadly wrong. The only difference is that they know it. They only pretend not to.

So what you get on television is shilling—as blatant as any sideshow barker's. The score is 42-0 in the third period, but the commentator expects the trailing team to make a brilliant comeback. "The game is never over until the last one out," just may be the cliché most often spouted by men who broadcast baseball games (many of which are one-sided and dull). But if you turn the dial, who will watch the commercials?

If there are empty seats in the stands, the cameras don't show them. If the cameras are there, the game is important. *Of course* the seats are all filled. Until very recently, television cameras turned away from on-the-field fights. They still daintily turn away when there is trouble

90

or obscenity in the dugout. "You slide into the habit of saying how great everything is," Arledge admits. "You get bland. Everything's wonderful. It's easy when you pay a fortune to televise an event."

Which brings us to the commentators. When Red Barber was fired by the Yankees, he said they had fired the wrong man. He said nobody cared anymore about the construction of an English sentence or the use of language. He said all anybody cared about was having nice things said about the ball club and airing ex-players, who thought syntax was a comment on the high price of sex. He put it this way: "Radio and television have forgotten all about the most beautiful thing I know next to human love, and that's the English language." Barber left it clear that he wasn't wanted anymore because the day of sports broadcasters being reporters and commenters was over; this was the age of the shill—come see our wonderful, great, marvelous last-place ball club.

The attitude of networks and ball clubs was expressed by CBS in a magazine ad not long ago:

Phil Rizzuto went through a tough training process before he made the CBS radio sportscasting team. Phil spent years at shortstop for the New York Yankees. For a sportscaster that's maybe coming up the hard way. But what an inside view he got—of baseball and all sports.

The theory can be expressed this way: the best drama critic is a former actor, the best writer on scientific subjects is a former scientist, the man most equipped to comment on our political scene is a politician, the best critic of architecture is a bricklayer. Sheer nonsense, and CBS knows it.

What the broadcast people are shooting after here again—you guessed it—is money. The average red-blooded American businessman grows up as a fan. Being allowed into the presence of a name athlete he has worshiped from afar for years brings tears to his eyes, sweat to his palms and openings to his wallet. He becomes easy to sell. Networks were charging 150,000 dollars a minute for Super Bowl time. It's a lot easier to extract that kind of money at a party attended by a half dozen football players who have just wound up brilliant careers. There is no more wooden, less articulate man in broadcasting than Frank Gifford, the ex-Giant back. Yet he is all over the dial, like a pall. And you haven't seen a soft-nosed reporter in action until you've watched the retiring Frank Gifford. If he had played football that way, he wouldn't be a broadcaster today.

Using jocks, as athletes are fondly called on Madison Avenue, is a great debasement of broadcasting standards, not only of voice and language, but of reporting.

It is one thing for Gerry Coleman, former Yankee second-baseman, who has only a minor speech defect, to say on the air, "We thought for a minute as though that might drop," or that "pandamanium [sic] has broken loose here," or to have to contend with Phil Rizzuto's abrasively aggressive voice, his inane "holy cow," and his strangled syntax. It's quite another to be told that these men are giving us an inside view. In fact, they are doing exactly the opposite. These men protect fellow athletes with a fervor undreamed of in the ordinary TV shill. They do less than report—they deliberately conceal.

Several examples leap to mind. In the 1967 NFL championship game, Green Bay Packers vs. Dallas Cowboys on frozen Green Bay turf, the Packers were three points behind with 20 seconds to go. They were, however, only a yard from the Dallas goal line. They had two downs left, but there was some question as to whether there was enough time for two plays. If there was time for only one, a safe play would be to kick a field goal, which at the distance was almost certain to be successful, and take the chances involved in a sudden-death overtime. A courageous play, if there was time for only one, would be to go for all or nothing—try for the touchdown. If you make it, you win. If you don't you lose. On the other hand, if you think there is enough time, you try for the touchdown and then, if you don't make it, you rush in your kicker in order to get the tie.

As it happened, Bart Starr, the quarterback, called a

92

running play into the line and, with the help of a marvelous block by Jerry Kramer, took the ball over. (The TV photography, by the way, was nothing short of exquisite.) In the clubhouse CBS had former football star Tom Brookshier, and plugged in was Frank Gifford. Neither of them thought to ask Starr if he thought he had enough time for two plays. Neither asked coach Vince Lombardi if *he* thought they had enough time for two plays. They just oohed and ahhed and made me want to, in the immortal words of Dorothy Parker, fwo up.

Eventually the truth came out, Starr and Lombardi were certain they *had* time for two plays. This made them only slightly lesser heroes than TV would have it. But they told the truth. TV didn't.

Another example. At the 250,000 dollar Westchester Classic golf tournament in the summer of 1968 twenty-five-year-old Bob Murphy was tied with forty-eight-year-old Julius Boros at the last of 72 wilting holes. Boros was playing just ahead of Murphy. The last hole was a 525-yard par five with a slight dog leg to the right. On his second shot, Boros picked up a wood and let fly. He landed in one of the traps which guarded the right side of the green. Then he blasted out to within 19 feet of the cup.

In the meantime, young Murphy had driven and, *before* Boros could putt, he picked up a short iron and laid up in front of the traps. It was a dumb play, no doubt brought on by the heat and the nervewracking possibility of taking down the 30,000 dollar first prize. What Murphy should have done was wait. If Boros sank the putt and made the birdie, he would have little choice but to try to reach the green. Even if he did not, he would have been no worse off than Boros. On the other hand, if Boros missed, he could have laid up, had a mild shot at a birdie, but be virtually sure of a tie. But when he laid up, giving up a stroke, Boros' eyes lit up with dollar signs. The old pro in him was oozing from every pore. He putted without a care in the world and sank it. Murphy put the ball 15 feet from the pin with a wedge and now he had a long putt he *had* to make in order to tie. Naturally he missed. Tied for second with two other players, Murphy took home about 10,000 dollars. All he lost was 20,000 dollars.

Now the first thing I, as a viewer, wanted to know from Murphy was what he was thinking of when he took out his iron and laid up before Boros' putt. Nobody on television asked him. He was, instead, asked how it felt to finish second. He said fine.

Sometimes the ex-athlete does worse than nothing. He is out of his depth when confronted with some of the complex disputes of our time and, if he attempts to apply some of his simplistic notions, the result is disastrous—especially if it's before a huge nationwide TV audience. Take Joe Garagiola. He is an ex-catcher who likes to kid about his lack of talent as a baseball player. Actually he was a pretty good catcher and not a bad hitter. Then he went into broadcasting and, despite a squeaky voice, wasn't bad at all. He could tell a funny story with anybody and built up a repertory of them. He became a busy after-dinner speaker and he became wealthy. Then he became ultra-establishment. "Why does everybody knock the game?" Garagiola would whine. "If you can't say anything nice about the game, don't say anything. We all make our living out of it." Also: "I'm a house man. That's what they're paying me to be." (A house man is one who blindly and obediently expresses what he hopes is management's point of view. See Chapter 1.)

So one day Garagiola got to interview Lew Alcindor, the large young basketball player from UCLA who refused to compete for the U.S. in the Mexico Olympics. This was the *Today* show and Alcindor was on it primarily to discuss his involvement with a New York City program to induce ghetto youngsters to remain in school and then go on to college. But the first thing Garagiola asked him was why he refused to compete in the Olympics. There were several reasons. One was that he did not want to miss so much school that he would have to remain an extra semester in order to get his degree. (As shown in a brilliant series of articles in *Sports Illustrated* by Jack Olsen, subsequently a book called *Black Athletes in Revolt,* too many colleges don't give a damn whether their black athletes graduate or not.) The other is that he is a bright and sensitive young Negro, so many of whom feel more and more alienated from American society. In either case, whatever action Alcindor took, it was a matter of right. But he said to Garagiola, "I live here, but I don't feel this is my country."

So Garagiola suggested there was only one thing he could do—leave.

Now this might have been fairly clever when Joe Garagiola played sand-lot ball on The Hill in St. Louis. "Nya, if you don't like it here, why don't you go back where you came from?" It was hardly fair to say this to a Lew Alcindor. Besides, it could only stir the hatreds which smolder so deeply in our country. But Joe Garagiola has his. He's all right, Jack. Let every discontented American go someplace else.

Me, I look at it this way. With a name like Garagiola, *he* ought to go back where he came from—catching. And leave broadcasting to professionals.

This is not to say that the only fools, knaves and incompetents in sports broadcasting are ex-athletes. Even a highly regarded professional broadcaster like Curt Gowdy will make himself famous with a line like, "He was originally born in Chicago." Old-timers, and even young men trying to make it in the business must decide early that the only way to do it is not to rock the boat, do it the way it was done before, refuse to ask the tough question, don't even *think* of the tough question, deal in the platitude and cliché. (The most prolific purveyors of clichés are the ex-athletes. As boys they listened to the clichés of broadcasters—and read them in the sports pages —and counted them as beautiful expressions of eternal truths.) It was, after all, some of the most respected baseball broadcasters in the business who changed the home run to Ballantine Blast, White Owl Wallop, a Case of Wheaties and a Case of Lucky Strikes until they were enjoined by the baseball commissioner. And even as I write this I listen to a man named Len Dillon from NBC radio ask Monte Irvin, ex-New York Giant outfielder and recently appointed promotion man in the office of the Baseball Commissioner, the first Negro to rise so high in

95

baseball, why he thinks it is taking so long for baseball to appoint a Negro manager. Irvin says: "I don't know." Dillion does not ask another question.

Not long after Barber was fired he was asked by a little boy what it took to become a baseball commentator. Said Barker: "Well, first you've got to bat .300."

I admire Barber for several reasons. It was pure corn, but when he talked about "tearin' up the pea patch," or "running like a bunny with his tail on fire," or described somebody as being as "wild as a chicken hawk on a frosty morning," I was delighted. And when he told the truth about a player's lack of ability, I chuckled. I often thought, however, that Barber had a tendency to take himself too seriously and that on television, he talked too much, like a lot of old radio men. Yet it upsets me to think that because advertising agency men and advertisers like to hoist a few with ex-athletes that there will be no more Red Barbers coming along in the broadcasting business.

Barber, Mel Allen (no matter what one thought of him in his compulsively talkative late years), Russ Hodges, Bob Prince, who broadcasts the Pittsburgh Pirate games, are originals. They are men who set out at a young age to become broadcasters. They broadcast high-school football games and worked at little stations. They learned their craft. Most important, they had *style*.

With the possible exception of Dizzy Dean, no athlete has any style as a broadcaster. It is a disgrace that in industry which claims to pride itself on professionalism should have turned itself over to amateurs.

I bow to no man in my admiration for Sandy Koufax as a man and as a pitcher. I think, however, he is a terrible broadcaster. And well he should be. Says Sandy: "I listened to all the games when I was a kid, but I never thought about becoming a sports announcer. That's not the sort of thing you think about when you're a kid. You think about growing up to be a fireman or a policeman or a ball player. I didn't really think much about radio and TV until I started thinking about retiring from baseball."

Yes. Now guess what Red Barber dreamed of being when *he* was a kid.

It cannot be said that television has never had before it an example of competent sports journalism. For when ABC is not actively promoting an event Howard Cosell can often be depended upon to ask the right, the difficult question. He will sometimes even mount a documentary that does more revealing than pandering. Cosell knows how to open little windows on sports which otherwise would remain closed.

I would not like to be misunderstood about Cosell. There are a great many things wrong with what he does on the tube. He sometimes lets his considerable ego get in the way of truth. He is occasionally less than reliable when his company is, overtly or covertly, promoting an event. His overblown language is annoying, time-wasting and often a disguise for pettifoggery. But Howard Cosell understands television sports journalism and, from time to time, gets it on the air.

It's interesting that no one has tried to imitate him. In television circles only his bombast is noticed. And then the other networks say, who needs bombast? Nobody, of course. Yet when Cosell is honestly reporting he does a fine job and why doesn't anybody take notice? Why is he allowed a monopoly?

CBS might say at this point that it has noticed that Woody Broun is doing an excellent job of television sports journalism every week. And this is true enough. For one thing, though, it's feature reporting, and although it's an excellent example of its kind, we do not see Woody Broun in the locker rooms after tough games asking hard questions. For another, Broun is sort of hidden away on Saturday afternoons and one must be alert to catch him. Each of Broun's segments is a gem, and CBS deserves credit for letting him do his stuff. It's hardly a substitute, though, for real enterprise.

No matter how one rails against the manner and mannerisms of television, the understanding remains deep that it is forever more a part of the sporting life. The major reason is that the technology of television is far ahead of its civilization. At the winter Olympics, for example, ABC

97

introduced a split-screen technique—involving live action on one half, tape rerun on the other—of two skiers apparently racing each other down the same slope, although they actually competed at different times. At the site a spectator at best could see a portion of a run, one competitor at a time.

The isolated camera has been a boon to the football fan. The isolated camera focuses on a single player. If that player is not involved in the play, then it's forgotten. But if he is, the tape may have caught the outstanding moment of a contest from its point of development. To the sports buff, nothing could be more beautiful, unless it's the instant replay.

In this, just as people in the stands are turning to each other to ask what happened, the switch is tripped and the play or knockdown or great moment of trouser splitting is run through again—in slow motion. Says one newspaper sports columnist, "It's gotten so that when I go to a game I keep waiting for the instant replays of plays I've missed."

At the Grand National Steeplechase at Aintree, England, there was a camera under one of the jumps. There are now cameras in the football end zones and atop 300-foot cranes at golf tournaments. Hand-held cameras—in color —once called "creepie peepies," can go places big cameras couldn't go before.

Says Arledge: "You take golf. If there are three golfers in contention, and one is on 18, another on 16 and the other on 15, there's no physical way you can see all of them. But you can see them on television. In a way, we can actually change the sport. At the U.S. Open in 1967 we had Billy Casper and Arnold Palmer, a couple of holes apart, putting against each other for the lead on a split screen. Now that's *rewarding*. There is no way you could see that if you were there.

"The way it has worked out, a reporter can cover a golf tournament best by sitting in the press tent and watching television. He may not like it, but it's a fact."

And if television ever grows up to the point where it asks adult questions of the competitors, there will be no function left for the newspapers except to enshrine what has already been said on television. Newspaper people don't expect that to happen. They tap their heads and say, "There's no money in digging up truth."

The money still seems to be in television events. And the danger there is always that eventually a point is reached where people would rather stay home and watch television than attend an event. TV has shown that it cannot, even when it tries, support events which do not draw at the gate. So when the going gets tough, TV collapses. It happened with boxing, it happened with soccer. And don't bet against it happening in a lot of other places. There is no law professional football has to be with us forever.

## 3  Let's Win One for the Gyppers

THE ITALIAN WALKED UP TO THE SMALL, HOTEL-TYPE desk in the main United States building in Yoyogi Olympic Village in Tokyo, in 1964. He had come a long way. In heavily accented English he struggled to make himself understood to the old man behind the desk sorting mail. The old man did not look at him.

The Italian said he was a newspaperman, from Rome, and that he would like to arrange an appointment to interview Bob Hayes, the U.S. sprinter, who was being billed as the world's fastest human. The old man finished sorting the mail and the Italian waited. Finally the old man turned around and said, "I don't understand ya."

Laboriously, the Italian went through his little speech again. "Cheez," the old man said out of the corner of his mouth to an American standing nearby, "I wish these guys would learn to speak English." Then he turned to the Italian.

"Hayes ain't here," he said.

When would Hayes be there?

"I dunno," the old man said. "I ain't his keeper."

Would Hayes be there tomorrow?

"Sure, he'll be here," the old man said. "Whaddaya think? He sleeps here. But I don't know if you can see him. There's a lot of reporters want to see Hayes."

Yes, but when . . .

"For cryin' out loud. I told ya I don't know."

The Italian turned on his heel and left. He walked a short way down the road to the Russian compound. At the desk there he was greeted by a pleasant, squarely built young Russian woman. She recognized his Italian instantly, held up a hand to stop him, made a phone call and, in a minute, a young Russian appeared who spoke Italian fluently.

The Italian newspaperman said he would like to interview Yuri Vlasov, the intellectual and champion weightlifter. The Russian interpreter made a phone call, nodded, told the Italian to return at 4 P.M., when both Vlasov and an interpreter would be available.

The Italian smiled, thanked the Russian and left. The USSR had made another friend. The US had lost one.

This incident typified to me amateur athletics in this country—crotchety, stupid, shortsighted and, in the end, self-defeating. Amateur athletics are not run for the amateur athlete. He is the most put upon, the least considered and, as long as he remains a true amateur, the most exploited man in U.S. athletics. The people who get the most out of amateur athletics are two willful groups of men in two self-perpetuating organizations—the Amateur Athletic Union and the National Collegiate Athletic Association.

To understand the AAU, one must start at the top, which is, no matter the protests to the contrary, the International Olympic Committee. This is the body that runs international competition and thus runs amateur athletics all over the world. Since the goal of amateur athletics is Olympic competition, the IOC holds life and death power over all national amateur groups. Withdrawal of recognition by the IOC makes any amateur organization *non persona*. Obviously then, when the IOC has a cold, the AAU sneezes.

Naturally the IOC is a democratic group. Since its

members are unpaid, it is made up of rich men who know what is good for all of us. To make sure it will always do what is best, it elects its own members. It elects them for life. If the founding fathers of our country had thought of anything so democratic, we would have been relieved of a great deal of trouble, like electing Presidents, for example.

The members of the IOC are of course jealous of their membership in what is, even more than the U.S. Senate, the most exclusive club in the world. They rule with an iron hand. There are 83 members. When one dies, the other 82 choose a successor. This means that if the French member of the IOC, having reached the most competent and effective age of ninety-three, dies, it isn't the French amateurs in his country who elect a successor. It is large group of foreigners who are, naturally, less interested in French athletics than they are in their own power. This is what is meant by self-perpetuation.

As one would suspect, the IOC often comes along with heavy-handed, light-minded decisions. They'll take it into their old heads to knock both Red and Nationalist China out of the Olympic Games and guns are cocked all over the world. The decisions of the IOC are old men's decisions, conservative, hard-arteried, often ludicrous. Early in 1967, for example, the IOC decided to demand that every Olympic champion sign a pledge that he would not, for a year, turn professional. This means nothing to skiers, weightlifters and swimmers. But boxers, for one, use the Olympics as a stepping stone to professionalism. So do some ice skaters, basketball players and soccer players. How can the IOC tell them what to do with a year of their lives? The absurdity is that the IOC has not been able to govern the amateurism of *any* of its athletes. Is an athlete supported by his government an amateur? Is an athlete attending college on a scholarship an amateur? But being absurd is a characteristic of the IOC—and by a sort of contagion from the top, the AAU. Its members, possibly because of a certain deafness which accompanies advanced age, march to a special kind of drummer. And Avery Brundage, eighty-one-year-old president of the IOC, has a drummer all his own.

Never was this more apparent than during the 1968 Olympic Games in Mexico. The heavy hand of Brundage was everywhere. Even before the games, completely misreading the passions loose in the world, Brundage made a clumsy but determined effort to allow racist South Africa to compete. He did so on the ground that great progress had been made because South Africa was willing to field an integrated team. What he refused to take into account was that the trials, held in South Africa, would have to be separate. Now it may be possible to judge track athletes on time alone (although it would be unfair, since time often depends on the quality of the competition), but how could South Africa select a boxing team or a wrestling team without contact between the races? Besides, the segregated selection of the team would be against Olympic rules.

Brushing law and logic behind, Brundage nevertheless championed the South Africa cause. Only a threat by most of the world to halt the games altogether forced him to relent. He did so, kicking and screaming all the way.

And it was Brundage, too, who became so enraged at the relatively mild and dignified Black Power demonstrations of Tommie Smith and John Carlos at the Olympic medal ceremony. Smith and Carlos finished first and third in the 200 meters. At the medal ceremony they each raised one black-gloved fist (one right fist, one left, suggesting they could afford only one pair of gloves between them) during the playing of "The Star-Spangled Banner." A sputtering Brundage demanded some kind of overreaction from the U.S. Olympic Committee. He got it. The committee picked up the credentials of Smith and Carlos and sent them home. This outraged the U.S. team and shocked the rest of the world.

Soon after, the U.S. Olympic Committee leaked a story that Black Power athletes were being investigated for taking money from equipment manufacturers. Names were named, although newspapers withheld them for lack of evidence. The implication was clear, however, that there was evidence of professionalism and that the Olympic medals would be taken away from the Black Power lads. In fact, there was no evidence. Not only that, but if the black athletes were guilty of anything, so were most U.S. track stars. It was a can of worms better left unopened and at the end of the bumbling officials were making denials of the stories they themselves had spread.

Finally, it was the International Olympic Committee that decided that only seven athletes from each country could march in the wonderful Olympic closing ceremonies. This is another clear example of throwing out the baby with the bath water. The whole thing came up because there was some milling and shouting fun by the athletes in Tokyo four years ago. Also some good-natured joshing of the Japanese Emperor by Australian athletes who may or may not have been wearing their trousers at the time. So in a meeting in 1965 it was decided to abandon the fine old tradition of massed marches at the close. In the end, in Mexico, many athletes leaped out of the stands and onto the field at the ceremony and everybody had a good time. What the old men had forgotten was that sports should be fun. This is only one more sign of arterial atrophy.

This dum-dum syndrome is epidemic in all amateur organizations. Some funny things have happened in the AAU, too. One of the more famous bits of nonsense dates back to 1959. It is said that this brouhaha in a teacup led to the first open break between the NCAA and AAU. Since the NCAA can, in its own special way, be just as stupid as the AAU, it must be guessed that the incident was as much an excuse as a cause.

It started when a Swedish amateur group arranged to bring a basketball team to play at a number of small colleges with Swedish and Lutheran traditions. In what amounts to a fit of pique, Daniel J. Ferris, the now seventy-nine-year-old secretary-treasurer of the AAU, refused to allow the Swedes to play on the ground they had not arranged their trip through the AAU.

This wasn't exactly the case. After Ake Nilsson, president of the Swedish Basketball Federation, had made arrangements with the colleges, he did write to the AAU and ask for their blessings. As proof, he had a curt, almost rude letter from Ferris:

Your undated letter [in fact it was quite clearly dated] requesting permission to arrange a series of basketball games is at hand, and will be glad to assist you in arranging such a series if you desire such assistance.

Naturally enough Nilsson assumed he now had AAU permission and proceeded with his plans. Suddenly, just before he and his boys were to leave Sweden, there was a flurry of letters involving the International Basketball Federation and the AAU. Nilsson was informed, finally, that his team would not, under any circumstances, be allowed to play in the U.S. He couldn't believe this was anything but a mistake and, having promised his lads a trip to the United States, he did not feel he could renege.

So here came this nice young group of fresh-faced Swedish basketball players and here came old Dan Ferris, waving his thou-shalt-not-play flag like a lance. Ferris prevailed. The Swedes went home without playing a game of basketball and American sports were saved from heaven knows what kind of disaster.

Just how foolish all this was the AAU admitted a year later when it not only reimbursed the Swedish Basketball Federation for its wasted trip, but it arranged another, free of cost.

This sort of idiocy, I submit, is the rule rather than the exception around amateur athletics. Athletes who must submit to the often mindless tyranny of amateur-athletics organizations become cynical and bitter in short order. It is, for example, the practice of AAU officials to conceal from athletes invitations to compete in foreign meets if these meets will conflict with minor American meets. Now, the rewards of track athletes, most of whom must do an astonishing amount of training, are few indeed. One of the major ones, though, is getting free trips abroad. To have the AAU withhold an invitation from Brazil in order to protect a minor meet in New Brunswick, New Jersey, is not only dumb, it's mean and unfair. It's also typical.

Many of the people in the AAU work without pay. This sounds rather sweet of them, but they extract their

104

share of rewards. Chief among them is the same thing that athletes get—free travel. As a result, there were 1,518 American officials in Tokyo in 1964. Thus 1.5 out of every seven Americans on the Olympic "team" was an official. It was the highest percentage ever. Considering that there were actually 326 fewer American athletes in Tokyo in 1964 than there were in Helsinki in 1956, it also illustrated one of Parkinson's laws, that the number of officials increases as the amount of work to be done decreases. The less work to be done, the more time it takes and the less joy there is in it. So we have surly attendants to greet the press at the Olympics. Inexperienced hacks are sent out to "coach" the athletes in the lesser events. (In Tokyo the "coach" of the long-distance runners and walkers was an assistant manager who knew as much about long-distance running as the AAU knows about public relations.) Relatives and hangers-on take up space and spend money that would much better have gone to experienced coaches and trainers. Jealousy is rampant, backbiting a kind of universal sport. ("If *he* can take *his* wife to Mexico City, why can't *you* take *yours?*")

Other charges that have, with a good deal of justice, been levied against the AAU (particularly by the NCAA) are:

1. There is complete mismanagement of international competition largely because the AAU plays politics in picking both coaches and competitors.

2. There is blackmailing of athletes. The AAU has been known to threaten with expulsion athletes who appear in NCAA meets. Also the AAU forces athletes to contribute to it the small sums they might earn appearing on television—that's if the AAU finds out. Also, unless an athlete is prominent, the AAU is chintzy about paying traveling and living expenses for big meets which fill AAU coffers.

3. The AAU fights to the death for control of track meets. When the NCAA balks at this control, the AAU will call off the meets, nobody suffering but competition and the athletes.

4. Under the AAU hierarchy, people not interested in

track—wrestlers, gymnasts and rowers, for example—
are put into positions of power where they make decisions affecting track out of pure-hearted but 100 percent
ignorance.

5. The AAU is run by an executive committee which is
dominated by past presidents (nine) and past executive
secretaries (two) who have lifetime membership on the
committee and rule with iron, albeit ancient fists.

Although the AAU is terrible, it is quite possible that
the NCAA is worse. An organization of colleges and
universities—or at least their athletics departments—the
NCAA seems to have as its major pursuit only money.
This is not true. It also pursues power. And with such
singlemindedness it sometimes leaves athletes drowning in
its turbulent wake. Sometimes it tosses back a small life
preserver. Sometimes it doesn't.

Here is the way things work. The colleges, as members
of the NCAA, make rules. Each college hopes all the
others will obey them. Each reserves the right to break
them if it wishes. When a college is caught breaking a
rule, who gets punished? The athlete, that's who.

The college caught paying an athlete, cheating on recruiting, luring away a coach, breaking practice rules, is
placed on probation. That means it can't play in certain
postseason games and otherwise has its wrist slapped. But
the boy who has had the money pressed upon him, the kid
who has allowed his head to be turned by a white con-
vertible, is barred from competition. This is a serious hurt
indeed. Especially since he is probably in college mostly
because he wants professional scouts to get a look at him.

Have a recent case. Early in 1967 the University of
Illinois was discovered to have a slush fund for its athletes
which was administered by the athletics department. All
an athlete is supposed to get in return for playing games
for a college in front of huge crowds is room, board, tuition and 15 dollars a month. Not that this is so little. Ask
any father who has had to pay his son's way through
college. But the slush fund was used to lure athletes to the
school with additional payments. (These slush funds are
usually set up by successful alumni who get some kind of

ckle—possibly sexual—from going out to see their alma ater win, win, win. What this leads to in basketball is iscussed in Chapter 11.)

The fund was discovered at Illinois because an assistant irector of athletics—Milt Brewer—got sore about being assed over for big jobs and blew the whistle. The fund, e revealed, had been in operation for at least five years. Illinois got the usual slap on the wrist. But five boys ere ruled ineligible for future athletics competition. One f them was Cyril Pinder, a nineteen-year-old Negro youth om Hollywood, Florida, who had been counted as an xtraordinarily talented halfback He was also a good udent, ranking eighth in his high-school graduating class. s a result he was much sought after by many of our great alaces of learning.

"Even Princeton was interested in me," Pinder said fter his athletics career had been nipped in the bud. They wanted me to go to some prep school first. An- over, I think." (The Ivy League does so stoop to con- uer.) Among other schools that wanted Pinder were Iichigan State, UCLA, Arizona, Indiana. "They offered ars," Pinder told reporters. "They offered checking ac- ounts, they offered charge accounts so I could go down nd buy clothes whenever I wanted And some of them, ostly the ones far away, offered to fly my parents to and om the games, all expenses paid."

Naturally young Pinder turned down all these offers or the Spartan life at Illinois. The only thing he did wrong ere, he said (and he was backed by an investigation ade by the president of the university), was accept irplane tickets to visit his Florida home, 1,645 dollars orth over two and a half years. "In his senior year in igh school," reads an official report, "[Pinder] had re- eived offers of 90 football scholarships and thought trips ome were a regular thing since all schools offered them."

"I know it sounds stupid," Pinder said. "I had read bout guys who got in trouble for taking money, getting ars and things like that. But I didn't think I was doing nything illegal as long as I wasn't taking any money."

Pinder was allowed to finish college and his scholarship

107

was not taken away. Colleges are not always that decent. Many freshman athletes understand from the beginning that, if they don't make the varsity, they will be invited to become dropouts. The NCAA frowns on this, as it does on red-shirting, the delightful practice of keeping a boy off the team for a year when there is not an immediate need for his particular skills and letting him stay in school five years so that he can play four. But boys still get red-shirted and kids lose their scholarships and the NCAA, bloated on television money, goes on and on, for God, country and the Big Ten.

A classic example of NCAA stupidity surfaced in the summer of 1969 when it suddenly refused to allow basketball players to compete in the Maccabiah games in Tel Aviv. Why? Because there was an NCAA rule that prohibited basketball players from playing in organized games during the summer. This isn't a bad rule. It was designed to keep college basketball players from playing in summer hotel leagues where they were exposed to gamblers, bookmakers and assorted black hats. Obviously, though, the Maccabiah games had nothing to do with this. Why wasn't the rule waived? Because nobody asked, because proper channels weren't used, because of red tape, because of stupidity.

The ugly thing about it is that supposedly intelligent college officials went along with this ruling. At the University of Pennsylvania, for example, the college allowed participants in soccer, track and fencing to go to Tel Aviv. But two basketball players were kept home.

Only one college man refused to be a party to this nonsense. DeLaney Kiphuth, the Director of Athletics at Yale, instructed Yale's Jack Langer, basketball player, to go to Israel no matter what the NCAA said.

As this is written, the NCAA has taken no action against Yale. I am guessing it will take none. In which case, how will the athletic directors who held back their basketball players feel?

In many ways money is a more important factor in the NCAA than it is in the AAU. Its top people make a lot more—30,000 dollars a year as opposed to 17,000 dollars —and while many people serve the AAU on a volunteer, no-pay basis, the NCAA is basically an army of paid college coaches. On the other hand, where is an athlete to go once he has used up his college eligibility? The NCAA has nothing for him. He has to go to the AAU. So does the man who never goes to college.

A man who sums up this situation precisely is a short, slight distance runner I know named Pete McArdle, a dandy little Irishman, who ran some good races for this country. McArdle has good reason to dislike the AAU. Running for Ireland as a boy, he caught the eye of AAU men here and was promised a marvelous job, an apartment, and a lot of loving attention if he would emigrate here and run under the banners of the AAU and the good old U.S.A. McArdle jumped at the chance. And all he ever got was a job washing buses and the opportunity to run his guts out like everybody else. Still, he couldn't go to the NCAA for help. "The college men don't give a damn for the likes of me," he says. "They want to make the trips themselves."

Ah, the trips. For coaches, officials, competitors, hangers-on and their wives, the trips are the things. Whether they are paid, like the NCAA men, or unpaid, like many AAU people, the reward they all expect is the trip. Trials in California. Pan-American games in the Andes. To Russia, with love, every other year. And every four years, in some favored far corner of the world, the Olympics. It's a jockstrap jet set. And all freebie.

Plus you get to wear all those medals and identification buttons. There were so many well-decorated sports officials in Tokyo they were soon being identified as gaily festooned pot-bellied bar flies. National borders mean nothing to that kind of bird. He is as apt to be Roumanian as anything else. One night in Tokyo an American official was encountered wearing a bright U.S. blazer, U.S. Olympic button, TV-Radio badge, Working Press medal, NBC emblem, Rhodesian Olympic button ("I had to give two NBC buttons for that," he said) and something that looked as though it said "I Gave" in Arabic. He was also wearing a pleased grin. "I feel safer walking around this town at night wearing all this stuff," he said. "I figure it makes me look important." To be a gaily festooned pot-bellied bar fly in Tokyo is a wonderful thing. (And in Mexico City in 1968 a spy of mine swears he saw a Yugoslavian wearing a button that identified him as a "Gringo.")

If this system of rewards—in college scholarships and airplane tickets to exotic places—seems to blur the meaning of amateurism, it's only because it does. Sometimes the amateurism becomes downright invisible.

An amateur, it has been said, is a guy who won't take a check. This is a canard, because he will. It is the custom, for example, during the indoor track season to pay top athletes transportation from their homes. A 100-yard-dash man who lives in Los Angeles might make a swing east during which he runs in Chicago, Detroit, Boston and New York. He will collect round-trip jet fare from each promoter. This amounts to a tidy profit, but he is not only expected to do it, he is encouraged. And just a year ago the U.S. Davis Cup team (tennis, you know) had its annual salaries raised from 7,000 dollars to 9,000 a man. They promptly complained the increase wasn't large enough and pointed to foreign tennis players in the U.S. who get as much as 500 dollars for "expenses." In the end tennis amateurs opted for "open" tennis, which means, "Get what you can, fellas."

The largest complaint of all amateur athletes is that they are not getting *enough*. And this is certainly true about the track athletes who compete in the less popular events —long-distance running, for example. Nobody offers to buy these fellows even a glass of milk and they have to work as hard, or harder, than any other track competitor. At this writing there was a move afoot to stage professional track events on television. This would no doubt prove a great attraction, especially to those track men who cannot become pro-football flankers. But what it will do to amateur footracing, God only knows. It can't do it any good, certainly, and heaven help us all if professional track should become so popular that people take to betting on the results.

The fact is that the effect of amateurism on college kids are bad enough. They don't all turn out to be basketball point-shavers, and so far nobody has been caught dumping a football game, at least it has never been proved in court. But what they see in college makes a deep impression on their view of morality. It would be both inaccurate and unfair to blame the sports programs at our universities for the huge rate of crime in the country, although one wonders if the breakdown in business ethics shouldn't be placed there. And what is in the mind of the student who must, at great difficulty, work his way through school, when he sees how well the athletes, most of whom are much less qualified as students than he, live on the campus? The snap courses. (Michigan State once offered a BS degree with a major in mobile homes; at Bradley University dumper Mike Chianakas received credit for courses in elementary badminton, elements of tumbling, golf and boxing; and when Syracuse had its great teams a lot of the players were majoring in Canadian geography.) The cars. The clothes. The girls. He couldn't be a very bright student if he didn't recognize them as the wages of sin.

As for the young athletes themselves, they are subjected to the values and the authoritarian rule of the coach who must, he understands, win at any cost. Who is that man who devotes his life to winning at children's games?

The Coach is middle-aged and has coached at four American institutions of higher learning, leaving each time, despite the fact that he had a signed contract, for a large increase in pay. He is white-haired and impressive-looking, attractive to women, but he is an ex-football player who didn't attend many classes and is considered a boor by the rest of the faculty. He is never invited to any of the faculty parties and this galls him. He tells his wife it's jealousy because he makes more money than all the professors. His wife, who was the daughter of the dean where the Coach played football as a boy, knows better. She has long learned to content herself with the drunken parties the alumni throw for her husband. And she is glad the professors aren't invited to those.

Through the years the Coach has built up a reputation as a genius and he likes to deprecate himself. "I'm such a genius," he likes to say, "that I only know three plays. With what I got playing for me, I got to keep it simple. We pass, we run into the line, we run around end. And I don't like to run around end much. The only genius around here is the Athletic Director. He got me five oxes for the line, four orangutans for the backfield and two giraffes for ends. And he kept that menagerie in school for four years. I ought to give him half my pay and they ought to give him half what they get for pro contracts."

In fact, though, the Coach views himself as a brilliant tactician. ("When he says he's not a genius," a friend comments, "he's lying in his teeth and he knows it.") The Coach also considers himself a consummate handler of men although the way he handles his men is he screams, "Ten laps around the field," at every imagined infraction. He also takes scholarships away. His players call him "sir" and they hate and fear him.

The assistant coaches contribute to making the Coach feel something more than mortal. They flatter him at every opportunity and, although he used to do the same thing when he was an assistant, he neither remembers nor sees through their tactics. Of course, it is understood that the assistant coaches will flatter him or look for another job.

It is not difficult for a man who spends most of his time bossing boys to get this feeling about himself. Power corrupts. And men who enjoy bossing other men or boys often take sadistic glee in maltreating those in their power. The Coach forces his assistants into demeaning tasks— spying on the players to see that they do not break curfew, demanding to know the number of dates the players have gone on, who the girls are, whether there have been any infractions of his stringent rules about sex. The Coach is very serious about sexual infractions.

The Coach likes to hang inspirational signs around the dressing room. "God, Country, School and Team," one of them reads. And underneath, in smaller letters, it says: "And during the season the Team is FIRST! What You See Here, What You Hear Here, Leave Here." This sign is designed to make sure the players do not tell newspaper reporters about his long, foul-language harangues about winning, winning. Trying is Not Enough—You have to DO! No Excuses, Especially Not for Failure. Obey the Three E's: Energy! Effort! Excellence!

The manifesto the Coach considers most important is the one he distributes to his players every season and makes them sign. It is a pledge that during the season there will be NO! smoking, drinking, staying out after ten o'clock, going to the movies, watching television, sex (including masturbation). He invoked an honor code, each player pledging that he would inform on any other he saw breaking any of these rules. "Remember," the Coach likes to tell his players, "your scholarship is at stake."

Since no one ever dares tell the Coach he is out of bounds, he finds it impossible to believe he ever does anything wrong, much less dishonorable. That's why he actually believes it when he says he has never broken a contract. In fact he has, three times. Each time he had a year or more to go on an old contract when he received a better offer. The coach has convinced himself that contracts are for the protection of coaches, not of universities. Meanwhile, his players are learning how to behave about contracts in the future. This is a nuance the Coach doesn't understand.

The Coach is a churchgoing man and many of his players have discovered that if they are seen in his church on Sunday morning it will go easier for them that week. But they snicker behind his back at what they consider his false piety and exaggerated view of his own abilities. (He let slip to an assistant while in his cups on an airplane—after he had been turned down by the stewardess—that he felt perfectly capable of running the whole university as its president. The assistant whispered this fantasy about and was fired when word got back to the Coach.)

The power of the Coach should never be underestimated. He indirectly controls the slush fund the alumni have set up for him to bribe athletes into coming into his college. (While he gives credit to the Athletic Director, it's the Coach who does the important recruiting of his animals.) There's a lot of money in this fund and money can mean power. The Coach can also threaten to quit and bring the alumni down on the college president. When professors protest that athletes are not showing up in class, he has been able to convince them to give passing grades anyway. He enjoys bringing pressure on professors, especially the ambitious ones. He has been responsible for certain contracts not being renewed and word is out on the campus not to cross him.

The Coach often bets money on his team to win, sometimes very large sums, and this makes him a vicious taskmaster. Players are afraid to tell him they hurt and he has ruined ankles and knees forever by having them injected with novocaine. He works his players unmercifully and boasts that they win because they are in such great physical condition. At the end of the football season most of his players go to bed for two weeks.

But the Coach is a happy man. He smiles all the time and he is never so happy as when he is playing demigod to young men over whom he has everything but life and death control. That he is paid well to do this, that he can live like a Croesus all the while, is so sweet that he sometimes chuckles in his sleep. His life is ideal. The only thing he can't understand is why his two strapping sons swore, when they were fifteen and fourteen respectively, that they would never, as long as they lived, touch a football.

The trouble with men like the Coach is that they touch people and change them, seldom for the better. One such was the Professor. He was a professor of sociology at a Midwestern university and he was a happy man. It was his theory he could accurately predict the trends of human events if he could learn the right questions to ask electronic computers. His calculations convinced him it would take him 50 years to check out the probability factors involved and he would then be able to write the definitive future history of mankind.

In the meantime, the Professor had become known as the nation's foremost expert on sociological computation. It was an ideal life for him, but his wife was not happy. Each day, and likely as not more often, she would carefully remind him that the football coach was making 10,000 dollars a year more than he. The Professor was getting used to this nagging and in truth seldom heard it. But in a sudden switch in the athletic department, the football coach was fired and another brought in at an even higher salary. The sociologist's wife increased the tempo of her nagging by 5,000 dollars a year and at last he could take it no longer. He gave in and went to work for a company which manufactured a totally useless product.

Through his skill with computers the Professor was able to increase the sales of this useless product to astronomical proportions. He put one in every home in America. He then turned his efforts to other useless products and people still buy them happily. Closets all over America are filled with them.

The Professor has, alas, had to give up his plan for the future history and is no longer happy. But his wife is. She loves to point out to all her friends, most of whom are wives of manufacturers of useless products, that her husband now makes more money than most football coaches.

## 4 The Flower of America

IT IS ONLY IN RECENT YEARS THAT THE PROFESSIONAL athlete has been looked upon as anything more than hired help. Not long ago golf professionals were allowed to compete at fancy country clubs but were asked not to use the main entrance or hang around the clubhouse bar. Baseball players were counted ruffians and part-time bartenders (and, indeed, they were often both). Professional football players, who came much later, were underpaid animals, fit for nothing but slamming each other around in the mud during poorly attended Sunday afternoon games. Even today Arthur Ashe, the renowned tennis player, may be capable of winning every tournament in sight, against professionals as well as amateurs (a line which is now so blurred in tennis as not to exist), but few of the clubs at which he plays would have him as a member. This same is true of Charlie Sifford, Pete Brown and Lee Elder in golf.

There is, indeed, an Anglo-Saxon tradition of derision of the professional athlete. An unfortunately anonymous author stated the case as long ago as 1870, in the August 13 issue of a British magazine called *Every Saturday:*

> Indeed, it may be doubted whether the modern system of cultivating athletes, namely by a fierce competition stimulated by heavy bribes, does not inflict positive moral injury, by developing animal intensity of the will—the root of one kind of cruelty—and a hungry greed for more money earned without toil, of all the passions that renders the heart most callous. Nobody is quite so "hard" as the professional sporting man, quite so incapable of pity, remorse or self-restraint in the pursuit of gain.

The author then went on to explore the professional athlete in Wilkie Collins' novel, *Man and Wife:*

> Geoffrey Delamayne, the typical modern Briton, with his features "as perfectly regular and perfectly unintelligent as human features can be," with his "expression of immovable composure," with his "brawny muscles showing through his light coat," "deep in the chest, thin in the flanks, firm on his legs," a "perfect human animal" as fearless as a bloodhound, and when first introduced as gently good-tempered as a Newfoundland when the fit of placability was on it, is nevertheless a brute, with capacities for becoming a criminal. He seduces because his training, while making him a fine animal, has given no hint of self-restraint; he cheats . . . because it has made him callous; he betrays his friend because he has been seeking all his life roads

of escape from difficulty; he lies because his will is so fixed that he would rather lie the trouble through than yield; he hates like a wild beast, and he plans a murder because his wife stands in the way to the gratification of his fierce greed.

Then the author adds a minor carp. "But we are not sure," he writes, "that he [Collins] has not attributed too much of the evil he describes to the pursuit of muscularity, and too little to the spirit of competition which has been permitted to intrude into it."

Whether it was the muscularity or the competition, the intellectuals at least were against it. Times have changed, however. It is a mark of ignorance not to have some basic knowledge of professional sports. Professional football has become the darling of both the business and the artistic communities. Baseball has become respectable and players make money endorsing products. Television has helped make golf stars wealthy beyond imagination; Arnold Palmer, for a small example, pilots his own jet airplane. Players themselves have changed somewhat. Basketball and football professionals acquire at least some polish if not a degree in the four years they spend in college. Baseball players have a tendency to remain in school longer than they did years ago. Golfers grow up around country clubs and construct the facade and absorb the values of the rich. It is no longer altogether disreputable to be a professional athlete.

This does not mean that the portrait sketched in *Every Saturday* outlives its validity. The plain fact is that being a professional athlete *does* mark a man. Some are marked deeply, some less so, but all bear the brand. Most of all, I suppose, the professional athlete understands that he is making a great deal of money performing a function that, at bottom, comes easily to him. Like the man who finds a wallet in the street and decides to keep it, he becomes suspicious and defensive because he imagines that everyone sees through him as easily as he sees through himself. He knows, in addition, that his moneymaking years are short, and thus he is nervous and antagonistic. At-

117

tempting to hide his nervousness and antagonism, he builds a veneer of manly aggression and civilized cool. Underneath, he boils with fear.

Bob Gibson, the really fine St. Louis pitcher, who was earning some 90,000 dollars a year, was approached not long before the 1968 World Series by a reporter from the *Wall Street Journal*. As Gibson tells the story, "He wanted to know what I do with all my money. I told him the only way he could find out was if he was with the Internal Revenue Service."

Mickey Mantle, particularly in his early years with the Yankees, would talk about money only to trusted friends. As a result, he was taken by a series of sharpers.

Bob Pettit, the former pro basketball player, has put it this way: "There's no easier way to make a living than being a pro athlete. It spoils people. You make more money than you'll probably ever make again, establish a high standard of living and get a lot of publicity. Then, all of sudden, you wake up and realize you have to go out and work for a living."

I do not believe, though, that professional athletes are ever surprised when they find their careers are over. I think they are haunted by the knowledge that they soon will be and, as a result, become ill-tempered and, often, penurious. It is said of a famous pitcher that not only was he a poor tipper, but that when he ate with other players he would hang back as they left and steal *their* tips from the table. They try to hide all of this, of course, and so profess generosity and great love of the game, God and motherhood. In fact, they care more about money.

Harold Charnofsky, himself a former baseball player grown up to become an assistant professor at California State College, wrote a report to the American Sociological Association meeting in San Francisco in 1967 in which he said, "Heroic considerations, such as service to the public, fierce love of the game, and the importance of competition and challenge, are clearly beneath matters of personal gain in the [baseball] players' hierarchy of values."

Charnofsky took a scientific poll of 73 major-league

118

players—57 white, nine American Negroes and seven Latin Americans. His poll showed that most of the rah rah notions fostered in much of the press, by ball-club ownership and, indeed, by the players themselves, are myths.

*Myth:* Baseball is a model of American integration.

*Fact:* Not one white player interviewed would willingly spend his leisure time with a Negro or Latin player. Nor would he willingly share a room with him. (A recent exception. Reggie Jackson and Chuck Dobson of the Oakland A's room together. Dobson is white.) In addition, white players said they believed that Negro players were poor team players, that they were more afraid than whites of pitches thrown at their heads, that they were both lazy and show-offs and were easily defeated because they would not hang on and fight back.

*Myth:* Baseball owners don't care about a player's color, only whether he can run, throw, field and hit.

*Fact:* Baseball teams have their own quota systems. There are times when you might see a team with eight or even nine Negroes on the field, but this is frowned on. In fact, if the Negro is only slightly more talented, the white player will get the job. One scout told Charnofsky he was looking for a white outfielder because the club had too many Negro outfielders.

*Myth:* Baseball players like fans, especially the kids, and enjoy giving them autographs, appearing at dinners and being in the public eye.

*Fact:* Charnofsky found that both management and players like to put forth this image, but in fact players believe that adult fans are squares who don't really understand the game, that kid fans are sweaty little delinquents and that fans generally are naïve, fickle and not to be trusted.

*Myth:* Baseball is a glamorous, exciting way to make a living and baseball players love every minute of it.

*Fact:* The players told Charnofsky that the game was difficult and demanding and that the only thing they really cared about was the money they made.

While Charnofsky did not survey other sports, his

findings apply to most professional sports performers. Although pro basketball has dropped what was once a rigid quota system, I doubt if you will ever see an all-Negro squad (except in pro basketball) even if that would be the best team. In pro football the St. Louis Cardinals and Cleveland Browns were torn by disputes between Negro and white players. In St. Louis the black players at last felt they had to present management with a petition of grievances. In Cleveland, a white and a Negro player, both stars, had to be traded after a dispute involving the Negro players not being invited to a golf outing. Possibly in an effort to stave off that kind of problem, the Green Bay Packers have announced that they will room their players alphabetically, rather than racially. None of the other teams rushed to follow suite.

Unquestionably it takes toughness to be a successful professional coach. This toughness is paid for in humanity. It's a high price. Vince Lombardi, long an extraordinarily successful coach at Green Bay, now running the Washington Redskins, makes his players respect him. They also despise him. Henry Jordan, Green Bay defensive lineman, liked to say, "He treats us all the same, like dogs."

After a stinking, sweating, mind-bending morning workout under a choking, hot, muggy Green Bay summer sun, Jordan talked about the coach. "Sometimes you hate him," he said. "He drives you until you know you can't go on. When we were doing the grass drill, my legs just wouldn't come up anymore. So when he walked by me, *he hit them.* He pushes you to the end of your endurance and then beyond it. If you have a reserve, he finds it."

Jerry Kramer, the offensive guard, who painted a brittle picture of Lombardi in his diary of a season, *Instant Replay,* tells a Lombardi story he treasures. "In 1962 I was banged up around the chest. I was out for about two plays. I didn't know it at the time, but I had two broken ribs. I played anyway. The next week, all I can remember is Merle Olsen of the Rams making cleat marks up and down me all afternoon. After that game we took X-rays and found out about the ribs. I went to Coach and told him I had been playing with two broken ribs and he said 'No shit? Well, they don't hurt anymore, do they?' "

Certainly a great deal of Lombardi's success stemmed from his ability to convince a player that injuries were not important. "No one is ever hurt," Lombardi would tell his players over and over. "Hurt is in your mind." Lombardi had a lot of slogans like that.

"You've got to be mentally tough."

"Winning isn't everything, it's the only thing."

"If you can accept losing, you can't win."

"If you can walk, you can run."

"What the hell are *you* limping around for?"

"Dammit, get up, you're not hurt."

These are more than slogans to Lombardi. They are a way of life, a way that leads him into a simplistic philosophy which enables him to understand football perfectly and life hardly at all. In a speech before the American Management Association in 1967 Lombardi said: "Unfortunately, it has become too much of a custom to ridicule what is termed 'the company man' because he is dedicated to a principle he believes in. . . . Everywhere you look, there is a call for freedom, independence, or whatever you wish to call it. But as much as these people want to be independent, they still want to be told what to do. And so few people who are capable of leading are ready and willing to lead. So few are ready. . . . We must gain respect for authority—no, let's say we must *regain* respect for authority because to disavow it is contrary to our individual natures."

Since this was not out of the memoirs of some South American general, but out of Vince Lombardi, American hero, I was glad of the opportunity, soon after, to ask him about these opinions. He did not back off. Indeed, he was willing to expand on them. "I think the rights of the individual have been put above everything else," he said. "Which I don't think is right. The individual has to have respect for authority regardless of what that authority is. I think the individual has gone too far. I think

121

ninety-five percent of the people, as much as they shout, would rather be led than lead."

A lifetime in athletics, most of the years spent commanding the soft, empty minds of young people, is nearly certainly bound to lead one down through the labyrinths of authoritarianism to Lombardiism. Certainly Lombardi's uniqueness among coaches is due more to his success than his attitudes. Patriotism, conformism, religion (many football teams kneel in prayer in the clubhouse before and after games)—these are the raw materials a coach demands. For after them, blank-eyed dedication to hard work, team spirit and the ignoring of painful injury come more easily.

There are differences in baseball managers, of course, for the game is less demanding physically. But it takes a certain kind of man to be a baseball manager and, whatever qualities he has, they do not make him superior to the football coach.

When the Manager was a player it was said he made up for his lack of talent with desire. In truth, the Manager's only desire was to spend more money than he was making. Before he became sophisticated enough to catch on the ways of the freebie, he usually succeeded.

He was a ball player because he couldn't make as much at anything else and he's a manager now because he's the only one who can keep up with the owner on a drinking bout. The only thing the Manager loves about baseball is his pay check.

One way he keeps his job is by never making a managerial move he can't justify by "the book." After he bunted with his best hitter in a tough ball game, he invariably told reporters: "Ask anybody who knows the game. It's the only move."

Finally reporters stopped asking him. Now they don't bother to lift their heads from their scorebooks to watch his moves. They know them in advance. So do the other managers in the league. Privately, the Manager says, "Let those other guys, the ones who get fired every year, be the geniuses. I need the job."

The Manager was fired twice, but was hired again on the ground that he's a sound baseball man. (A sound baseball man is anybody who has been fired twice.) Another reason the Manager gets along with his present owner is that they have a tacit understanding about Negroes. It's never said right out, but the Manager knows he's never to play more than three Negroes in the lineup at the same time.

In the dugout the Manager will look up and down the bench and, if there are no Negroes present, he'll say out of the corner of his mouth, "Those guys don't have the heart to play this game." He really believes it and makes mistakes managing against Negro players because he does.

The Manager chews tobacco and his idea of a joke is to spit thick brown juice into the inside of the glove of an unsuspecting rookie. He says the funniest sight in the world is the look on the face of the kid when he puts his hand inside the glove. Once a young player grabbed him by the shirt front and offered to beat him bloody if he did it again. He didn't, but he got the owner to trade the kid the next season.

In three years the kid was most valuable player in the league, but every time the Manager talks about him now, he taps himself on the heart and says, "He hasn't got it here. Believe me, I know." Even so, the Manager gave up surreptitiously urinating on the legs of rookies in the shower. "They don't make kids the way they used to," he grumbles.

The Manager's ambition is to hang on for just five more years. Then he can start collecting a respectable sum from the players' pension fund. The rest of it will come from slum property in which he's invested heavily in Chicago. He doesn't talk much about that, not because he's ashamed, but because he doesn't want anybody to know he's got an outside income. The Manager doesn't like to pick up tabs.

That's why he enjoys being on the road. The ball club picks up the tab. Besides, although he's married, the Manager has a wealthy girl friend who flies to meet him in most cities. She pays her own way. Everybody knows about her, but the Manager likes to think nobody does. Once two newspapermen who cover the club encountered him at the bar of an obscure restaurant. He was with his girl friend. In a few moments the woman left and the Manager came over to the two newspapermen and told the bartender to give them a drink. They were shocked. "There I was sitting here having a quiet drink and this hooker sat down next to me," he said. "Fifty bucks. I might have gone for it, but she was so fucking ugly."

He finished his own drink quickly and left. The very next day, again by coincidence, the newspapermen met the Manager walking on a crowded street in the theatrical section. He was with the same woman. The Manager had the good grace to pretend not to see them.

Lately the Manager has begun worrying about losing his lady friend. He gets loaded and swats her around somewhat and recently she's been saying that the coast-to-coast trips are becoming too expensive. He's even thinking of sending her some flowers. He's giving ball-park passes to the girl who runs the hotel flower shop in anticipation of the event.

The Manager has never won a pennant and ridicules those who predict, in the spring, that they'll win. He says that's the easiest way to get fired. "I think we'll be better than we were last year," he tells the local papers. But he tips out-of-town columnists that he's got a bad ball club. Then he tells them it's off the record. So he's never picked higher than fifth and, when the owners wonder what's wrong with the club, the Manager points to the clippings. "Hell," he says, "we're so bad even these dumb newspapermen can see it."

Fifth place is the Manager's home. It's a good place to be, he tells his wife. "You always got something to shoot for and it's not quite bad enough to get your ass fired." Given the outlay of cash and the extensive scouting staff, a high-school coach could get into a fight for the pennant. But the last time the Manager got into one, he finished second and blew his job. He swore it would never happen again.

Despite everything, the Manager commands great loyalty from his older players. It's because his club is called "the country club." The Manager makes few demands on his players. That's why there are more out-of-shape players on his team than on any other. It's the talk of the league. Any time a pitcher comes off that club, his new pitching coach, just for fun, runs him in the outfield until he vomits. Then the coach reminds him that he has left the country club. That's baseball. And that, by the way, is the Manager's favorite expression.

Faced with the guidance of these single-minded men right from the start of their careers, it is no surprise that the values of professional athletes are not those of most of us. Athletes mistrust the man who seems to be thinking differently, indeed thinking at all. Until very recently professional athletes dressed the same, wore identical crew cuts and counted as flakey anybody who read a book. In a recent season, however, there has been a trend to sideburns, longer hair, higher education and, just as the fashion world ruled they were going out of style, Nehru jackets. But most athletes remain, generally, what they always were—narrow and suspicious of change or even involvement. Those who do not conform are made to feel acutely uncomfortable. I quote here from a column written in 1967 by Vic Ziegel of the New York *Post*.

Jim Bouton . . . ran a gallant campaign for player-representative when the Yankees voted last week. Clete Boyer decided to step down and Bouton and Steve Hamilton were the candidates.

"Before this year," Bouton explains, "we used to get together and somebody would say 'Awright, we gotta get this player-rep business out of the way, let's cut it short. OK, you wanna be player rep? OK, everybody, he wants to be player-rep. OK, let's vote. OK, you win.' "

This year, with the Baseball Players Assn. spending $150,000 to set up an office and having Marvin Miller as the new director, the job of player representative becomes more than finding a man who needs the courtesy car that comes with the post.

Bouton came up with three pages of questions and answers and passed the sheets around the clubhouse. ("I would like to be our team player representative. Before you make up your mind, please read this," were the lines on top of Page One. "Two guys threw it away without looking at it," says Bouton, much too outspoken to be the most popular of Yankees.)

One of the questions is: "Why do I want to be our player representative?" The seven answers are typically Bouton.

"A. I'm very interested in the welfare of the present and future ball players on this team and in baseball in general.

"B. I like to be part of the decision making.

"C. It's an excuse to get out of the house in the winter.

"D. I like the responsibilities that go with the job.

"E. I get to fly in a great big airplane to some of the meetings.

"F. I think we should have someone interested enough to represent us at *all* the meetings and I think I can do the best job for our team.

"G. I get to write "Player Rep" on all my underwear and sweatshirts with a marking pencil."

Another question was "Why would I be a good player representative?" This was one of Bouton's answers:

"As a pitcher working every fourth day at best, I would have more time to devote to the job than someone playing every day. This year I could have made it a full-time job."

So the Yankees balloted and Bouton ended up with four votes and Hamilton romped. And Mel Stottlemyre was named the alternate representative.

Of course, the Yankees do not count themselves as anything but intelligent for picking the best player-representative. But they could not vote for Bouton because he

126

was *different*. And anything *different* is *bad*. Ball players deal in stereotypes. It's all they know.

Two examples, both from some time I spent with the Boston Red Sox. But it could have been *any* professional team.

Gene Oliver, a heavy-legged reserve catcher, tried to make up in exuberance what he lacked in talent. In the bullpen he was always pretending he was a broadcaster and described the action on the field, loudly and often obscenely. And one day in the dugout Al Lakeman, a coach, was telling Manager Dick Williams about Oliver's antics. "You know what I said to him?" Lakeman said. "I said, 'Hey Oliver, you a Jew?' And he said, you know, surprised, 'No, I'm Catholic.' And I said, 'That's funny, you talk just like a Jew. Talking all time, just like a Jew.' " Lakeman was very pleased with himself. He laughed. So did Williams.

Another time Williams was talking about the small crowds the Chicago White Sox were drawing at their home ball park in the South Side Negro ghetto. "It's not really bad around the park," a young reporter from Chicago said. "The riots were miles away. The park has a bad rap."

Williams guffawed. "You kidding?" he said. "Where'd they move that park to? You sure you're talking about the same one?" He guffawed again. "I remember when I played for Kerby Farrell. We lost a tough game there and he just sat around the clubhouse until the bus was ready to go. He said, 'Hell, let it go. I'll walk back.' " Another guffaw. "Imagine walking from that ball park all the way back to the hotel. They'd have to go out looking for him in the morning and they'd find him all over the place—an ear here, a leg there."

The Red Sox coaches, who were listening, nodded wisely. They knew you can't walk on the South Side. They knew because they had never tried. Pro sports are like that. The people in them have only a filmy understanding of the world outside. Stereotypes are their only connection with life out there.

One of the best examples of the overpaid, overexposed,

overidolized athletes in this country is Wilt Chamberlain. Just because he grew to be probably seven feet four inches tall, thus attaining a certain advantage in a game where height is important, Chamberlain has been showered with wealth from the time he was a teenager. It would be a miracle if the bribery of his elders and the adulation of his peers did not spoil him. There has been no miracle.

Wilt Chamberlain is a millionaire. His salary from the Los Angeles Lakers is reported to be 200,000 dollars a year. His income from other ventures, trotting horses, a restaurant, real estate, may add another 250,000 dollars. His tax position is undoubtedly difficult. But Wilt Chamberlain does not have what he wants. What he wants is to be six feet tall. Tough.

The colleges started out spoiling Chamberlain. They socked it to him. Scholarship. Car. A no-work job. Wilt the Stilt, a name he grew to despise, chose Kansas. But the itch for money was upon him. The scholarship was nice. So was the car and the no-work job. But the job didn't pay much. And Wilt Chamberlain was in the process of building up some expensive tastes.

So he chucked college and went with the Harlem Globetrotters until his class graduated. That made him eligible for the National Basketball Association. After that it was, well, a giant among pygmies. One year Wilt Chamberlain averaged 50 points a game. He could do it all. Except he couldn't shoot fouls, still can't. But then, being tall doesn't help a man shoot fouls.

In the process of doing it all, Chamberlain began to think that he could do *everything*. That includes coach better than anyone who happened to be getting paid for the job. He humiliated Dolph Schayes, his coach in Philadelphia, missing practices, ostentatiously sitting on the bench and not paying attention while Schayes lectured his players during time-out, going over the head of Schayes to whine to the owners about how the coach didn't understand him, until at last one of them had to go, Chamberlain or Schayes. Guess who went. Chamberlain was so surly to his next coach, Alex Hannum, the large, mostly amiable coach of San Francisco and later the Philadelphia

76ers, that only an offer by Hannum to fight it out with fists enabled them to live together in a sort of armed truce. Chamberlain's next victim was Bill Van Breda Kolff at Los Angeles. It wasn't hard. All Chamberlain had to do was get into a dispute about exactly how he should play the game and then say, "Either he goes or I go." And even while the NBA was in the process of making Chamberlain as rich as Croesus, he signed an article in *Sports Illustrated* (for about 15,000 dollars) titled "My Life in a Bush League." This wasn't just biting the hand that fed him, it was taking it off at the elbow. And when an outraged cry went up, Chamberlain courageously denied he had said what his name appeared over.

Since it was the practice of magazines to obtain manuscripts in these cases, *Sports Illustrated* was justifiably smug. So Chamberlain made another flip-flop. He said, well, he hadn't seen the *title* of the story. That was no doubt true, and the phrase "My life in a bush league" did not appear in the body type. But the word "bush" was there many times, as plain as the beard on Chamberlain's face, and no one took him very seriously. It is one of the things that has turned Chamberlain crabby and sour with sportswriters.

What Chamberlain has learned most about life is that he has to take orders from nobody. He has supreme, lofty and total confidence in his own omnipotence. He believes that he is not only the best basketball player in the world, but the best football player, the best cook, the best lover. He believes he could have been heavyweight champion of the world or the decathlon champion. Says Willis Reed of the New York Knickerbockers, a 6' 11" center who has to look up at Chamberlain the way most men have to look up at him, "He swears he can beat anybody in the whole world at *anything*. I don't know if he can, but he talks a good game."

What a lot of this is, of course, is defense. Even about his height. He has been like a fat lady and her weight. He has lied about it. According to Chamberlain he is either seven feet and one-sixteenth of an inch tall or seven feet one and a sixteenth inch tall. There is ample evidence that

129

he is closer to 7' 5". Most impressive is the fact that his fans in Philadelphia once gave Chamberlain a trophy that was seven feet one inch and a sixteenth. Chamberlain was able to look down on the top of it.

The point is that Chamberlain is afraid of being considered a freak. So he lies about his height and fantasizes about accomplishments. This is all understandable, if not reasonable. One must wonder, though, what Chamberlain would have been if there were no professional basketball. Is it possible that without basketball there would have *been* no Chamberlain? Or that he would have been down in the trenches with Martin Luther King instead of campaigning for Richard Nixon? Alas, we shall never know.

What we do know is that despite his braggadocio Chamberlain was never even as great a basketball player as he wanted to be. He always let himself be defeated, in the end, by Bill Russell of the Boston Celtics. And at the last, he caved in altogether. This was in the final game of the 1968-69 NBA playoffs won, of course, by Boston. In the last minutes of the game Chamberlain took himself out of the lineup because, he said, his knee hurt. Then he ripped Van Breda Kolff for not putting him back into it.

This all proved to be too much for Russell. For years Russell had maintained a stony silence about Chamberlain. But now he was so furious he opened up. Chamberlain didn't deserve to be put back into the game, Russell said. He shouldn't have been out of there in the first place. Nothing short of a broken leg would have been an excuse to leave. "Chamberlain copped out," Russell said.

Russell also said that Chamberlain talks a good game of basketball, but that it's a team game and he wondered whether Chamberlain thinks he brought out the best in his Los Angeles teammates, Elgin Baylor and Jerry West. "Chamberlain thinks he's a genius," Russell said. "He's not."

That kind of tongue-lashing coming from a man Chamberlain must respect above all men, a man who is a demonstrably better basketball player than the great Wilt, might have a salutary effect. Then again, it might not.

The personality of a player usually undergoes a certain amount of revision before it is implanted in the public mind. One reason is that the public mind does a great deal of its own image building, being less interested in truth than comfort. It is comforting to believe that athletes are kind, upright, gentle and truthful, and sportswriters have learned that the image they project of the athlete that will be believed is the one the public wants to believe.

When this smooth current is disturbed, the reaction can be violent. Jack Johnson, the heavyweight champion, might have been better accepted had he held his hat in his hands and bowed meekly in the direction of his public. Instead, he lived flamboyantly and took white mistresses and wives. The public bared its teeth, turned on him and, in the end, destroyed him, bringing to the language, in the process, a new phrase: white hope (and eventually a hit Broadway play, *The Great White Hope*).

This is why everyone knows that Babe Ruth was a sweet soul who spent all the time he wasn't hitting home runs in hospitals making happy the last hours of children with terminal cancer. In fact, he was a gross man of gargantuan, undisciplined appetites for food, whiskey and women. One of his famous illnesses, indeed, "the great American bellyache," was actually a venereal disease. J. G. Taylor Spink, founder of the *Sporting News,* has written:

[On the road] Ruth did not usually do his sleeping in the hotel. . . . When Ping Bodie joined the Yankees, he was assigned to a room with Ruth and on the club's Western swing an old friend asked Ping, "Who are you rooming with?" "A suitcase," answered Ping.

In St. Louis he usually was to be found at Busch's Grove, an eating place in St. Louis County. He frequently would go there in the morning for breakfast. It was not unusual for him to eat two fried chickens and wash them down with goblets of beer.

Spink also described one of Ruth's famed eating and drinking bouts. "Ruth ordered a double porterhouse steak, a double order of head lettuce and Roquefort dressing, a double order of cottage-fried potatoes, a double order of apple pie à la mode, and a large pot of coffee. When he called the waiter and asked for the check there was not enough left to feed a sparrow." And that was only the beginning. From the restaurant Ruth and his party went to Coney Island, where the Babe promptly consumed four hot dogs and four Cokes. Two hours later he duplicated this performance. On the way home Ruth again stopped at the restaurant where he had had dinner and promptly went through it all again—double everything.

Paul Derringer, a National League pitcher, has described the first time he met Ruth. It was in a dining car on a train. "I was eating at a single table and the seat opposite me was the only vacant one in the car. In came Ruth, alone, and seeing the empty chair he sat at my table.

"The Babe called over the waiter and ordered a pitcher of ice, a pint of ginger ale, a porterhouse steak garnished with four fried eggs, fried potatoes and a pot of coffee. He told the waiter to be sure and bring him the pitcher of ice and ginger ale right away.

"A few minutes later the waiter set the pitcher of ice and pint of ginger ale in front of Ruth. The Babe pulled a pint of bourbon out of his hip pocket, poured it over the ice, poured the ginger ale, shook up the mixture and that was his breakfast juice.

"Sometime later I happened to meet his roommate and related to him what happened in the diner that morning. He told me that it was nothing more than a daily habit. Ruth generally drank a quart mixture of bourbon whiskey and ginger ale at breakfast, before attacking a steak, garnished with four or six fried eggs and potatoes on the side."

Ruth lost enormous sums at racetracks and left large IOUs unpaid. Perhaps he didn't remember them. Certainly he found it difficult to remember the names of even close friends. All young men he called "kid." Older men were

"Doc." As Roger Kahn wrote in *Esquire* in 1959: "Once when he accidentally spiked a Yankee named Ray Morehart, he apologized profusely, then said to a veteran, 'Hey, when that guy join the club?' Morehart had been with the club for months."

Ruth was never the playful, outgoing man he was supposed to be. In fact, he was keenly aware of his fame and popularity. "Paris ain't much of a town," he once said, largely because he was unrecognized there. He began to believe that he was a law unto himself, ignored club rules, battled with umpires. When he was suspended for five days for "shameful and abusive language" to umpires, Ban Johnson, president of the American League, said in a letter to him: "It seems the period has arrived when you should allow some intelligence to creep into a mind that has plainly been warped."

Little of this was available to the contemporary public. The Babe was thoroughly protected by the news media. Yet the truth rises eventually. It does not take much research to find out what the Babe was really like. It doesn't matter. The fake Babe Ruth is more palatable than the real one. As poor currency always drives out the good, so does the fake drive out the real.

There are other famous Yankee players whose public images bear little relation to the kind of men they actually are—Joe DiMaggio, Yogi Berra and Mickey Mantle, to name three.

Suave, sure, husband of Marilyn Monroe, Joe DiMaggio holds a unique place in Americana. He is super-hero. Sixteen years after he completed his remarkable feat of hitting in 56 straight games he was immortalized (if a god can obtain new immortalization) by Simon and Garfunkel in "Mrs. Robinson."

Where have you gone, Joe DiMaggio?
A nation turns its lonely eyes to you.

In fact, the nation has not turned its lonely eyes to Joe DiMaggio. As Gay Talese showed in a remarkable article in *Esquire* in 1966, DiMaggio is a vain, lonely man, who is a tyrant to the sycophants who surround him. Wrote Talese. "His friends [know] . . . that should they inadvertently betray a confidence . . . [he] will never speak to them again." Talese then described a scene in a restaurant called Reno's in San Francisco which DiMaggio would often drop into.

They may wait for hours sometimes, waiting and knowing he may wish to be alone; but it does not seem to matter, they are endlessly awed by him, moved by the mystique, he is a kind of male Garbo. They know he can be warm and loyal if they are sensitive to his wishes, but they must never be late for an appointment to meet him. One man, unable to find a parking space, arrived a half hour late once and DiMaggio didn't talk to him again for three months. They know, too, when dining at night with DiMaggio, that he generally prefers male companions and occasionally one or two young women, but never wives; wives gossip, wives are trouble, and men wishing to remain close to DiMaggio must keep their wives at home.

His friends fawn on him, call him "Clipper" (one must wonder why a grown man would tolerate that), introduce him to mindless young women and pick up his tabs. At her death he turned a marriage to Marilyn Monroe that didn't work (she complained that all he wanted to do was watch television) into a maudlin lost love. He held a permanent grudge against Robert Kennedy because he once spent a lot of time at a party dancing with Marilyn. This was *after* their marriage had disintegrated.

And in the end he took a coaching job—not a managing job, a *coaching* job—with Charles O. Finley, the erratic owner of the Oakland Athletics. It was the act of a lonely, probably bitter man. No one had offered him a job as manager. In the fall of 1968 Joe DiMaggio was in Japan to teach the batters there how to hit. One suspects he had more difficulty communicating with them than he did with American batters.

Yogi Berra is a particularly glowing example of an

image which has outstripped the man. Of course, it is not his fault. It is not his fault that he is not a lovable gnome bubbling over with *bon mots*. Nor is it his fault that he is a narrow, suspicious man, jealous of the man other people supposed him to be and which he knew he was not. He was supposed to be a humorist because he said things like "Bill Dickey learned me all his experiences," and "I want to thank you for making this award necessary." In fact, there is severe doubt that Yogi Berra ever said anything intentionally funny in his life. The late Tom Meany used to tell this possibly apocryphal story about Berra which, at the least, illustrates the breadth of his knowledge. Berra was introduced to Ernest Hemingway at a party in a restaurant. When he returned to his table, he was asked what he thought of him. Said Berra: "He's quite a character. What does he do?"

Well, he's a writer.

"Yeah? What paper?"

After a while Berra and his wife, Carmen, came to believe that he was indeed something of a man of the world, raconteur, sophisticate. After all, weren't they rich? (Berra has had enormous financial luck. He sold his interests in a bowling emporium at a great profit shortly before the bottom dropped out of the bowling business. And he took a block of stock in return for endorsing a little-known chocolate "drink"—which means no milk and very little chocolate. The stock skyrocketed.)

There was an autobiography called *Yogi*. It was a typical baseball autobiography, all shiny and bright for the kiddies, naturally written by somebody else, a man who could have done better. But by the time the world was ready for a book about Berra, the Berras were not interested in reality. They wanted the book to be about Berra as they would have liked him to be. So it turned out to be a terrible book, cheap and phony and transparent. I reviewed it that way.

It was a lovely spring day in St. Petersburg. The palm trees waved shiny green against the high blue sky. Yogi Berra saw me as soon as I arrived.

"You son of a bitch," Berra said. "You cocksucker."

135

He never said that in *Yogi*.

But that is not what I remember about him most. I remember most that the other ball players always complained that Yogi Berra would stand naked at the clubhouse buffet and scratch his genitals over the cold cuts.

Mickey Mantle is a quite different man. He was never shoehorned into a role which, like Berra, he was unprepared by nature and intellect to play. Mantle was a country boy, ill-educated, frightened, convinced at an early age by a series of deaths in his family that he was doomed to live only a short life.

He was simple, naïve and, at the very first, trusting. It did not take him long to misplace his trust. He soon found that he was trusting the wrong people and, when this cost him money, it made him withdrawn and sullen, as well as poor. Fortified by Yankee tradition—watch out for outsiders—Mantle was soon responding only to his teammates and the glad-handers and celebrity fuckers who flocked around him. (Mantle is almost universally liked by his teammates because he goes out of his way to be outgoing and friendly with them. He vigorously denies that he decided to behave that way after he, as a rookie, was ignored by the aloof, morose DiMaggio, but a young ball player I trust swears Mantle told him this and I have no reason to disbelieve him.) Pretty soon, as his skills blossomed, it became Mantle and his hedonistic enclave against the world.

And obviously the world didn't count. The world was made up of crowds of sweaty, smelly little kids who demanded autographs and smeared ice cream on your new shantung suit, middle-aged slobs who accosted you in restaurants in mid-forkful to simper about getting an autograph for their little kiddies at home, and cloddish newspaper and magazine people who never got anything right and only wanted to hurt you anyway. When he was playing poorly or when he was especially plagued by one of his numerous injuries, Mantle would become particularly withdrawn and sulky, turn his back even on well-wishers. A great deal of this was sheer self-protection. For Mantle always doubted himself and, most of all, his knowledge of the game.

He had reason to. Mantle was never much of a student of baseball. Born with marvelous skills, he played it intuitively, never having to pay much attention to what was going on. More than once I heard him ask a teammate about a rival pitcher, "What's he th'ow?" This is not an unusual question around a ball club—except if the pitcher had been in the league five years and pitched against the Yankees maybe 30 times.

It is possible that Mantle was incapable of even the minimum amount of concentration the finer points of baseball require. Certainly he refused to work on his own physical conditioning during the off-season, a refusal which, if it did not actually shorten his career, obviously did nothing to prevent the pulled muscles in legs and groin which plagued him during almost every season. Year after year Mantle was told to go home and lift weights with his legs. He was begged to keep in good enough physical condition so that he would at least not disarrange a hamstring, as he did so often, in the opening days of spring training. But Mantle's idea of keeping fit was to have an active social life and play golf out of an electric cart which was outfitted with a bar. He had fun. He also had pulled muscles.

It has become a cliché to wonder how great Mantle would have been had he been physically healthy during his career. What I wonder is how great he might have been had he even *tried* to keep physically healthy.

In the early years of his career Mantle was booed by the fans because he refused to live up to his promise. Later on the boos turned to cheers as he became known as a man who made a gallant effort despite enormous physical pain. I'm not sure the fans weren't right in the first place.

Sometimes one is provided with a brief glimpse into the character of the famous ball player. I recall an incident involving Warren Spahn, when he was at the end of his great pitching career. He had just been knocked out

137

of the box by, of all people, the new New York Mets and I thought I might write a compassionate column about the old pro who knew he was losing it and about what he thought as he was being beaten by the worst club in baseball. At the same time I thought it would be interesting to ask him about a suit he had going against a man who had, without his permission, written a book about his life.

My conversation with Spahn went like this.

Hi, I wanted . . .

SPAHN: I don't want to talk about the game.

You don't?

SPAHN: No I don't. I'll talk about anything else, but I won't talk about the game.

A thought flashed through my mind of General Custer saying he would talk about anything but the battle.

Well, let's talk about that suit . . .

SPAHN (enraged, veins in the neck standing out, etc.): Get the fuck out of here. Get the fuck out of here before I punch you in the mouth.

I added the threat to my collection and, after a suitable interval, I got the fuck out.


It is necessary here to point out another aspect of the life of the professional athlete in America. Perhaps it can best be done by relating a true story, an incident which took place some years ago, well before the sexual revolution which is supposed to be sweeping through our young people today.

The tale involves two baseball players whom I shall call Great Ball Player and Ordinary Ball Player, though they were not brothers, only roommates. It was ten o'clock in the evening, on the road, when the telephone rang. Ordinary picked it up. It was a girl, wanting to know if Great was in his room. No, he wasn't, but since curfew time was 11 P.M., he should be there shortly. At 11:05 the girl called again. Had Great arrived? Er, no, well not exactly. In fact, since he had not, and since it was now past curfew, there was no telling what time he would show up. Well, it so happened that the girl was in the

138

lobby of the hotel and it was kind of creepy. Could she come up to the room and wait? Ordinary hesitated. It would be against the rules. Come on up, he said.

The girl was pretty, young, under twenty, and it turned out she had never met Great. But she had heard Great was great and she just had to, er, meet him. Don't worry about me, she said. You go to sleep and I'll just sit here in his chair.

It didn't work out exactly like that. One thing led to another and with only minor delay, the poor little waif agreed to share Ordinary's bed, just to be comfortable. Of course. And so came the dawn and Great still had not arrived.

A day game was scheduled and Ordinary got down to the lobby just in time to catch the team bus to the ball park. So did Great, arriving from another direction. Ordinary couldn't help gloating a bit. Sorry you're so late, he said. There was this little girl . . .

GREAT: Where is she now?

ORDINARY: She's still in the room.

GREAT: Tell the manager I'm going to be a little late.

He sprinted up to the room.

At the ballpark later Great winked at Ordinary and said, great. Then, after being out all night, after his quick visit to his hotel room, after huffing in late to the ballpark, Great played a great ball game. That's what greatness is.

It's also what shortens careers, why some men can make a living in athletics until they are forty and others are has-beens at thirty-two. As Casey Stengel always said, it's not the catching that hurts an athlete, it's the chasing. And there remains the nagging question about what this quick success in catching the girls, the money, the fame does to a man. At the least it turns his head. At the worst we have Wilkie Collins' wild beast. The fans put in their money and crank out their man. They never get any worse than they deserve.

Finally there is the athlete who can be called, for lack of more precise designation, the Goody Two Shoes type.

139

Goody is a fine athlete, a Southerner and a member of the Fellowship of Christian Athletes. This means he sells God and Country and makes money in radio and television. Goody says things like "golly" and "swell" and "oh gosh" and nods wisely at the new militant separatist Negro because he always knew the nigras didn't really want to live with white folk. Goody Two Shoes will tell you, if you have gained his trust, that he grew up with nigras and therefore understands them better than any Northerner. He'll point out carefully that nigras do a lot of things better than white men, because of the way they are built. But they simply do not have as much physical courage or brains. It's not their fault, mind you, it just happens to *be* that way.

When he's not talking about Negroes, Goody Two Shoes can be terribly persuasive. He has big, penetrating, icy-blue eyes which always register Sincerity. He is *involved*. A good piece of his life is devoted to talking to kids at church meetings, holding clinics, speaking up for God. He is widely respected by his teammates and the press and his forthright manner, friendliness and self-assurance make him an ideal television commentator. He always said he would devote his life to young people but finds that there is always time to make big money in communications. If there is anything Goody Two Shoes can do, it's *communicate*.

Goody Two Shoes doesn't drink, smoke or swear and he is faithful to his wife, smugly faithful, even on the road. That is, he *was* smugly faithful. Then he met this airline stewardess. He managed to keep it secret for a long time, but it all came out into the open when the airline stewardess tried to commit suicide in his hotel room because he wouldn't get a divorce and marry her. Goody Two Shoes is still holier than thou, but now he has fewer disciples.

His good looks and sincerity have made Goody Two Shoes friends wherever he goes. He is himself convinced that people instinctively understand that he likes them. Somehow, though, the men who become his closest friends are the ones who throw things his way—real-estate deals,

140

stock tips, business ventures to which he contributes his name and little else in return for a large block of stock.

Goody Two Shoes is the very model of the new athlete, educated, articulate, owner of all the social graces and nearly a million dollars. He is grateful to God and country and says it in every one of the many speeches he makes at church suppers and Rotary stags. He also says that if everybody would work as hard as he did, instead of asking the government for help, they too could raise themselves by their own bootstraps. This is always very well received. Goody Two Shoes is now thinking of going into politics. He got his feet wet getting out the vote for George Wallace. He liked it.

# 5 The Losers

BY PROFESSION BUDDY EDELEN WAS A MARATHON runner, which is to say a masochist. The loneliness of the long-distance runner doesn't have time to develop in depth in a mere four-or-five-mile race. For bedrock loneliness, for sheer departure from sense, for the feeling that one is in a world apart and damned be he who is not, there is the marathon—26 miles and 385 yards of excruciating, lung-bursting agony.

The training, the dedication it takes to prepare one's body to run this distance in world-class time cannot properly be imagined unless one has lived a long time alone with pain. Buddy Edelen endured that pain, reveled in it even, and gave the marathon his life. In the end he failed. But what a beautiful failure he was! His was a failure that brought no shame, only a kind of glory. If the measure of a man is not how well he succeeded, but how hard he tried, Buddy Edelen was a giant.

A man does not become a marathon runner by design. He sort of falls into it. In Edelen's case, he sort of failed into it. When he was asked, as he often was, why he became a marathon runner, he said: "I found everybody was beating me out at the shorter distances. I'm virtually devoid of natural speed. I can't run a mile in under 4:18."

This would have clued in anybody else to forgetting about footracing as a sport. But Edelen was a tenacious young man, stubborn and strangely prideful. He was still in high school when he signed his personal declaration of independence. It should be illuminated by monks and hung in the office of every expense-account rugged individualist in the land.

Leonard Graves Edelen IV was born on September 22, 1937, in Harrodsburg, Kentucky, the son of a salesman. His mother was institutionalized when he was six and he lived with an aunt in Alabama, later in a boarding school and with his father again when he remarried. Young Edelen didn't, as he says, "get on" with his stepmother and the marriage, at any rate, was brief. By the time his father married for the third time and settled in Sioux Falls, South Dakota, where he became advertising sales manager for a TV station, Buddy Edelen was a most self-reliant young man.

Edelen never went to his father and said Daddy, send me through school. He went to Minnesota University without any help. Indeed, since his father's financial position was healthy, Buddy was not eligible, as he might have been, for a full scholarship. He worked as a busboy in a sorority house, watered the indoor track and roomed free upstairs at the fire station in return for running errands and closing the doors to keep the snow out when there was a fire call during the night. It took him five years to get through school. "Too many Americans go hand in cap to their parents," Edelen says. "If I wanted help from my father, I'd have asked." Then he smiles his boyish smile. "At the same time, he didn't offer."

With no God-given natural speed, which is what Edelen liked to call it, he found himself entering longer and longer races. In 1960 he went to the Olympic trials to take a crack at the 10,000-meter race and failed miserably. In a last-ditch effort to make the team, he worked his way

142

to Finland on a freighter, chipping paint, swabbing decks. When he got there, though, the gates were shut. In an Olympic year foreigners were not eligible for Finnish races. He worked his way back to England, where he had a letter of introduction from his coach pen pal, Fred Wilt, ex-track man and FBI agent, to a man named Derek Cole, who was interested in track. "I can pinpoint the moment when I became a long-distance runner," Edelen says. "It was the day I stepped on British soil."

The reasons for that are many. English climate is particularly suited to long-distance running. More important, this is a nation which takes long-distance running seriously. So Edelen became an expatriot. "I had a dream," he says. "I meant to fulfill that dream in the best way possible."

That way involved a teaching job, obtained with the help of Cole, and a gloomy, ill-lit, one-room flat in Westcliff-on-Sea, a clammy seaside resort some 50 miles east of London. The teaching job was at the King John School in Thundersley, four and a half miles west of Westcliff along London road. It was an ideal distance, Edelen ran it every morning. He ran it back every afternoon.

For almost four years his routine varied little. After his run to Thundersley, past the stores and garages, the neat British row houses, each with its tiny garden of roses and hollyhocks, past the commuters with bowler hats and rolled umbrellas going to work the way normal men do, unseeing of it all, only an eye out for the dogs who liked to dash up and nip at his heels, Edelen did 30 sit-ups in the gym and took a shower. The shower was usually cold. The British are proud of their poor plumbing. At noon Edelen was on the grass track to do wind sprints, 110 yards fast, 110 yards at a jog, over and over, ad nauseam. The important thing was not to even breathe hard. He took a lot of pride in that. Even after his four-and-a-half mile run to school, accomplished in 20 minutes, Edelen breathed no harder than a commuter reading a newspaper while he waited for his train.

After school, most days, after running back to Westcliff, Edelen would turn down Chalkwell Avenue to the sea. In the summer the area was crowded with "trippers" down from London. But in the winter the Esplanade, where Edelen did his repetition quarters, was bare of humanity and naked to the elements.

The training involved a fast quarter mile, jogging in a circle for recovery, then another quarter at top speed. In wind and fog he ground it out. "You do one quarter and you know you have to do one more," Edelen once said, explaining his training. "You just go back and forth, back and forth, all alone. It takes a terrific amount of perseverance."

Saturdays during most of the year Edelen competed in cross-country races in England and on the Continent. These were true cross-country events, ten miles up and down the hills and often through the mud. Edelen liked the mud. He felt it built up his legs.

And pretty soon his rugged training program began to pay off. He started accumulating a tableful of dusty trophies. Sometimes a portable radio was the prize. He had three of them.

On Sundays, the day God rested, Edelen went to his toughest grind, his 30-mile run at racing pace. On the road from Westcliff to Chelmsford, a route Edelen often used for his Sunday run, there is a steep hill he made famous. That was where he caught up to and passed a heavily loaded truck. The driver, Edelen remembers, had a funny look on his face as he ran by. A local paper found out about the incident and printed it under the headline: "Edelen Overtakes Lorry." The clipping is one of Edelen's prize possessions.

The sacrifice did not stop with the training grind, the 130 miles a week. There was a financial sacrifice. An English school teacher made 130 dollars a month at the time. And there was the sacrifice of the food. He never looked it, but as a boy Edelen had a tendency to flesh. For a while he was even called "Butterball." So he was convinced that he was a deep and incurable glutton. He kept his weight at around 140 pounds, which means his skin was always stretched tightly over his 5' 10" frame. So in

144

addition to living sparely—he never felt he could afford a telephone—he ate sparely. His daily menu would have driven the average sedentary worker to distraction. Yet Edelen always felt he was eating too much. He would not, for example, keep any food in his cold little apartment. "I can't keep it around," he would say. "I might eat it."

He was tightfisted with money, but when I visited him in Westcliff, he would not go out to dinner with me. It made him nervous to be under one roof with that much food. His dinner usually consisted of a bit of fish—half the size of a normal portion—and a tomato. Rarely, a potato. He never spent more than 40 cents on his main meal. Then he might allow himself tuppence worth of salted peanuts. But he never bought more than that at one time. He could have saved money buying a tin of them, but he was afraid to keep them around.

At the same time, Edelen developed an important involvement with his pulse. It was his theory that the slower he could coax his pulse to be at rest, the less rapid it would be under strain. And the way to get it to go slow he reasoned, was to make the blood vessels very large by giving them a lot of work to do. A normal at-rest pulse is 78. Edelen got his down to 38. He said he knew one man who had a slower pulse. Only one thing wrong with the fellow. He was dead.

This requires effort that is almost beyond comprehension. During a race Edelen would often run right out of his head. He would hurt all over; legs, arms, lungs. "When you get that tired," he explained, "you're preoccupied with pain. People would shout things at me, nice things, really, shouts of encouragement and I'd just tell them, 'Fuck off.'" Sweet, gentle, Buddy Edelen, fuck off.

Eventually Edelen began to win important marathon races. Marathon courses vary so widely that there is no official time record for the race. But Edelen set an unofficial world record when he ran the Polytechnic Marathon, from Windsor to Chiswick, in two hours, 14 minutes and 28 seconds. When he ran over the original marathon course in Greece, he broke the time of Abebe Bikila, the

145

barefoot Ethiopian, who was to win the Olympic marathon twice in a row. (The legend of the marathon, of course, is that the first—and unknown—marathon runner, who ran the distance from Marathon to Athens to bring news of the Greek's victory over the Persians died of effort. "I don't think that guy did his 130 miles a week," Edelen liked to say. "You have to respect that distance.")

In October of 1963 Edelen ran a race he'll never forget. It was in Kocise, Czechoslovakia. He won the marathon, the most famous in Europe, in a record two hours 15.09.6, beating the Russian Sergei Popof by half a mile. The year before at Kocise Edelen had run a thrilling marathon against Dr. Pavel Kantoorek, the Czech, losing by an unbelievable, sweaty nose at the tape. The crowd remembered that well when the American came in all alone with his record the next year.

There was a lot of emotion and many tears as Edelen went around those last two laps. And at last 50,000 voices rose in a great measured chant: "Ee-da-len, Ee-da-len, Ee-da-len."

"It was," Edelen says, "a feeling that will take some beating."

But all of this was mere preparation. Buddy Edelen's driving dream was to compete for the U.S. in the 1964 Olympic Games in Tokyo and, in order to do that, he had to come back to this country to qualify. (It did not altogether please him that the money for him to travel home had to be raised by public subscription in Sioux Falls. It was the only time I ever heard Edelen complain about his lot. "You look at the money professional baseball players and golfers make," he said. "You know you put in as much work or more. You can't help but be envious." Then he went out for a run.)

The qualifying race was the Yonkers (N.Y.) marathon. It was run starting at high noon on an unseasonably hot day in May. In brain-frying temperatures Edelen set himself a blistering pace. Pretty soon he was running all alone, but he was convinced his footsteps were being dogged. Wilt fed him sugar water, poured cold water over his head. But Edelen was out of his mind with the heat.

146

"Dammit, Fred," he kept saying. "How much longer? Why don't you tell me how much longer?"

"I was angry," Edelen was able to say the next day. "He didn't tell me how much to go without my asking. That's foolish, of course, but that's the way you get."

Edelen finished the race in 2:25.6. His nearest rival finished *20 minutes* behind him. That's roughly comparable to winning a baseball game 64-0. At that point Edelen immediately became a favorite to win the gold medal in Tokyo. If he had, he'd have been the first American in 56 years even to come close.

But between Yonkers in May and Tokyo in October Edelen developed a severe sciatic-nerve condition. The constant pounding on pavement had taken its toll. Edelen was a mass of pain from the small of his back down to the back of his knee. Pain or no, he kept on training, going to doctors who couldn't help him, osteopaths who thought they could, charlatans who must have known they couldn't, paying the bills himself from his meager savings.

In Tokyo Edelen battled the pain with blind intensity. He drove himself harder than ever. One reason was the pain. The other was the Japanese. This is an event which, unlike Americans, they care about. They call it the "flower event" and treat marathon runners as heroes. Edelen couldn't believe it when Japanese kids ran after him during his practice runs, shouting, "Buddy, Buddy." Then one night I prevailed upon him to come with me to a Japanese restaurant. We had not yet been seated when a lovely Japanese waitress, dressed in a bright kimono, bowed to us and said to Edelen, who was wearing his Olympic blazer: "Marathon?"

There was surprise on his face. "Marathon," he said, nodding.

"Edelen-san?" she asked in that tinkly voice Japanese women have.

Edelen flushed happily. This could never have happened to him in his native land. "Edelen," he said, nodding and grinning. The waitress let out a tiny squeal of delight. Soon there was a flutter of kimono-clad young women

147

around him, clamoring for his autograph. He signed everything in sight, wearing a look of great glee.

In his last long run before the race, Edelen ran over the marathon course and then five more miles for good measure. He must have psyched out a goodly number of runners who noticed that he completed the course and now was going around again. He ran the distance at an unvarying pace, moving like a machine, uphill and down, taking two hours and 52 minutes for the 31 miles. He was in pain all the way. When Pete McArdle, the gnome of a man out of Ireland and New York, who had been training with Edelen, gave up after 25 miles and climbed into the following jeep, he said: "He's a madman. An absolute madman."

At the end, with the salt of his sweat caked hard in streaks down his dehydrated skin, Edelen gave his prerace prediction: "I shall run my bloody guts out."

And he did, he did. No moment in sports has ever moved me so much as the sight of Edelen's slight figure coming into the range of my glasses in the great stadium, his head wagging back and forth in pain, his fingernails digging into the palms of his hand so furiously he had drawn blood. The marathon was over. Abebe Bikila had won it in a record time of two hours, 12:11. Perhaps there was no way Edelen could have won that race. His own personal best had been two hours 14:32. On this day, with the pain sitting on him like a ton of knife, he ran it in two hours 18:12.4. He finished sixth. To this day he is certain that, were it not for the pain, he would have taken the silver medal. It would have meant a great deal to him.

What Buddy Edelen did about all of this was go back to work. He intended to run his guts out in Mexico City in 1968. Except he never got the chance. He left England after another year to take a teaching job at Adams State in Colorado, not so much because he wanted to return home but because of the altitude. He had three years to train at an altitude approximating that of Mexico City.

Yet once again he was defeated. The pain of his sciatica became so great he could not train. He did not even try

148

to qualify for the Mexico City marathon. He will never be an Olympic athlete again. But he will never stop running. He once bet a friend that he would still be running the marathon in under two hours and 30 minutes at the age of sixty. I have no doubt he will. Buddy Edelen is a determined man.

There are many other athletes like Buddy Edelen, young men who give of themselves constantly and in return get only the satisfaction of their accomplishments. Most of them are amateur track athletes, of course, but there a great many poorly paid professionals in sports who keep trying just because it's there. Hockey players, for example, most of whom make miserable wages for most of their active playing days. These young men are the pure of sports, the men who make the words of the man who is supposed to have fathered the modern Olympics —Pierre de Courbertin—seem more important than pretentious. Said de Courbertin: "The most important thing in the Olympic Games is not to win but to take part, just as the most important thing in life is not the triumph but the struggle."

Somehow, the sacrifices these men make turn them into better people. My own theory is that earning your living— or fame—with pain is a gentling experience. It's as though pain sensitizes nerve endings, the way a safecracker alerts his finger tips on sandpaper and makes you understanding of and responsive to the world around you.

I have seldom met a prizefighter I didn't like. With certain outstanding exceptions, they are the gentlest of men. The quiet, rueful courage of Jim Beattie, a large young man with all of the desire but none of the equipment to be a heavyweight champion, will always be remembered by people who knew him. And Dick Tiger. He was middleweight champion and then light-heavy-weight champion and for years he carefully saved his money and made investments in Nigerian real estate. But he is a Biafran and, when the civil war came, he was wiped out, stony broke, scrounging for money to pay for food for his family and friends, some of whom were

149

literally starving. Dick Tiger showed no bitterness. He took those losses the way he took pain in the ring, with scarcely a blink, as part of his life, as though pain and deprivation were his due.

There are fighters who turn arrogant and difficult in their late years. I count Jack Dempsey and Rocky Marciano among them. (After he had retired, I called Marciano for a quote a magazine editor wanted. He was friendly and affable, and made it known that in return he expected a subscription to the magazine. Jack Dempsey would not answer the phone.)

But these are exceptions. Even Muhammad Ali, who had more cause than anyone since Jack Johnson to rail against the treatment he received from newspapers and boxing commissions around the country, somehow never betrayed the innate decency I believe he possesses. Like Malcolm X, I have had severe doubts about the sincerity of Elijah Muhammad, founder and leader of the moribund Black Muslim movement with which Muhammad Ali so involved himself. But I never questioned for a moment that Muhammad Ali believed intensely that this was the way the black man had to go.

In return for sticking to his beliefs against impossible pressure from almost every quarter, including even the Black Muslims themselves, Muhammad Ali was denied permission to earn a living during the years his battle against being drafted was being fought in the courts. One can only guess that some important person in Washington said, "Get me that nigger," for the vendetta against him went to teeth-gnashing lengths.

It was one thing when the hack politicians who are the boxing commissioners of the country, men never noted for lack of patriotism or depth of intelligence, first stripped him of his title, then refused to sanction any fights involving him. It was quite another when the supposedly sound-minded people in Washington prevented him from going abroad to fight, on the ground he might elect to avoid prosecution by becoming an exile. "That's crazy," Muhammad Ali said. "Where am I going to go? How can I leave my mother and my father and my brother and my

150

little wife and baby and all my friends?" If Muhammad Ali wanted to become an exile, he could have fled to Canada long ago. It should have been obvious even to the most dense that he *welcomed* going to prison, that he saw himself as a martyr to his cause and embraced this martyrdom. When Dr. Benjamin Spock and Rev. William Sloane Coffin of Yale were convicted of conspiring to help young people avoid the draft, no one attempted to prevent them from earning a living while they appealed. Yale did not stop Coffin from preaching to its students. Dr. Spock's license as a physician was taken away by no state.

In the face of this kind of rancid discrimination men turn to revolution. That he did not shows, I believe, the inner strength Muhammad Ali commands. I have encountered few men on the sporting scene who have displayed this much courage and restraint.

Not that Muhammad Ali doesn't understand what has been done. I quote him from an article I wrote in *Esquire:*

> The power structure seems to want to starve me out. I mean the punishment, five years in jail, ten-thousand-dollar fine, ain't enough. They want to stop me from working, not only in the country but out of it. Not even a license to fight an exhibition for charity. And that's in the twentieth century. You read about those things in the dictatorship countries, where a man don't go along with this thing or that and he is completely not allowed to work or to earn a decent living. That's what they're doing to me here, right now.

Yes, they were. But at least Muhammad Ali could solace himself with the thought that he was a great fighter, maybe the greatest champion who ever lived. Most men I have admired in the little world of sports never had even that cold comfort. What I mean is that I believe I have detected a connection between performance and—what can I call it? Personality? Humanity? Soul? How do you measure a man when you can't put his performance on a chart or count it against a clock? Call it what you want, I believe this (and its converse) about athletes,

151

particularly professional athletes: the better the man, the worse the performance.

It's as though the gifts had been given out one for you and one for you and nobody got both. Perhaps the wherewithal that accrues so rapidly to the super athlete prevents him from being the man I would like him to be. Perhaps it's the other way around—the kind of man I admire, a man with intelligence and values that go beyond his next girl, his next drink, his next pay check, his next endorsement, a man with some awareness of the world in which he lives, one who knows enough to leave brutality behind when he comes off the athletic field, cannot be a super athlete. And perhaps, alas, it's the struggle to succeed without the talent that builds the man rather than the performer.

Whatever the sequence, the men I have known in sports who pleased me most as *people* often had to battle fiercely to make up for a lack of physical skills. Most times it was a losing battle. And Jim Beattie was one of the biggest losers.

He shouldn't have been. Beautiful people seldom become losers, and Jim Beattie was a beautiful man. Only rarely do beautiful men stumble into a profession they can't handle. The reason is that beautiful people are often good at a lot of things. If the Kennedys hadn't been born into wealth and politics they could have done as well selling refrigerators to Eskimos. Muhammad Ali didn't have to be a boxer. He could have been the best halfback in professional football. Suppose Humphrey Bogart couldn't act, or Marlon Brando. Would they have had to stand in breadlines? But Jim Beattie was a beautiful man who chose to become heavyweight champion of the world. It was a mistake. He couldn't even become champion of James J. Woody. It was a sad and lonely thing.

Jim Beattie was 6' 8" tall, clean and smooth of limb and his face was handsome in a craggy, masculine way. He was as bright as he was big, had been exposed to college for a while and he bought and read books. His wit was so quick and sparkling it very often went over the head

152

of boxing journalists. "I only weighed nine pounds when I was born," Beattie would tell them, "but I was five feet seven inches tall." Or "My father isn't very tall, but Mom is eight foot six." Or "One thing about being this big a boxer. I could go into a ring with Sonny Liston and he could have a gun in one hand and a knife in the other and he'd be the underdog." The kid knew a lot, but he did not know how to fight and he never learned.

Jim Beattie came to New York via Wisconsin, where he was a college boxer. He responded to a publicity-stunt ad placed by a restaurant man named Gene Schoor and set out to become champion. He really believed he could. He married a girl from back home, had a baby, lived in a walk-up on the West Side and trained and trained and trained. He was dedicated and hardworking and never spared himself in the gym. The only thing you could have said against him was that he didn't appear to have the reflexes of a good fighter, but you felt it was possible he could make do with his great height and natural 240 pounds.

Early in 1964, though, he was exposed, stripped naked. He went up against a hard young man named James J. Woody, who had a large family and small ambitions. He was a maintenance man in a housing project and his ambition was to be a fireman. He never even thought about being heavyweight champion. It was an amazing fight. At six feet Woody appeared, in the ring with Beattie, to be a midget. Yet the two of them tore at each other like a couple of fighting cocks for eight rounds. There was no boxing. Just the two of them throwing and landing heavy blows. Blood dripped from both of them until their chests and trunks were stained crimson. They staggered each other repeatedly. In the end Woody got the decision and Beattie discovered his nose had been broken in 17 places.

The next day, wearing bandages and two eyes the color of a Grand Canyon sunset, Beattie was rueful. "All it proves," he said, "is that I got a lot of guts. I hate to keep having to prove it."

So it was back to the drawing board. It was a year before he was ready again—not for the title, of course, for

James J. Woody. Beattie didn't particularly want to fight him. He had managed to knock off a few guys named Dick Greatorex and Tom McNeeley and Orvin Veasey. He thought he was entitled to bigger game than Woody. But that's all Madison Square Garden would offer him. Besides, he admitted, the defeat by Woody rankled him. He did not think Woody was a good fighter. So he agreed to try him again and, as a preliminary to an Emile Griffith fight, Woody and Beattie went at it once more.

Beattie looked good enough for three rounds. He kept Woody away with his long arms and hit the smaller man enough times to score points. Several times he had Woody stupid and rubber-legged. Suddenly, though, it all turned around. Beattie came unglued. He looked as though he was fighting underwater. He had to hold on to the ropes with one hand to remain erect. Woody seized this opportunity to beat the hell out of him. The referee stopped it after the seventh round. It had been a show, but a sick one, and was appreciated the way one appreciates a sick joke, with a shudder and a nervous laugh.

What it looked like was that Beattie was in no kind of fighting shape. It looked as if he was able to stand up for no more than three rounds. It looked as if he had disgraced himself. Even Schoor scurried to desert the sinking ship. "How could he peter out after three rounds if he was in shape?" Schoor asked reporters.

"He was in great shape," insisted Freddy Fierro, Beattie's trainer. "He was in the greatest shape of his career."

That's what Beattie said, too. He said it was something else. He said he had this lung-congestion problem, see, and he took this shot before the fight and all of a sudden his legs went out. "I was flabbergasted," Beattie said. He used words like that naturally even under tension. "In the third round my legs just went out from under me. I could hardly stand. I'm positive it was the shot I took. Doc Campbell said so."

In fact, Dr. Edward Campbell, Boxing Commission doctor, had said no such thing. What he did say was that, if Beattie had a breathing problem, he should have taken

154

a shot of something called Depro Medro. "It's a type of cortisone," the doctor said. "An anti-asthmatic. If you can't breathe, your legs go out from under you."

Beattie was damned either way. When a man has a fight like that, even a beautiful man like Beattie, he doesn't have much choice. He has to start looking around for another field. Yet right after the fight, boxing was all Beattie could think of. "I'm ten times the fighter I was out there tonight," he kept saying. "Ten times. Now I'll just have to start over again and prove it."

Actually there was nothing to prove. If he really was ten times as good as he looked, he wouldn't have been good enough.

Soon after, the New York State Boxing Commission lifted Beattie's license. He went home to St. Paul and back to the drawing board. He fought a few more fights, got beat by a couple of nonentities, and had to hang the gloves up. It was a nice dream while it lasted, a painful one, but nice nevertheless. Guys like Beattie would make great, gracious champions if they ever made it. Somehow, though, they almost never do.

Of course, neither did Woody. He got a few fights on the strength of having twice beaten Beattie, but then he started to get beat up a lot and at last became what is called an "opponent." He's still working in maintenance. When the family is tight for money, his wife goes back to work as a practical nurse. They're making it, sort of.

Jim Bouton made it for a year . . . well, two. In 1963 he won 21 games for the Yankees and lost only seven. In 1964 he won 18 games and lost 13. After that he just hung on. Then in the spring of 1968 he seemed to have found it again. It may have been an illusion, for the way Jim Bouton threw, it was a wonder he lasted as long as he did. He had a reputation as a cute pitcher in the minors, but when he came up to the Yankees, he started to throw hard with this huge overhand motion that involved so much effort he finished with the top of his head aimed at the ground. Naturally, he lost his hat on almost every pitch. I do not know why he did not lose it on every pitch.

155

After his good year, he had had a salary squabble with Ralph Houk, who was spending his brief time as general manager, a job that ill-suited him. Houk threatened to deduct a hundred dollars from his best offer for every day Bouton was late to spring training. This was not only immoral, it was against baseball law, which is most relaxed where the rights of players are concerned. Bouton caved in, but Houk was made to look ridiculous in the press. So it did not come as a surprise to Bouton that after his good spring, Houk, now a manager again, would give him little opportunity to pitch once the season started and then send him down to the minor leagues. Bouton, apparently washed up at twenty-nine, took it in good spirit. He understood the game of baseball better than most.

Three stories about Jim Bouton. The first has to do with when he was a boy and lived in New Jersey, just the other side of the river from New York. He was a Giant fan and made the trip to the Polo Grounds whenever he could. He'd sit out in left field and hope somebody would hit a Chinese homerun, a Polo Grounds specialty, in his direction. "Actually, we'd get there real early," he once explained. "We'd put our lunches on our seats and wander around the park. Mostly we'd go behind the dugout trying to get autographs. We never got any."

I can imagine Bouton as a little boy. He is blond and not very tall and, of course, wears his hair in a crew cut. He has blue eyes, but they are deeply set and squinchy, so he looks almost Oriental. But when you can see his eyes, you see the intelligence in them and the mischief. He smiles a lot and, when he laughs it is pleasant, because his voice is throaty, a little hoarse. He must have been a fine little boy, because he became a fine man, too.

Once Bouton and his brother and a couple of their friends got a bright idea. They got a long bamboo pole, hung a fishnet on the end of it and decided to go into business catching baseballs at the Polo Grounds. Bouton was twelve at the time. "We tried it out and it was hard to catch a ball in it," he remembers. "But we practiced for a week and got real good at it."

But when they got to the park, the gatekeepers wouldn't

let them in with their contraption. This called for more strategy. They went around to another entrance, lining up and marching in like Our Gang, the baseball trap concealed under clothing and arms on one side while they presented their tickets with the other. "But we never caught a single ball," Bouton says, chuckling.

With this background as a Giant fan, Bouton moved to Chicago with his family. "I used to go to Wrigley Field when the Giants played the Cubs," he recalls. "I'd hang around the visiting dugout and when the Cub fans yelled at the Giants I defended them. Al Dark [later to become manager of the Giants with a reputation for near-sainthood which was somewhat tarnished just before he was fired] was a player for them. I remember once, after I defended them, I leaned out and asked him for his autograph. Alvin said, 'Take a hike, kid!'"

That's one story. The next is about a couple of kids named George Saviano and Albert Gornie, who lived in the Bronx. This was 1964 and they were fourteen, and the founders of the Jim Bouton Fan Club, which even had its own newspaper, called *All 'Bout Bouton*. Each year they had a fan-club dinner which Bouton and his wife attended, without fail. I asked George how he had picked Bouton, among all those big and famous Yankees. "He was the only Yankee who would *talk* to us," George said.

The third story is set in 1968. Bouton has been playing with the minor-league Seattle team. He and his wife have two children by now, one a boy, five years old, the other a girl, three. Despite life in the minor leagues, they felt affluent but helpless to do anything concrete to improve the world around them. So they adopted a child, a Korean child, fatherless and with a mother who could no longer care for him. It wasn't a lot, they thought, but it was *something*. He was four years old when he arrived at the Seattle airport and was escorted from the plane. The first thing he did was squat down, put his hands behind his head and cringe, as though he expected to be struck.

The Boutons had gone to school to study Korean before the boy arrived. Even so, he crouched there a long

157

time before he was willing to go home with them. And learning English came hard to him at first. The Boutons arranged for the Korean teacher to visit them. She had a talk with the boy. He said the Boutons talked too much— and too fast. In a matter of months, though, the lad was pounding Jim Bouton on the shoulder when they drove along in their family car, and pointing. "Dad," he would say, "car." "Dad, truck." "Dad, dog."

The boy is doing fine.

"He looks like me," Bouton says. "Except maybe with these eyes I look a little more Oriental than he does."

Toward the end of the 1968 season with Seattle, Jim Bouton started fooling around with a knuckleball and won four games in a row, fast. The knuckleball was something he had even when he was much younger, in the days when he counted himself a young junk man. And, of course, Seattle got a major-league franchise. Bouton counts himself the ace of the staff. And with his knuckleball he says, chuckling, that he can be a star for the next ten years. Somehow, I doubt it. But the important point is it won't make a great deal of difference. Jim Bouton doesn't need to be a great pitcher. Being a man will be quite enough.

Then there was Mark Freeman, the loser's loser. He tried and tried, spent years in the minors and never even came close. Somehow he even managed to be of the wrong religion. While he was still fresh in the Yankee chain, the esteemed Dan Daniel, then of the New York *World-Telegram,* told the interested New York public that Freeman would be the first 6' 6" right-handed Jewish pitcher ever to become a star at Yankee Stadium. Freeman was, of course, Presbyterian. That was only the beginning.

We now switch to a vital moment in the life of Mark Freeman. It is the spring of 1960 and the Yankees have run out of options on Freeman. They must now keep him or trade him. When this happened, the Yankees would turn warm and cuddly to a player. The propaganda mill would start grinding and virtues would be found that even the player didn't know he had. The idea, of course, was to get a good price for him when he was traded. So now Freeman was getting his big start of the spring against the Detroit Tigers.

Things started off a bit rocky. Freeman got two strikes on Eddie Yost, but gave up a single after five straight pitches, presumably strikes, were fouled off. Frank Bolling walked. Harvey Kuenn followed with a hit-and-run single that scored Yost. Freeman then walked Al Kaline to fill the bases, and here is Mark Freeman sweating through one of the supreme moments of his career. Will he get out of it? Will he throw one pitch for a swift double play? Or will he earn immortality of a sort by throwing a one-pitch home run, clearing the bases and clearly disabusing the Yankees of their wisdom in keeping him in the chain for nine long, unsatisfactory years? Neither. With two balls on Steve Bilko, Freeman suddenly staggered off the mound, a hand to his eye. He had committed a balk. One runner scored. The others advanced.

What happened was that at the moment a bug flew into his eye. A bug would not have flown into the eye of Bob Gibson or Denny McLain. A bug would not have flown into the eye of Warren Spahn. But a bug flew into the eye of Mark Freeman. In the land of the losers, losers always lose.

Casey Stengel, who was manager at the time, and always unforgiving of failure, suggested that, instead of allowing the bug to fly into his eye, he should have snapped at it with his mouth, caught it and eaten it. Failing that, the old man rasped, "He shoulda rolled the goddam ball up there."

Later on, Freeman, who had a bachelor's degree with a psychology major, analyzed his action. "The thought flashed through my mind that I should have thrown the ball anyway. But I had two balls on the hitter and didn't want to risk another ball. The only thing I could think of was to back off. After thinking about it for a while, I decided I should have continued pumping with my eyes closed until the hitter got tired and backed off. Then I could have stepped off the rubber and called time."

Although Euripides is credited with a first, saying,

"Second thoughts are ever wiser," it is a record tied by many. On first thought, poor Mark Freeman should never have tried to become a baseball player.

"I was a momma's boy," Freeman has said, explaining the route he had taken. "I took to baseball because it was my way of proving my masculinity, of impressing my father. I've been trying to impress him all my life. My case is the classic one. As long as I can remember, my father—he played some Class D baseball—was throwing a baseball to me. He's always pushed me and supported me. He wants me to make it as much as I do."

When Freeman did not do well on the mound, he got angry, and did worse. "I hurt myself that way," he explained. "And in hurting myself I hurt my father. I suppose I wanted to. Of course, it's only a theory."

Freeman read books and had a firm command of the language, which didn't make him especially popular with the other ball players. He was, indeed, counted as something of a large oddball. Nor could he understand other players particularly well. "I think too much on the mound," he said once. "I've asked guys like Mickey Mantle what they think about when they are hitting and they say, 'Nuts.' This is completely foreign to my way of thinking. I'm always looking for a rationale.

"Actually, I'm a dumb pitcher. Half of pitching is instinct and I get a minus rating in that. Whitey Ford, for example, picked up the important things about pitching almost immediately. I've been pitching for eight years, but it's only in the last two seasons that I've mastered anything about pitching. In anything else, I think I'm a quick learner, but not in this. It's been slow and painful. It's not the kind of thing you can lay out a syllabus from which to proceed."

Still I don't think that's why Mark Freeman never made it. I think it's because of something else he believed. It came out in a conversation about a society which attaches so much to baseball but so little to things which should count more. "The important thing," Mark Freeman said, "is love—with all its connotations; selflessness, creativity and everything that's inherent in the golden rule." He

160

wasn't trying to impress anybody. He said what he thought. Guys like that never finish very high up in the wonderful world of professional sports.

The Yankees kept Freeman the year his options ran out, but by the trade deadline on June 15, he was gone to Kansas City. Less was demanded of him there, but it didn't matter. Mark Freeman never won a game in the major leagues. He retired to Denver to sell mutual funds. I don't suppose the years in baseball hurt him very much. Perhaps they even made him a better mutual funds salesman. I wonder, though, what Mark Freeman would have been if he hadn't tried to please his father. Once he was asked what he would like his son to be, and Mark Freeman said, "I would love for him to be a creative person." Well, perhaps Mark Freeman would have been that.

When Freeman came along, he was sort of an underground Jim Brosnan. In fact, Jim Brosnan was a sort of underground Jim Brosnan. He was the only baseball player who ever admitted in public that he (1) read a book; (2) drank martinis; (3) drank stingers; (4) liked foreign movies; (5) knocked hitters down; and (6) wrote a book. In the end he was undone by number six.

Perhaps it isn't fair to include Broz, as he was called lovingly by the handful of teammates who would talk to him, in this collection of failures. Yet despite a couple of good years—Brosnan had a 10–4 record with Cincinnati in 1961 and managed to qualify for nine years' worth of major-league pension—Brosnan never made it very big as a player. Nor was he terribly happy playing the game. Often he sounded just like Freeman. "Sitting on the bench between innings, the tiredness is compounded," he wrote in *The Long Season*. "Unfortunately I sit there thinking, 'Only three outs to go' instead of 'How am I going to pitch to the next man?' Worrying about your last mistake seems to bring on a rash of them, too."

Another time, Brosnan had this to say about the art of pitching:

Pitching is a simple, and simple is the word, physical

161

experience that has simple limitations. You have to stay in the bounds of these limitations. You can afford neither experimentation nor relaxed reflection. It demands your mind to this extent—you have to stay up. You have to be tense. The ability to handle tension with cool is difficult. Poise in the face of your knowledge of your limitations isn't easily maintained.

Maybe so, but I'll bet Whitey Ford never had any trouble. And still another time:

Pitching, playing baseball, is a simple aspiration, but I tried to make it too complicated. It was too simple, I felt, it couldn't possibly be that simple. So I'd make it complicated. If I get back to thinking instead of pitching, I'm in trouble.

In fact, Brosnan always did a lot more thinking than pitching. His *The Long Season* provided probably the best look ever at baseball as seen through a mature mind. It was a unique contribution to the literature of sports. It was revealing of baseball and of Brosnan. It was well and amusingly written. It was so good that Solly Hemus, who had been Brosnan's manager at St. Louis, said: "If you think his book was funny, wait till you see his pitching." It was one of Brosnan's best reviews.

*The Long Season* was a tough, honest book. (He even knocked baseball reporters: "San Francisco writers describe the baseball scene with all the precision of three-year-old children finger-painting on the playroom wall.") So tough and honest that it was the beginning of the end for Brosnan.

James Patrick Brosnan was 6' 4", big for an author, blond, and affected the demeanor of a scholar. He recorded the events around him with an accurate if somewhat jaundiced eye. When *The Long Season* was followed with a second book, *Pennant Race,* the story of the Reds' run for the pennant in 1961, the baseball men around Brosnan were upset. He had written with candor about the foolish machinations of the front office, the pomposity of managers and the peccadilloes of players. They began to look at Brosnan as though he were some kind of bug.

In 1962 the Reds finished only three games out of first place and it was endlessly and vividly recalled that Brosnan had thrown two home-run balls at crucial moments. Of course, Brosnan remembered those pitches pretty well, too. "Two bad pitches," Brosnan said the next spring. "Felipe Alou hit one and Sawatski [Carl] the other on a nothing and two count. He hit a hanging slider. It was all I had. He missed the first two hanging sliders."

So Brosnan was traded—to the Chicago White Sox. For some time, of course, he had been pitching in relief and he didn't have a great season for the White Sox. Still, his earned-run average was 2.84 and he had every right to think he would pitch again the following year. The White Sox offered him a 24,000 dollar contract—6,000 less than he had made the year before. But this time they wanted to clamp down on his outside activities. He could drink as many martinis as he wanted, the White Sox said, but he could write nothing more than a letter to his wife as long as he was under contract. To a writer, which by this time was how Brosnan thought of himself, this was an impossible affront. I mean do you promise a bird food only on condition it doesn't sing?

When he refused to sign a contract containing such a demoralizing restriction, the White Sox offered him out on waivers. To the surprise of practically nobody, Brosnan included, no one picked him up. There isn't a general manager alive who wants to see his side of a salary discussion with a player appear in the public prints. Of course, it probably didn't help Brosnan any that he put an ad in the *Sporting News* which read in part:

> Situation sought. Bullpen operator, experienced. Attentive observer, open-mouthed admirer of skillful baseball.

That was 1964. After that Brosnan tried to make a living as a writer. He had no enormous success. A novel he was writing while he was still playing has not yet been published. Nor has his favorite short story, one about a pitcher who, ordered by his manager to knock down a

163

hitter, hits him in the head instead and kills him. In the end Brosnan took a well-paying part-time job with ABC. He's on television, not exactly telling how baseball really is. And when he's fifty, or sixty-two or sixty-five, he'll collect the pension that's due him for the nine years he played in the major leagues. Even so, Jim Brosnan will always be an outsider.

The first time I met Rod Kanehl he was a rather elderly rookie getting his first trial with the still-winning and thus ultra-staid Yankees. The rule was that rookies were not to bring their families to spring camp. I'm not sure of the reason, but probably the Yankees felt that rookies were supposed to suffer. The man who had to make sure they did was Bill McCorry, a crochety old road secretary who was called "Mom," for "Mean Old Man." And it was McCorry who verbally assualted Kanehl in the clubhouse for showing up in St. Petersburg with wife, kids and station wagon. Kanehl listened to McCorry for a while and then said, "Either you were gonna get mad at me or my wife was gonna get mad at me, and I got to live with my wife." While McCorry spluttered, the Yankee players laughed.

That was Rod Kanehl—brash, tough, never so talented as he was tenacious. He didn't make it with the Yankees, but when the new expansion Mets were created, Kanehl found himself in their first spring camp. There was an immediate affinity between Kanehl and the Mets. They were both losers.

But with the Mets Kanehl managed to attain a fame of sorts. To this day, at the drop of a suggestion he'll play a game of baseball trivia. What *other* utility infielder can play the harmonica? Who was Marvelous Marv Throneberry's roommate on the Mets? What Met was removed for a pinch hitter in the second inning of their historic 23-inning game? Who got the last pinch hit in the Polo Grounds before it was torn down? Who was the first man to hit a grand-slam homer for the Mets? The answer to all is Rod Kanehl.

Not only that, Rod Kanehl is the first man who ever

had his name on a Met banner. (Banners have since become a trademark of Shea Stadium.) That first banner read:

We Love the Mets'
Rod Kanehl

It was hung out in left field of the Polo Grounds for the Mets' first home exhibition game.

"You know why they had my name up there?" Kanehl was saying as he sat in motel room in his home town of Springfield, Missouri, some years back, his feet up on the bed, glaring holes in his shoe soles. "Because I was a hero, and I'll tell you how I got to be a hero."

It was spring training and the Mets' exhibition game with the Dodgers was being televised back to New York. The Dodgers were still hero-devils in New York, having left New York with no team to love until the Mets were created out of nails and snails and puppy dogs' tails. The Mets were behind by two runs in the last of the ninth and Sandy Koufax was pitching for the Dodgers. There were runners on second and third.

"Don't ask me how they got there," Kanehl said. "I was asleep in the dugout. I'd had a rough night and it was one of those sleepy days in St. Petersburg."

"Kanehl!" Casey Stengel, the manager, shouted suddenly, waking him. "You want to win it for me?"

"What could I say? I said, 'Sure.' It's the same thing I said the first time a guy asked me if I could play first base. I'd never played there in my life. That's what utility men have to say, 'Sure.'"

Kanehl picked up a bat, stepped out of the dugout and thought he had been struck blind for his sins. The sun hit his purple eyeballs like a flashing mirror, and he had to feel his way to the plate.

"The first pitch," Kanehl said, "zap! Strike one. I didn't even see it. The next one was another fast ball, I guess. The umpire said it was a strike. I wouldn't know. Strike two.

"Now Casey starts hollering from the bench, 'Butcher boy! Butcher boy!' He meant take a short swing, meet

165

the ball, don't strike out. Well, the next pitch I can see. I start going for it, then I realize it's too high, so I pull back. But it turns out to be one of Koufax's big curve balls. I'm pulling back, and the ball is curling down over the plate. It's also curling down into my bat. Damnedest thing. It hits the bat and goes between the first baseman and the bag. Two-base hit, tie score."

Koufax, who later was to say ruefully that his biggest problem with Kanehl was to get him to hit the ball well, was so unnerved he allowed the next batter, Felix Mantilla, to hit the first pitch. Kanehl scored the winning run. And that's how Roderick Edwin Kanehl got to be the first Met hero.

Kanehl never got much better as a player, but on the soporific Mets, even though he was always a utility man and often on the bench, he became a symbol of the Met's effort to get better. Rod Kanehl, Hot Rod Kanehl, he came to be called, never quit hustling. So there are some things that will be remembered about him. Like that first day in the Met camp when the veteran Richie Ashburn called for a fly ball in the outfield and then let it drop and Kanehl snarled at him, "If you call for it, goddam it, catch it." Or the time he strolled from first to second base against the Giants because they had forgotten about him (it was easy to take the Mets for granted). And it was Kanehl who scored from second on a short passed ball and Kanehl who, as a pinch runner, scored the winning run in nine of the first 12 Met wins and Kanehl who played seven positions—not well, but with a memorable élan.

As a reward he was quietly dropped out of baseball. Not kicked out, just sort of discarded. In 1965, after three years with the floundering Mets, not even enough time to become eligible for the players' pension plan, Kanehl was simply not invited to spring camp. Nor was that the final indignity.

When the Yankees heard that Kanehl was at liberty, they called and offered him a choice of two jobs: third baseman and coach at Toledo, or manager of a rookie-league team in Florida. The offer was not unusual. Players

166

like Kanehl who, in the words of one general manager, go further than their skills, make good managerial material. Kanehl wasn't sure he could take either of the jobs. He was involved in a small construction business which was doing well and didn't feel he could leave it for less than 15,000 dollars a year. He called the Yankees to tell them that, but he never got the chance. Sorry, he was told. George Weiss (then president of the Mets), who didn't think enough of Kanehl to invite him to the major-league camp, wouldn't give him up for less than two Yankee players. The Yankees were not, naturally enough, about to give up two players for a minor-league manager. Career over. Eleven years in the business, and nothing to show for it except a lot of scars on his shins inflicted because he played second base a lot even though he could not make the double-play pivot very well. He got the outs though, simply by letting the sliding runner slam into him spikes first. "There isn't anything to the pivot," Rod Kanehl always said, "if you have guts enough to stand there."

I think the most touching story Kanehl ever told me had to do with finding himself, in the spring of 1958, in Monterrey, Mexico, on loan from the Yankees to the Cincinnati organization, living in screenless barracks with a spring towel supply of one, unable to get an offer of more than 400 dollars a month for his fifth season in baseball. He decided to chuck it all and go home. First, though, he went out to take on a barrel of tequila, and when he returned to camp late that night, he ran into the man who was running the club for Cincinnati. He proceeded to lecture him loudly on the social concepts of baseball. "In this goddam game," Kanehl said, "they're always telling you to sacrifice yourself, hit behind the runner, play for the team. But nobody does it, not on the field and not in the office. And at the end of the year, all you look at is the averages. You don't have a column for the times you hit behind a runner or the times you play when you're hurting. If my boy wants to play baseball, I'll tell him one thing: be selfish. Don't worry about

167

anything but yourself. That's the way *everybody* plays this game."

Eventually Kanehl got 600 dollars a month and resumed his mediocre baseball career. But when, years later, he told me about the incident, he added, "You know something? I never did believe that stuff I said. I can't play this game selfish." He laughed his infectious laugh, dimples appearing in his firm-jawed face. "Maybe I'm just not good enough."

After a while rising interest rates turned Kanehl's construction business sour. He went to work for a trucking firm. But the passion was still upon him. The game gets into some men like a cinder in the eye and it won't wash out. Especially men who don't play it very well. So a couple of evenings a week Kanehl flew from Springfield to Wichita, to play semi-pro ball with something called, appropriately enough, the Dreamliners.

But no dream lasts forever. And when that one was over, Kanehl had to settle for pick-up softball and, well . . . he said his heart was never broken. And maybe it wasn't. For it was Rod Kanehl who once said, "Baseball is a lot like life. The line drives are caught, the squibbers go for base hits. It's an unfair game."

There are exceptions to what I have come to think of as Shecter's Law of Diminishing Persons. Stan Musial was a great player and a marvelous man. Al Kaline, so far as I know, has never done or said a single offensive thing. Whitey Ford very often managed not to take himself seriously. A lot of professional football players, linemen, particularly, seem to have gone through some sort of gentling experience in the painful game they play. Phil Linz, the harmonica rascal, struck it rich not in baseball but in a bar and manages to laugh at himself for it. There are men, like Rocky Bridges, the coach, who have through the years made themselves wealthy beyond their dreams but who retain a sense of perspective about their true worth. Bridges, for example, gives his off-season occupation as sanitation engineer—"I dig sewers." And there are Negro players who made it big and never forgot their roots, men like Bill Russell, Curt Flood and Bill White, and some, like Ernie Banks, whose good nature is so great, they are incorruptible. But few men are able to resist the twin blandishments of money and fame. Somehow, though, those who come best equipped to do it, seldom achieve the fame or the money. As John F. Kennedy and Rod Kanehl have said, life is unfair.

# 6  The Man I Love

CHARLES DILLON STENGEL MANAGED A LOT OF LOSING baseball teams, many of which, he points out, are now defunct. And once, while he was managing the Boston Braves, he was struck by an automobile and suffered a broken leg, which prompted a Boston newspaperman to write that this was the best thing that had happened to the Braves in years. But Casey Stengel was never a loser. He was a winner and he made an enormous amount of money and, according to my prejudices, he should have become a wretched man. He did not, because, I like to think, Casey Stengel was no ordinary man. I never met an immortal who was.

One of the few non-imagined privileges of newspapermen is the opportunity to work in the presence of greatness, an opportunity few others can enjoy. Political reporters, I would guess, must have felt this about Franklin D. Roosevelt, John F. Kennedy, Adlai Stevenson. But the only great man I ever knew was Casey Stengel. When he limped out of baseball, he took with him, I suddenly realized, the last part of the sports business that had any meaning for me.

He gimped away, leaning on an eccentrically shaped cane, seventy-five years old, a steel ball where the bones of his hip should have been, and I wanted to reach out and call him back. I had known this day would come,

169

and I had dreaded it. I didn't want to let him go. Dammit, Casey Stengel, I wanted to say, now wait a minute.

I remembered watching him, seventy years old and more, sprinting after buses, his lumpy legs churning, and I would think, don't get old. I listened to him, his seamed old face breaking into pantomimes of fury, horror, sadness or shock, his ears so enormous they were comically fascinating, haranguing crowds of slack-jawed bumpkins in hotel lobbies in places like Kansas City and Cincinnati, and I would think, don't get old. I watched him talk young men senseless in barrooms and then lecture sleepy elevator operators into obscene hours of the morning only to bustle into the dining room for breakfast at 9 A.M., bright-eyed, alert, energetic, and I would whisper to myself, don't get old; please don't get old, you old bastard.

Then he broke his hip in a senseless fall and suddenly he was old. His back, which only weeks before had been so broad and strong and permanent, seemed thin and bent. Suddenly he was old and it was as he had always said. He didn't need anyone to tell him. He stopped being a manager and he leaned on his crazy cane and walked away from it and a piece of my life went with him. And *I* felt old, older than Casey Stengel could ever be. When he left, he carried with him a large slice of the little world of sports and what he left behind didn't seem worth caring about.

The first time I met this man who was to come to mean so much to me, he confounded me so badly I lost a night's sleep. This was back when Joe DiMaggio was at the beginning of the end of his career with the Yankees. I was covering my first Yankee game. I'll remember always being in Casey Stengel's presence for the first time. He was sitting in his little office off the Yankee clubhouse and he was pulling the socks off legs which were lumpy even then. He was, as usual, talking. He said that "he" was having trouble with his legs and that "he" couldn't run anymore the way he used, nor get the bat around so quickly and that "he" could probably use a few days of rest. It seemed to me entirely logical at that moment that he was talking about Joe DiMaggio and I went home and wrote, as my first Yankee story, that Joe DiMaggio was going to be benched. I sent it to the paper and, content that I had done a good job, went to bed.

I was just drifting into sleep when, suddenly, I was startled sleepless. I had been struck by one of my rare thoughts. Who was "he?" Could it have been Charley Keller? Hank Bauer? Joe Collins? Good God, suppose he wasn't talking about DiMaggio at all?

This was the way Stengel talked, understand. He would refer to "he" and "the fella" and "the left-hander" and "their second baseman" and "my outfielder" and while his logic was at all times impeccable, his arguments always entirely lucid, one had to be *au courant* with his team, all the other teams in the league and his problems of the moment and the past, to understand his references. This is why wretches all over the country have written that Casey Stengel spoke a species of double-talk. This is a canard, and nonsense besides. They just didn't know enough about the game of baseball. About that, Stengel knew *everything*.

Having made my initial acquaintance with Stengel on the sports pages, I was ignorant of all of this. So I spent the night thinking what I would do for a living once it was discovered that Stengel had no intention of benching DiMaggio at all, but some aging supernumerary instead. What did my years in the newspaper business qualify me to do? Dig ditches? Become a civil-service clerk? Drive a truck? By the time the Yankee lineup was announced the next day, I was a quivering wreck. Of course, my fears were groundless. The old man *did* bench DiMaggio, just as he had said he would, and we both went on to bigger and better things. I like to think, too, that I never misunderstood the man again.

My next highly personal encounter with Casey Stengel was some years later when I was again contemplating the civil service as a career. This was after my revelation of the earthshaking, one-slap civil war between Ralph Houk and Ryne Duren and around the Yankees I was a leper. Not even Frank Crosetti would talk to me. But then Crosetti hadn't talked to me *before* this incident, either.

*Time* was still calling me to find out the inside story when, by chance, I encountered Stengel at the bar of a hotel in Baltimore. It was one of those sudden but total encounters. We both looked up and there we were, shoulder to shoulder, nose to nose, the great man of sports and the outcast rookie baseball writer. The old man's blue eyes were clear and luminous. He stuck a nubby forefinger into my chest. Silently I recited a prayer for the dead. The only thing I knew for sure was that he didn't know my name and what I expected was abuse, a tirade about my unimaginable stupidity, unmitigated gall and unfortunate parentage, which is what one learns to expect from people around the sporting business who think they have been wounded. At last the old man spoke. "You can do that to me three times," he said, poking three times for emphasis, "because that's your job." He let that sink in for a moment, then he turned to the bartender and said, "Give the man what he wants." I was too speechless to thank him, but I don't think I've ever been more grateful to anybody.

What's more important about this story than my feelings is what it revealed about the old man. His greatest genius lay in his willingness to adjust to the problems of other men, other times. Despite great age, which is often beset by rigidity of mind, Casey Stengel remained pliable, understanding, willing to adjust, to change. "Baseball is changed," Stengel once said, "and so is the writing profession." He knew the newspaper business, understood better than most that the afternoon newspaper reporter could not, as he once put it, "write the box score." He got along easily with young reporters. He knew that the world exists on change. He never resisted.

When he was fired by the Yankees in 1960, set aside like some rusty overage destroyer, he was angry and churlish. The Yankees thought they had talked him into saying he was retiring, but when the question was put to him directly, he blurted out the truth. "You'd have to say I was fired," he shouted at the great horde of reporters, "because my services were no longer required." And it was at that farewell address that he talked of a Yankee "youth movement" and rasped, "The youth of America is for kids."

Yet a year later he was exhorting the "youth of America" to seek a career with the "amazing Mets," a widely used phrase he coined, by the way, in his first speech about the expansion ball club at a time when it still lacked its first losing ball player. The following year, while the great Rogers Hornsby, who felt nothing but contempt for modern ball players, was telling the world that the mold for a good ball player had been broken years before, Casey Stengel was saying: "I'll tell you about youth. Look how big it is. They break a record every day."

One has to have known the many men around sports who are very like Hornsby to appreciate the large adjustments Stengel was able, even eager, to make. Take a small thing like the bunt. To some of the young-old men of the game, the bunt is as sacred as the family Bible. But I recall an important game the Yankees won in Cleveland because Bob Turley, the pitcher, hit away in a bunt situation. The man who changed the face of baseball, the man who invented platooning, was asked how come he had let Turley hit at that point. And it was then he let loose his definitive line on the modern bunt. "Because it's run sheep run," he said, succinctly describing a charging infield, "and you can't bunt the lively ball." Lesser men spent lifetimes in the game and never learned that.

Stengel never stopped learning. He even adjusted to having Jimmy Piersall on his ball club. This was no small thing, Piersall, who had suffered a couple of nervous breakdowns, had driven more than one manager to distraction. He was the kind of man about whom it may be said that he was born to be a Met. There are not many like that. In the end he had a terrible year with the Mets and was traded, whereupon he needlessly, undeservedly and, I add happily, with no effect, vilified the old man on the air and in the public prints. But at the beginning Stengel was always being asked how we managed to get along so well with this man who ran around the bases backwards when he hit his hundredth home run. ("He didn't run to third base first, did he?" Stengel said. "He touched all the bases, didn't he?") Stengel's answer was always that he had no trouble with Piersall because he was willing to forgive and understand. "Even the government lets people out of any place they've put them in," the old man said about Piersall. "The man's got eight kids. He don't drink. He gets the red ass when you smoke around him. That's all right. After my wife quit smoking, she was like that, too. Why, I know people who can't stand the smell of booze." He was even willing to understand that.

Part of the old man's genius was in his quick ability to recognize and obliterate (yes, that's the word; he sort of x'd them out) the sycophants who like to flutter around the aura of the famous. I once observed a well-known representative of the type (species: arm around the shoulder and whisper into the ear) get turned off like a light switch. He had thrown his arm around the old man's shoulders and was just about to offer the first sweet nothing when, in one quick swoop, Stengel ducked, flung his own arm back and fetched the sycophant a sharp rap in the biceps. The sycophant retreated in confusion. The old man had made another enemy, but he knew exactly what he was doing.

I think one of the great Casey Stengel paragraphs illustrating his mental and verbal shorthand was delivered in connection with another bit of his intuitive understanding—the reason baseball was no longer getting the *quantity* of young men from whom to pick and choose (and make a lot of mistakes) while deciding which were good enough to be major leaguers. "Nowadays," Stengel said, "it costs 30,000 dollars to send a man through a university. How can you hold him back [meaning, how can you ask him not to take a football or basketball scholarship which gives him such an expensive education gratis]? There used to be only ten tennis courts in the whole country [and now kids are playing not only tennis, but golf]. You could buy a drink at the Biltmore bar for 50 cents [everything changes, especially values]. The whole world lights up at night [there are many distractions for the young man].

174

In the old days there wasn't anything to do but get up in the morning and play baseball."

Nor did Casey Stengel ever stop teaching, and in a most vivid manner. In his first year with the new Mets he went out of his way to teach the nation's sports columnists about the game of baseball. Each time a new one trooped into camp he would tell him to keep an eye on Dawes Hamilt who, the old man would say with a serious, intense look on his face, was the greatest prospect since Mickey Mantle. The columnists looked, were impressed and marched off to their typewriters to write about Casey Stengel's new Mickey Mantle. What Stengel wanted them to see, however, was that poor Dawes Hamilt, an extraordinarily amiable young man, was leaden-footed, uranium-assed and titanium-headed and had less chance of playing baseball for a living than he had of dancing up a moonbeam. The very few who recognized this were rewarded by one of Casey Stengel's shyest smiles.

Then there was the way he instructed his players. In 1958 the Yankees were winning everything in sight. One day, though, the old man, old even then, but ageless too, spied Andy Carey, one of his musclemen, pounding the ball into the seats in batting practice. The old man shoved his hands into his back pockets and trundled out to Carey. "I understand you got some kind of record for hitting the ball into the bleachers," he said. "That right?"

"Yes, sir."

"Did you get a bonus for hitting that ball into the bleachers?"

"No, sir," Carey said.

"That's right," Casey Stengel said. "You don't get a bonus for that. But you might get a bonus if you get 40 hits."

Players hated Stengel because he criticized them that way, pungently, and often in the public prints. Of Jerry Lumpe, the second baseman, he once said, "He looks like the greatest hitter in the world till you play him." Of the muscular but fragile Moose Skowron who, when slumping hit into double plays in grape-like bunches: "The way he's going I'd be better off if he was hurt." And

175

of Bobby Richardson, the second baseman: "Look at him. He doesn't drink, he doesn't smoke, he doesn't chew, he doesn't stay out late and he still can't hit .250." Stengel was wrong about Richardson. Before he retired, he helped the Yankees enormously and one year he even hit .300. But the old man wasn't wrong about much and one of the reasons Carey never amounted to anything was he never stopped swinging for the bleachers.

One of the ways Stengel managed to be right all the time was by noticing everything. Nothing escaped him. He brought to baseball the mind of a chess-playing trial lawyer who had become a private eye. And he was never afraid of the truth. In the second year of the Mets, when great things were expected, he came into his Polo Grounds office after the first game, slammed down his baseball cap and said, "The attendance was robbed. We're still a fraud."

Rod Kanehl recalls that it always puzzled him how Stengel knew which ball players were staying out late. The call would come to report to Stengel's office and the conversation would go like this:

STENGEL: What kind of hours you been keeping, Kanehl?

KANEHL: Good hours, Case.

STENGEL: Good hours my tit. You better start getting in on time.

But how did the old man know Kanehl had been out late without a bed check, which he refused to use? "I finally figured it out," Kanehl says, chuckling. "Every-time we took an early-morning flight—and it seemed like we were always getting to some airport at eight in the morning—the old man would take a walk up and down the aisle of the plane. Anybody that was asleep before the plane left the ground would be called into his office for the talk. Good hours my tit."

Tony Kubek, once a Yankee shortstop, also has a story which illustrates the memory and keen eye of the old man. When Kubek was married, Stengel gave him a check for 25 dollars as a small wedding gift and suggested he take his wife out to dinner with it. Kubek folded

176

it into his wallet and forgot about it, until one Sunday in the winter when he was going to church and realized he had no money for the collection. He did have the check, though, and stopped at a drugstore to cash it. The druggist was so pleased with the check he wrote to Stengel and asked if he would mind if the check were never cashed. Stengel, never less thrifty than the next man, told him indeed not. But in the spring the first time he saw Kubek he said, "That was a funny place to take your wife to dinner."

Of course there was always Stengel the teller of tales. Traveling with him was like camping out with mummers. One should have had to pay for the privilege.

He let his stories drop at the most unexpected moments. Like this one on the bus to the ball park on the Mets' first trip to Cincinnati. The story went back to the days when he was playing right field for Pittsburgh.

"In those days," Stengel said, "when they got a new fire engine they liked to take it around so everybody in the city could see it."

So it was that the shiny new red engine was to be shown off at the ball park that day. In honor of the occasion a mock house was erected of two by fours in center field. At the proper moment the house was set afire and the fire engine was supposed to dash out and douse the fire.

"Only they forgot to measure the bullpen," Stengel recalled. "The engine was too big. They couldn't get it through."

The house flamed merrily, finally tumbled upon itself. When it had burned to the ground—and still no fire engine—Stengel could stand it no longer. "I filled a glass with water in the dugout," he said, "and I ran out like Charley Chaplin and shoosh! I threw the water on the fire. It was almost out anyway. And you know something? The fire department was mad as hell at me."

Still, these are not the things which made Stengel so important to me. What will make him live forever to those of us fortunate enough to have known him was that he was a man—irascible, selfish, a poor winner sometimes and a bad loser, but a man for all of that. He was a fascinating raconteur, an enchanting curmudgeon, a tireless bon vivant, a man cut down in the prime of life at age seventy-five. He is out of the game now and all I could think to say as he went, leaning on that foolish cane, was goddamit, Casey Stengel, now wait a minute.


## 7  In Introduction to the Dump


AS MUCH AS WE WOULD LIKE TO TAKE CREDIT FOR IT, the sports fix is not an American invention. At a guess, one could put the first dump to the Sumerians of Mesopotamia, who, archeological evidence indicates, made a big thing out of wrestling. And everybody knows about wrestlers.

Admittedly there is no proof about Sumerian wrestlers. But it is doubtful that even then the First General Theory of Sports—Larceny Abhors a Vacuum—could have been violated. Earliest proof that it was not comes to us from the first days of the Olympic games, which began in 776 B.C., the athletes competing for laurel wreaths. It is written that, in the 98th Olympiad, Eupolus of Thessaly was convicted of giving bribes to three boxing opponents to take dives. It is not written if he was doing it all for laurel wreaths. Eupolus was fined and disgraced. He could not have been the only Olympic transgressor, however, for a whole series of statutes called "Zanes" have been dug up. These "Zanes" were paid for with money collected by fines levied on Greeks like poor old Eupolus who broke the code of honor in the games. They were placed on the field of honor in such a way that they were the last things the athletes saw as they marched into the stadium. The statues were like cops at the door; at least that's what they were supposed to be. They couldn't have done a lot of good, though. They had to keep building the damn things.

In less than 200 years of the Olympics, the Greek ideal

of the all-around athlete began to disappear under the burden of specialization. And specialization almost always leads to professionalism. The Olympic games tried to stick to their laurel wreaths as prizes, but at other festivals more valuable prizes—ranging from tax exemptions to army deferments to pensions and even "lulus," the modern political trick of paying expenses which need not be accounted for—were awarded.

Once the Romans conquered the Greeks, the games really went to pot—or at least to Nero. This cat created events he could win—like music and acting—and then brought in 5,000 bodyguards as a claque while he competed. Once he was so drunk he fell off his chariot but, surprise, was declared winner of the race ayway. It was like Big Julie rolling dice in a hat in *Guys and Dolls*.

The Romans thought there was something homosexual about competing naked the way the Greeks did (possibly there was) and derided most of the Olympic events. They themselves leaned toward gladiatorial contests to the death and soon included them in the games. If you're going to fight for those stakes, you'd better be a pro. Soon all the athletes *were* professionals and, after a long period of increasing commercialism and scandal, the Olympic games were ended in 392 A.D. They were not resumed for 1,500 years. This was a somewhat longer time than it took for college basketball to recover from *its* scandal.

American frontier life was not much given to organized sports, the rigors of daily existence precluding much frivolity. In *American Sports 1785-1835* Jennie Hollman writes:

> Until after the War of 1812 the growth of recreation and sport were hampered by the prevailing opinions. . . . Ben Franklin recommended swimming because it led to cleanliness [but] thought any recreation or sport should be a school for character building.

Then she quotes Dr. Benjamin Rush:

> The common amusements of boys have no connection with their future occupation. Many of them injure

179

their clothes, some of them waste their strength and impair their health, and all of them prove more or less the means of producing noise or exciting angry passions, both of which are calculated to beget vulgar manners. The Methodists have wisely banished every species of play from their school.

There were, nevertheless, some rough-and-ready adult frontier games that were frequently indulged in. Among them were bull baiting, cockfighting and a little thing called gouging. "Gouging was performed by twisting the forefinger in a lock of hair near the temple and turning the eye out of the socket with the thumb nail, which was allowed to grow long for the purpose," Jennie Hollman writes.

Then there was horse racing. There is little question that this sport of kings has deep roots in our monarchless republic. Again Jennie Hollman:

> Despite the evils that were attended to horseracing (it was alleged that people who could not or did not pay their grocery bills bet money plentifully on the race course) the most prominent men gave it encouragement. George Washington was a patron of the races as of nearly every other outdoor sport. Henry Clay was fond of horses, and his thoroughbreds became famous the country over. . . . John Quincy Adams during his presidency . . . found relief from the throngs of visitors by attending the races near Washington. . . . John Randolph had a strong attachment to the sport, while Chief Justice Marshall was honorary member of the jockey club at Fairfield, Va. Thomas Jefferson gave his enthusiastic support and James Madison owned an interest in a race horse. Andrew Jackson owned some distinguished racers whose fame spread over the country, and even after he became president, he entered his horses and lost heavily on his wagers.

By the late nineteenth century horse racing had become something of a fine art in this country. A British observer of the period, John C. Hutcheson, wrote in the

London magazine *Belgravia* of June, 1872, that "Americans, as a rule, show far greater prescience and aptitude in the study of the equine race than ourselves and exhibit their natural keensightedness in this respect in a more business-like and practical manner than is practiced on the English turf." Hutcheson wrote that he had visited Long Island (where the mosquitoes were large but not so huge as in New Jersey, "where, it is said, they *bark!*") and noticed that the Americans had appointed a special "Clerk of the course" to make sure that no weights were altered, no burrs inserted nor "any other advantage taken between heats." He was also shocked to observe that men with less well-endowed trotters would deliberately make false starts in order to "weary out" the better horses.

Next to trotting matches [Hutcheson went on], I should say that gambling at cards was the principal resource of those in want of something wherewith to get through their spare time in America. . . . I remember, in the winter of '66, just after a great razzia [raid] by the police on some of the alleged chief gambling dens of Manhattan, reading a few mornings afterwards in the columns of the leading papers of a great "sitting" held at "Faro" wherein chief Magistrate Ben Wood lost the sum of $200,000 to Congressman John Morrissey, the ex-prize fighter . . . and now law-maker of the United States."

This was a bawdy, rollicking era. The gambling exploits of the infamous John Morrissey were finding their way into admiring print and, despite the "Clerk of the course," there were often betting coups in the trotting races. Indeed, until the lip tattoo was instituted in 1946, it was a matter of intricate gamesmanship to alter markings on horses, substitute good ones for platers and cash large bets. The fast pills, the slow pills, the tickling of horses with electric batteries, all are in the noble tradition of this great American sport. It is a tradition which goes back to our earliest days.

Would you believe 1674? This is the date of the first documented fix scandal in America. It was dug out of court records of York County, Virginia, by John R. Betts, who refers to it in his Columbia University Ph.D. thesis of 1951, *Organized Sports in Industrial America.* The record reads:

James Bullocke, a Taylor, having made a race for his mare to run with a horse belonging to Mr. Mathew Slader for two thousand pounds of tobacco and caske, it being contrary to Law for a Labourer to make a race, being only a sport for the Gentlemen, is fined for the same one hundred pounds of tobacco and caske.

Whereas Mr. Mathew Slader and James Bullocke by condition under the hand and seale of the said Slader that his horse would runn out of the way that Bullocke's mare might winn, *wch* is an apparent cheate, is *ordrd* to be putt in the stocks and there sitt the space of one houre.

In the chapters that follow I have explored the history of dumps, fixes and other unsavory aspects of the major sports of America—baseball, football, boxing, basketball. For historical interest I have included a brief chapter on professional rowing, a passion for which swept this country before the turn of the century. But I have gone no further into the scandals of horse racing—though they be legion—for two reasons. The first is that it is only too obvious that any pastime designed to exploit the public's propensity for wagering will soon be the rallying point for every sharpshooter in the country. To chronicle the known scandals of horse racing is to encounter the distinct possibility that there is hardly any honesty in it at all. Second, as explained in Chapter 2, I do not consider horse racing to be a sport. A spectacle certainly, a vehicle for taxing the impulse to gamble, of course. An exciting lure which can, with a sort of Dostoevskian fervor, lead one into a delicious debauch of debt, yes. But a sport, no.

For the same reasons I have not explored jai alai, a popular gaming device in Florida, or dog racing. I have also left the recounting of soccer treacheries to any European who understands the game better than I. As for the other major American sports—track and field, golf, tennis, swimming, ice hockey—none has had a tradition of wagering and thus no impulse toward the sure bet. And why no wagering? "Because," says a bookmaker, "you can buy a hockey goalie with a bag of lollipops."


## 8  Of Rounders and Bounders


IT IS THE VANITY OF THE BUSINESSMEN WHO RUN WHAT they like to call the "game" of baseball that, despite the long history of this money-drenched sport, there has appeared only a single blot on its escutcheon—the Black Sox scandal. To which it would be fair to comment in the colorful vernacular of the game: bullshit.

The history of baseball is a history of double-dealing unparalleled in American sport, if not in American enterprise. The sleight of hand, the lie, the fix are so ingrained in the traditions of the game that one need only study its history to understand the depths of the corruption which has pervaded it. One of the very foundations of the game, the story that it was invented in Cooperstown, New York, in 1839 by a man named Abner Doubleday, is a patent and deliberate fraud.

It is doubtful that Doubleday, then a young cadet at West Point, was even *in* Cooperstown, that year. And it is a fact that the game had been played in this country as long ago as 1778 and in England long before that. This is no knock at Doubleday, by the way. He became a general and was a hero at the battle of Gettysburg. He never tried to take credit for inventing baseball and died in 1893 without knowing he would be saddled with this misdemeanor. How this happened to him while he lay peacefully in his grave is a story of American enterprise.

The entrepreneur was Albert G. Spalding, who founded the well-known sporting goods company. (Growing up in New York, you call the lively pink rubber balls his company still makes "spaldeens." To this day when I see "Spalding" I consider it a misspelling.) In 1889 Spalding had been in business ten years and was making money hand over spaldeen. In order to increase his profits even further, he took his baseball team, the Chicago Club, and a group of all-stars on a world tour. There were stops in England, Egypt, Australia and the Hawaiian Islands. It was his purpose to sell the "American National Game" as a vehicle for international competition (although an International Base-Ball Association with teams in London and such other large cities as New Bedford, Lynn and Hornellsville had failed in 1878). Naturally Spalding's only stated motive was that he loved baseball.

On the team's return here, there was a celebration at the famed Delmonico's restaurant in New York (Mark Twain was present), and Abraham G. Mills, the third president of the National League, which had been formed in 1876, made a speech saying that research had established the game as American in origin. This made everybody so happy he got a lot of applause and no back talk.

But to those who knew anything about it, his statement came as a surprise. It had long been assumed that baseball was an outgrowth of the children's game of rounders, which was a centuries-old English invention. Since anti-British feelings were strong at the time, few argued against Mills' little distortion. In 1903, however, a dastardly sportswriter named Harry Chadwick raised the specter of rounders again and a furious A. G. Spalding announced he was going to settle the question once and for all. So he handpicked a commission to study the question and decide in his favor.

The commission appears to have relied more on verbal testimony than documentary evidence. (Whatever documents it *did* accumulate were fortuitously lost in a fire.) It labored for three years and brought forth the opinion that "according to the best evidence obtainable" baseball was invented by General Abner Doubleday at Cooperstown, New York, in 1839. Apparently this astonishing discovery was based solely on the testimony of an old man

184

named Abner Graves, who relied on his memory for what had happened at Cooperstown almost 70 years previously. Hilariously, even Graves' testimony is less than convincing.

Graves said that Doubleday had put the game of town ball (a version of rounders) into shape. He said Doubleday had cut the number of players down from an unmanageable 20 to 50 ("many were hurt in collisions") and had designed the game to be played by definite teams or sides. Then Graves added the sentence that should have ruined the whole scheme: "Anyone getting the ball was entitled to throw it at a runner between bases, and put him out by hitting him with it."

Hell, that was the major difference between rounders and baseball. Being able to put a man out by hitting him with a thrown ball meant that the ball had to be *soft*. Baseball didn't become the game it is today until it began to be played with a *hard* ball and that couldn't be done until the tag was introduced.

All this pseudo information was allowed to kick around for 26 years, until 1939, when baseball decided it could use some kind of promotional gimmick. What would be better than a centennial? And if Doubleday had invented the game in 1839, this was it. The old Spalding commission report was dug out of the archives, the dust blown off the top and the promotional wheels set grinding. It was about this time, though, that Robert W. Henderson, a librarian at the New York Public Library, began digging around in the mass of material available to him. One of the things he discovered was that there had been many references to baseball *before* 1839.

Among the early references he and other people have unearthed are:

1. In the *Letters* of Mary Lapell, Lady Harvey. Date: November 8, 1748. "The prince's family is an example of cheerful and innocent amusement. . . . They divert themselves at baseball, a play all who have, or have been, schoolboys, are well acquainted with."

2. Jane Austen in *Northanger Abbey*, published in 1798: "It was not very wonderful that Catherine, who

185

had by nature nothing heroic about her, should prefer cricket, baseball, riding on horseback, and running around the country at the age of 19, to books."

3. A children's book published in England in 1744 titled *A Little Pretty Pocket Book* listed 26 sports and games, one for each letter of the alphabet. B was represented by Baseball.

4. Oliver Wendell Holmes, after he became a Supreme Court Justice, told an interviewer he had played a lot of baseball in college. He graduated from Harvard in 1829.

5. A Revolutionary War soldier named George Ewing wrote in a letter dated April 7, 1778, that the soldiers at Valley Forge occupied their time playing a game of "Base."

6. A Princeton student has left us a diary in which there is an entry dated 1786 describing a game of "baste ball."

7. Thurlow Weed, the upstate New York political boss, wrote in his biography that in 1825 Rochester had a baseball club of 50 members, aged eighteen to forty, and they played baseball every afternoon during the ball season.

Besides, Henderson noted, there was probably a great deal more evidence to support the theory that it was a man named Alexander Cartwright who came closest to "inventing" American baseball. Cartwright, a fireman, but apparently a member of the upper crust anyway (as distinguished from A. G. Spalding, who just had crust), had played baseball a great deal around New York with his society friends. In 1845 he organized the Knickerbocker Base Ball Club of New York, and set about to write a set of clear, precise rules. In these rules he eliminated "soaking," or hitting the runner with a thrown ball, in favor of the tag. As far as we know this is the first set of written rules to do so. It unquestionably paved the way for the hard ball, the key to modern baseball. But Cartwright admitted readily enough that he had leaned heavily for his rules on *The Book of Sports,* published in Boston by Robin Carver in 1834. Carver, in turn, had lifted his rules from *The Boys Own Book,* published in London in 1838. In this book the game was called "rounders."

With all this information now available to them, the baseball moguls plowed grimly ahead with their plans for a 1939 centennial. And after all of that, they blithely staged a second centennial in 1969. This one was based on the 100th birthday of the Cincinnati Reds, the first professional baseball team in America. In fact, the Red stockings, as they were called then, were formed some years before 1869 as an amateur team. In those days, like our very own, the line between amateurism and professionalism was never closely drawn, but baseball doesn't need very much excuse, or much historical reality, to give itself a centennial.

It's noteworthy, though, that while baseball was able to get the U.S. government to issue a postage stamp commemorating its nonexistent centennial in 1939, Washington, which is not noted for being much preoccupied with historical truths, balked at General Doubleday. He does not appear on the stamp. He is also not on the stamp issued in 1969 to commemorate baseball's second centennial in 30 years. I don't believe he would have cared. Considering what went on in those early years of baseball, one might guess that the General would have been delighted not to be identified with the game at all.

Once the Knickerbocker club established stable rules—a four-base diamond, 90-foot bases, three outs, throwing runners out or tagging them, batting in rotation, nine-man teams—the game grew rapidly in popularity. The growth was interrupted by the Civil War, but by 1870 it was estimated there were 1,000 club teams in the country. None of the members, by the way, was Negro. Nor was it any accident that organized baseball had no Negro players until Jackie Robinson came into the game. That's because the 1867 convention of the National Association of Base Ball players, an amateur group, but the first national association of baseball players, specifically barred Negroes.

With all these clubs in operation and increased betting on games leading to ever more pressure to win, it was only a matter of time before clubs would start stealing each other's best players and attempting to keep their own by paying them salaries or giving them jobs they didn't have to work at, a system still happily traded upon by today's college athlete. Although the National Association was supposed to be amateur, it did not long remain so; indeed, it probably never was. In 1860 the Brooklyn Excelsiors were charged with paying a player named Jim Creighton. Al Reach was being paid by the Brooklyn Eckfords in the early 1860s. The Philadelphia Athletics were supposed to be paying 20 dollars a week to three players named Pike, Dickney and McBride. Al Spalding is said to have received 40 dollars a week from the Chicago Excelsiors, ostensibly for selling groceries, but actually for playing baseball.

A *cause célèbre* in 1867 involved George Wright, a shortstop now in the Hall of Fame, leaving the New York Gothams to play with the Washington Nationals. Wright seemed to be an out-and-out professional, listing his business address as a park on Pennsylvania Avenue, but other players on the team were given jobs as clerks in government. Obviously they didn't do much government work. This process of switching teams (jumping contracts, actually) was called "revolving." It was against the rules of the association, but widely engaged in anyway. Bonuses were not exactly in the class of Joe Namath's 400,000 dollars, however. A player named William Fischer, for one example, agreed to play for the Philadelphia Athletics in return for a suit of clothes and 115 dollars. Unlike Namath, he did not live up to his agreement. When next heard of, he had accepted another suit of clothes from the Chicago Club.

Control of the baseball clubs was soon slipping into the hands of men who were regarded as less than gentlemen. Boss Tweed, who was running New York with a greedy fist, grabbed the New York Mutuals for his very own. He was president of the club from 1860 to 1871 and ran the team as he ran the city. He stole players from all over, luring them with large salaries which he paid by putting them on the payroll of the Sanitation Department. These were, then, the first garbage dumpers. Tweed had, up to then, the highest payroll in the history of baseball. It ran to 30,000 dollars a year and the city paid it.

An even more swinging organization was the Troy Haymakers. Talk about making hay. They were controlled by a group of New York gamblers headed by none other than the ubiquitous John Morrissey. Morrissey at one point in his checkered career was proprietor of the best gaming houses in New York and he used the Haymakers like loaded dice or marked cards. The practice of losing deliberately, either to build up a close but fraudulent rivalry or to cash a bet at good odds, was so prevalent that it got its own name. It was called "hippodroming."

As one would guess, there were out-and-out betting scandals. One had to be pretty brazen to be caught and no one would have accused the New York Mutuals of being anything else. At any rate, three players—Thomas Devyr, William Wansley and Ed Duffy—were convicted by the judiciary committee of the National Association of throwing a game to the Brooklyn Eckfords on September 28, 1865. They did it with a vengeance, too, the Eckfords winning 28-11.

Not that it mattered much. Devyr never missed a game. That's because he was only supposed to have offered the money to Wansley and Duffy. Besides, the Mutuals were desperate for a shortstop, which Devyr was. (And one can only guess at how Boss Tweed reacted. Probably with admiration.) Wansley and Duffy didn't suffer much either. Duffy missed less than a full season. Wansley had to wait until 1870 to be restored to active status.

The first admittedly professional team was organized in 1869 in Cincinnati. They called themselves the Red Stockings. All the players had to moonlight, however. The payroll to a jeweler, an engraver, several insurance agents, a hatter, a bookkeeper, a marble cutter and a piano tuner amounted to only 9,300 dollars for the season. Nevertheless, playing from March 15 to November 15, they compiled a 69-0 record. This added great impetus to professionalism in baseball. Americans love to love a winner.

In 1871 the National Association of Professional Base Ball Players was formed, sounding the death knell for amateur or club baseball. By this time, admission, at first ten cents but gradually rising as high as a half dollar, was being charged. The first thing the professional association did was to ruin the flavor of the game. It told its players to stop screaming at umpires, not to make fun of an erring teammate and to try to cultivate a "gentlemanly demeanor."

At this point in the history of baseball one of the most skillful raiders in the game was William A. Hulbert, an officer of the Chicago Club. He practically took over the Boston Red Sox team, luring away such luminaries as Al Spalding, Cal McVey, Deacon White and Ross Barnes. He also bribed the famous Cap Anson away from the Philadelphia Athletics. This sort of thing meant that the players were starting to make some real money and Hulbert knew this was bad for business. So was the blatant gambling. Gamblers wandered through baseball crowds selling pools. Players in uniform openly made bets. They were supposed to be betting on their own team, but what was to prevent them from having a confederate get them down the other way?

So in 1876 Hulbert organized the National League, the first organization of *teams,* and his first thought was the now famous reserve clause. By 1879 he had rammed it through the league's constitution. That eliminated the problem of revolving, but it did not mean instant success for the league. Most teams lost money and many slipped out of existence. From 1876 to 1900 there were 21 cities represented in the league.

One of these cities was Louisville and it collapsed because in its second season it collected the dumbest group of dumpers the baseball world has ever known. It is axiomatic now that it doesn't take much intelligence to be a dumper, especially one that's going to get caught. But this was ridiculous. The Three Stooges could have done it better.

The culprits were James A. Devlin, pitcher, William H. Carver, shortstop, George Hall, outfielder, and Al Nichols, third baseman. The first clever thing they did was start showing up around town wearing shiny diamond stickpins and expensive spats. Sometimes they allowed themselves to spend a whole dollar for a meal in a restaurant. This was about as unostentatious as a masked burglar lurking under a street lamp in front of a bank idly toying with a steel drill.

To call even more attention to himself, one of the players, Hall, had imported his own personal dumper. When Bill Hague, the third baseman, was hurt, Hall suggested Nichols be picked up. Nichols had been a member of the defunct New York Mutuals and now was playing with an independent team in Pittsburgh. As soon as Nichols showed up, the team started to lose games in Marx brothers style. In game after game, errors by Hall, Carver and Nichols and sometimes poor pitching by Devlin (in those days pitchers pitched every day) led to one-sided losses.

The boys were being so obvious that a sportwriter, who traditionally will not notice this kind of thing if it is done with any dexterity and subtlety at all, thought he noticed some funny things. So the man, John Halderman of the Louisville *Courier-Journal*, confronted Devlin and Hall. They denied all. The fact that they didn't punch him in the nose, though, must have told Halderman something.

Meanwhile, Charles E. Chase, the owner of the club, was getting anonymous telegrams from Hoboken, New Jersey, warning him that his boys were up to no good. He did not take them seriously. However, at the prodding of Halderman, he began intercepting telegrams to and from the players. The codes were brilliant.

BROOKLYN, SEPT. 19—A.H. NICHOLS, LOU. B.B. CLUB, BURNET HOUSE, LOUISVILLE.—IS CINCINNATI SURE? JAMES MCLOUD LOUISVILLE, SEPT. 21—JAMES MCLOUD, 141 BROOME ST., NEW YORK—AT CINCINNATI TOMORROW. SASH. D. & H.

After a few blown ball games it didn't take much effort

to figure out that SASH meant the fix was in. So Chase finally steeled himself and confronted Devlin. The dumper collapsed like a sack of suet. He admitted all but pleaded for mercy on the ground that he hadn't been dumping league games. (The schedules were looser in those days and teams played a lot of exhibition games.) This started a chain reaction. Without any prodding, Hall showed up demanding to be allowed to confess. Years later, writing in *The Sporting Times*, Chase recalled this plea from Hall: "I know I have done wrong, but as God is my judge I have never thrown a league game. If I tell you all I know about this business will you promise to let me down easy?"

So Chase, who by this time was getting a bit sly, said: "I know everything you have done [He didn't.], and I can't make any promises." Hall being made of stern stuff, this broke him down completely and he spilled his guts about every fixed game he knew about. It was enough to get all hands barred from baseball for life and this time the ban stuck. Not that the players didn't do some tall crying, particularly Devlin, who insisted he got 100 dollars for throwing one measly game and from then on was blackmailed into compliance. There is available a bitter, brooding letter he wrote to Harry Wright, then president of the league. The spelling is his:

> I can assure you Harry that I was not Treated right and if Ever I Can see you to tell you the Case you will say I am not to Blame I am living from hand to mouth all winter I have not got a Stitch of clothing or has my wife and Child . . . the Louisville people have made me what I am to day a Begger.

In the end Devlin's excuse was that he did it all for the wife and kids. He thus beat Ed Cicotte of the 1919 Chicago White Sox to the punch by 42 years.

The press of the time seemed to take these little peccadilloes in stride either through lack of interest or because they were so common. There were, nevertheless, some doom criers. Among them was a fellow named Casper W. Whitney and I put him down as one of the world's great writers of sporting copy. He wrote with style, élan, great knowledge and was totally wrong all of the time. He was, in addition, a glorious snob and years ahead of his time. Here is Whitney on baseball in the *Fortnightly Review* of September 1893. The italics are mine:

Baseball thrived all through the 70s and in the 80s the crowds that attended the games were simply enormous while the star players commanded salaries in proportion. [I'm not sure what Whitney's idea of enormity was. In 1888 the Philadelphia club raised its attendance to an average 4,010 by lowering the price of admission to twenty-five cents. And in 1885 few clubs paid an average salary of more than 1,500 dollars a year.] But like all professional sport, the greed for aggrandisement proved to be its ruin. Just a few years ago a rival professional organization [the one-year Players' or Bolshevik League] was formed and the people were so bored with newspaper recriminating and tiresome warfare that so thoroughly disgusted them, the two organizations failed to draw nearly as many spectators as had the one in its pristine days. It went from bad to worse, until, in the last year or so, the better class of American sportsmen appear to have lost all interest in professional baseball; in fact, *professional sports in the United States is dead.*

. . . The [baseball] contests every May and June between the teams of Harvard and Yale and Princeton attract great crowds, and of the *best people.* Probably I ought to qualify my comments on professional baseball by saying that in many parts of the country it does today attract a fair number of people, *but the quality of the attendance has undergone an absolute change. Now it is composed largely of the same class of men as those that play ball. Formerly it attracted men of breeding.*

With the coming of the National League and then the reserve clause to baseball, salaries of players stabilized, and at, as one might guess, quite low levels. The reserve clause binds forever a player to the team he signs with.

He does not *have* to play baseball for that team, but if he doesn't, he can play for no other. This gives him the right to remain poor. With nowhere to go but home if they would not accept the pittance clubowners were paying—seldom more than 1,500 dollars a year—baseball players scouted around for methods of bettering their poor lot. One thing they did was form a union, or brotherhood as they called it. The other thing they did was make bets.

The union, the Brotherhood of Professional Base Ball Players, was the idea of a Philadelphia sportswriter, William H. Voltz. He tried to get it going in 1885 and was met with vast mistrust and almost as much disinterest. The relationship between ball player and newspapermen was even more difficult than it is now, since reporters were often quite directly involved with team management, often on a salary basis, and were entertained on a scale players couldn't afford and couldn't help noticing. But on October 22 of that year, nine New York Giant players got together to form a branch of the brotherhood. A year later there were chapters in every National League city and the brotherhood had some 90 members. Even so, by 1889 the brotherhood had accomplished so little that it was decided it would have to form its own league if it was going to get even to first base. Then as now, the thing baseball magnates understood best and quickest was a cocked revolver pressed firmly against their skulls.

Under the leadership of John Montgomery Ward, a *rara avis* in that he was a former baseball player who not only had a college education but a law degree as well, the brotherhood raised capital, built ball parks (not a difficult thing in those days: all you needed were a flat, empty field and wooden benches) and organized an eight-team league—Boston, Brooklyn, Buffalo, Chicago, Cleveland, Philadelphia, Pittsburgh and New York. Many players owned stock in their teams and were, in addition, represented in a "senate" that governed the league. The league was called the Players' National League of Base Ball Clubs but, sportswriters being a conservative lot, it came to be called the Bolshevik League.

194

In his scholarly book on the early history of baseball, Dr. Harold Seymour quotes a newspaper attack on the Players' League which ridiculed the appearance of the players at a league meeting. It said they were dressed in fur-lined overcoats, silk hats, patent-leather shoes, carrying gold-headed canes, wearing 5,000 dollar diamond stickpins and garish rings and smoking 25-cent cigars. "Don't mistake them for the poor, miserable, overworked, underpaid, haggard, starving slaves of the [National] League tyrants," the account read. "Nor is it a meeting of the Vanderbilts, Goulds, etc. It is but a gathering of the Brotherhood men."

The Bolsheviks almost put the National League out of business. They took with them most of the star players of the league and almost all the players who had any real talent. But the attendance war hurt both leagues and, at the end of the season, the Bolsheviks went around looking for some one they could surrender to. They found A.G. Spalding, who still owned the Chicago Club. Prepared to make some important concessions himself, Spalding was surprised at the abject capitulation of the Bolsheviks. This did not prevent him from taking advantage of it, however. He appeared to make some concessions to the players (one was that they could not be sold without their permission), but in short order it was business as usual. It was that for the players, too. Some of them even went to work as independent contractors for bookmakers.

"This thing of betting on games was a common condition previous to the 1919 World Series," said Ban Johnson, president of the American League, after the Black Sox scandal. It was so common no one wanted to do anything about it, for fear of wrecking the game. No one even wanted to talk about it. After the Black Sox were hung out to dry, though, the old aw-that-was-nothing boys came out of the woodwork. Horace Fogel, one-time president of the Philadelphia Phillies, revealed that in 1905 gamblers approached Rube Waddell, the Philadelphia Athletic pitcher, and offered him 17,000 dollars to miss the World Series against the Giants. Waddell actually did miss the Series, giving as an excuse that he had hurt his arm when he tripped over a suitcase on a train. No doubt he was walking on his hands at the time. The Giants won the Series, but Waddell, Fogel said, collected only 500 dollars. It is very hard to trust a fixer.

During the period after the Black Sox dump hit the papers, there was also a story quoting Charles "Red" Dooin, once player-manager of the Phillies, about how brazen the gamblers were. He said the Phillies had been offered all kinds of money to throw the 1908 pennant. "All we had to do was name a price," Dooin said. "Why the gamblers opened up a satchel, must've had over 150,000 dollars in it, told our pitchers to help themselves. At the first game at the Polo Grounds a man handed me 8,000 dollars, told me there was 40,000 dollars more waiting for me. He was a big man, so I called big Kitty Bransfield, who threw him down the stairs."

Fogel seemed to know even more about that than Dooin. He pinpointed the briber as "a former New York National League player [Giant], now [1920] a magnate in a western town in a minor league." He said this former player had offered Dooin, Bransfield, Otto Knabe, Mike Doolan and Sherwood Magee from 1,000 to 5,000 dollars each to miss a big series against the Giants.

Nobody took any money, it says here, and the team that won the NL pennant in 1908 was neither the Phillies nor Giants, but the Chicago Cubs.

What is certain is that few players had the fortitude to resist the sweet whispers of gamblers' gold. From 1917 through 1920 there are so many records of bribery that one has to be suspicious of *all* games of that era. The Black Sox scandal, in which eight players of the Chicago White Sox conspired to dump the 1919 World Series to the Cincinnati Reds, is the one even school boys today are familiar with. But there were a staggering number of other well-documented instances of player gambling, bribery and dumping, some of them involving the biggest and most sacred names in baseball. Some of these names were so important that the great and incorruptible Baseball Commissioner Kenesaw Mountain Landis felt it necessary to join with his baseball brethren in kicking them under a convenient rug.

One of the best-known player-gamblers of the time was Hal Chase, the man they called Prince Hal. He had two gifts: one for playing first base, the other for larceny. He was so insolent he would manipulate the score at first base, nonchalantly missing easy grounder after easy grounder until enough runs scored for him to cash his bet. He also was adept at corrupting his fellows, buying his own or opposition pitches for prices which ranged down to 50 dollars. Although there had been many charges made against him, Chase seemed to lead a charmed life. Then on August 9, 1918, the Cincinnati Reds suddenly announced that Chase had been suspended "indefinitely." The club wouldn't say why, but Chase freely admitted he had been accused of gambling (actually, it wasn't considered a bad thing to bet on your own team to win) and denied all. He even had the gall to sue the Cincinnati club for back pay.

The National League got around to having a hearing on the case on January 30, 1919. There were two complaints against Chase, both by pitchers. One was Pol Perritt of the Giants. He said that on the day of a doubleheader Chase had asked him which game he was going to pitch. Perritt said he didn't know, so Chase said, "I wish you'd tip me off, because if I know which game you'll pitch, and can connect with a certain party, you will have nothing to fear." What Chase was saying, apparently, was that Perritt would be allowed to win his game. Perritt told his manager, John McGraw, about the conversation. McGraw, who came to win, did nothing.

The other pitcher was named Jimmy Ring. He pitched for the Reds. He testified that in 1917 he was asked to pitch in relief with the score tied and two runners on. As he was warming up, Chase came over from first base and, smiling insouciantly, said, "I've got some money bet on this game, kid. There's something in it for you if you lose."

Ring said he told Chase to go jump from a high tower

197

into a shallow pool, but as sometimes happens, the good guy lost. He blew the game by one run. In the lobby of the Majestic Hotel in Philadelphia the next morning, Chase strolled by him and dropped a 50-dollar bill in his lap. Ring told his manager, Christy Mathewson, about it. But for a year the Reds took no action.

More incredibly, John A. Heydler, president of the league, found the evidence against Chase insufficient to warrant expulsion. To top it off, the Reds were able to trade him—*and to John McGraw's Giants*. Chase went right back into business. He played for the Giants for most of the season and then suddenly disappeared. McGraw said Chase had been taken sick. A lot of people guessed he was no sicker than McGraw.

Early in 1920, after the artistic 1919 World Series but before the beauty of it all became public, a player named Lee Magee was suddenly given his unconditional release by the Chicago Cubs. Magee had played second base for the Reds in 1918 and been signed to a two-year contract after being sold to the Cubs in 1919. When he was fired, Magee brought suit against the Cubs. Their defense was that he was a proven gambler. The trial began in the U.S. District Court in Cincinnati on June 7, 1920. Before it was over, not only Magee, but Chase as well, stood convicted as dumpers.

Magee told an interesting story. He said that Hal Chase had come to him one morning on a train headed for Boston and suggested that they bet on their team (the Reds) to win the first game of a scheduled doubleheader the next day. Magee said he thought this was a fine, upstanding idea and gave Chase a check for 500 dollars. The Reds won 4-2 in extra innings and Magee asked Chase for his winnings. Sorry, baby, Chase said, the money was bet on the Reds to lose, not win. This so incensed him that Magee, in a blind rage, stopped payment on his check. Cool.

A lively little tale that. Except there was a fellow named Jim Costello involved. He ran a pool room in the Oxford Hotel in Boston. He took the stand and told an entirely different story. He said that on July 24 Magee

198

came looking for him with a proposition to dump a base-ball game, and that he expressed a small albeit definite interest, "although I never bet on baseball myself." The next day Magee showed up with Chase and an agree-ment was hammered out. Magee and Chase were to sign checks for 500 dollars which would be bet against their team. If they lost, they would get their checks back, plus their winnings, plus one-third of all the profit certain gamblers made. "I never bet on baseball myself," Costello said.

A funny thing happened in the ball game, though. It was played on July 25, 1918. With two out and the score tied 2-2 in the thirteenth inning, Magee reached first base when an easy ground ball he had sent to short hit a pebble, jumped up and broke the nose of Johnny Rawlings, the Boston shortstop. Then Magee was ordered to steal second. He started out to do so, in slow motion. Halfway down he even stopped. But Art Wilson, the Boston catcher, made a wild throw to second and Magee had to go all the way to third. Talking about it years later, Heydler said, "He might have scored with the winning run, I think, but you can see why he didn't." Then Ed Roush of the Reds hit a home run and Magee had to cross the plate with the run that cost him 500 dollars of his own money and heaven knows how much more.

The next day Chase showed up at Costello's wearing a straw hat and egg on his face. The conversation, Costello testified, went like this:

CHASE: It was a tough break we had, Jim; we tried awful hard.

COSTELLO: Yes, the gamblers are satisfied you tried, both of you.

CHASE: (grimly): Put them checks through.

Grateful for the honor among thieves, Costello put the checks through. Magee's bounced, though, for the reason that he had stopped payment. Outraged at the dishonor of it all, Costello came to New York for the express pur-pose of telling Magee he knew somebody would be happy to break both his elbows. Costello's testimony reads:

199

... I says [to Magee], "What are you going to do?"
"Well," he says, "the best I can do is send you reports
of different games we are going to fix. You can do
business on them." I says, "That don't satisfy me."
I says, "I don't gamble on baseball myself." He says,
"That is the best I can do." I says, "If you don't take
this check up immediately, I will take it up with the
club." Chase and Magee got a little ways away and
talked the thing over among themselves. They says,
"Why not stay here in New York today? We are going
to play New York and that game is fixed." I says, "I
don't gamble on baseball." They talked the thing over.
He says, "I will tell you what I will do, Jim. You go
back to Boston and we will send you half of that check,
and the other half when we get home to Cincinnati."
I says to Chase, "Will you stand good for that check
and make Magee pay it?" He says, "Yes." I says, "I
will take your word, Hal."

Possibly because Costello never bet on baseball, not
himself, the jury found for the Cubs and against Magee.
Neither he nor Chase ever played in the major leagues
again. It is important, however, that all this happened in
a court of law rather than inside baseball. The people
who ran the game didn't seem interested. Indeed, Charles
A. Comiskey, The Old Roman, as he was called on the
sports pages, had a lot of reason to be certain that the
Chicago ball club he owned had dumped the 1919 World
Series, but instead of investigating, he spent his time
denying that this could be so. He even offered a 20,000
dollars reward for information proving that the Series
was anything less than 100 percent American. He got it,
eventually, in the neck. But he never paid the 20,000
dollars, although a couple of gamblers claimed it. His
reasoning, obviously, was that what was bad for baseball
was bad for Charles A. Comiskey. It may be difficult to
believe, but it is possible that Comiskey himself was involved in fixing baseball games; at least when his team
collected 45 dollars per man in 1917 ostensibly to "tip"
the Detroit Tigers for beating contending Boston in an

important series, but more likely to pay them off for dumping two doubleheaders to the White Sox, it was with the full knowledge of the redoubtable Mr. Comiskey. This "tipping" practice was so common that one of the first things Landis did when he took over after the scandal was to prohibit it.

In any case, that was baseball in the first quarter of this century. And if it were not for a runaway grand jury in Chicago little of this gambling and payoff activity would ever have been prosecuted. A lot of money was being made, both by professional gamblers and by the players. Gambling on baseball was so popular that Costello told Magee he could get down "any amount" on a routine Cincinnati-Boston game. During the 1919 World Series gamblers were able to wager a quarter of a million dollars without anybody so much as blinking.

The Chicago grand jury got underway on September 7, 1920, after almost a year of rumors about the 1919 Series. One can only guess why a year went by before anybody undertook a serious investigation when, on the day after the Series ended, Dan Daniel was able to write in the New York *Sun:* "After the series of startling defeats of the White Sox early in the Series it was said here that Eddie Cicotte had been bribed to throw his games. It was also said that five members of the Chicago club had been given 100,000 dollars by a gang of gamblers to throw the Series." He had it almost exactly right. Yet when the grand jury was finally convened it was not to investigate the White Sox, but a report that a game between the Cubs and the Phillies on August 31, 1920, had been fixed. Presiding, however, was a Judge Charles MacDonald, a politically ambitious man who soon saw the advantages of probing into the 1919 World Series. The national pastime was to be saved in spite of itself.

There was a sudden shift in odds before the August 31 Phillie-Club game. The odds dropped from 2-1 on the Cubs to even money and then the Phillies became favored. Before the game, William L. Veeck, president of the Cubs and father of Bill Veeck, received a telegram from Detroit

201

warning him that the game was fixed. Veeck did what he could. He switched pitchers from Claude Hendrix to Grover Cleveland Alexander and offered him a 500-dollar bonus for winning. The Cubs lost anyway and, during the course of the grand-jury investigation, Hendrix was quietly dropped by the Cubs.

The grand jury heard some other interesting things. John "Rube" Benton, New York Giants pitcher, testified that "Buck" Herzog of the Cubs and Hal Chase had offered him 800 dollars the year before to throw a game to the Cubs. He said he had refused the bribe and won the game. McGraw was supposed to have heard about the bride attempt, but once again nobody did anything about it. Brought back to testify again the next day, Benton, confronted by affidavits of two ball players he had told about it, admitted that Chase had tipped him to the White Sox Series dump. He said he won 3,800 dollars betting on the Cincinnati Reds. And that Chase had won 40,000 dollars. This sent the grand jury off howling in the direction of the 1919 Series. It didn't take long for names to start dropping—Ed Cicotte, Arnold "Chick" Gandil, Oscar "Happy" Felsch, Charles "Swede" Risberg, "Shoeless" Joe Jackson, Fred McMullin, Claude "Lefty" Williams, George "Buck" Weaver, the men who were to become known as the Black Sox. If Daniel had had the dope the year before, it couldn't have been hard for the grand jury. Meanwhile, from other parts of the country, there were stories from gamblers who seemed to know all about it. They named names and amounts. Baseball had tried to sit on the story but the lid had bubbled off. Jackson, who had been trying to confess to Comiskey for a year, told the grand jury all. So did Cicotte.

The Black Sox scandal has been blurred by time and three major misconceptions about it have been generally accepted. One is that the players wound up dumping for nothing, or virtually nothing, that they were so stupid they let themselves be cheated out of the money they had cheated to earn. The second is that it was a gambler who thought up and organized the fix. The third is that Ed

Cicotte and Joe Jackson, particularly the latter, were ring-leaders of the fix.

In fact, the players received at least 80,000 dollars (only the distribution was inequitable), the fix was the idea of a player, not a gambler, and that player was Chick Gandil, not Cicotte or Jackson.

The reason Jackson is accepted as such an important figure in the fix is that he was immortalized by these paragraphs in the Chicago *Herald and Examiner*:

> As Jackson departed from the Grand Jury room, a small boy clutched at his sleeve and tagged along after him.
>
> "Say it ain't so, Joe," he pleaded. "Say it ain't so."

Scholars have since decided that the kid really said, "Say it ain't true," and maybe he did. But one of the great satisfactions of this world is that alliterative euphony can be counted on to triumph over nit picking.

Despite this most memorable phrase, the moving force in the fix was unquestionably Gandil, a nervy first baseman who, after arranging the World Series fix and making off with what probably amounted to 35,000 dollars, was a salary holdout the next spring.

In *Eight Men Out*, Eliot Asinoff's brilliant study of the big fix, it is pointed out that it was Gandil who played upon the penuriousness of Comiskey (Jackson, the second-best hitter in the league was making 6,000 dollars) to talk the player into the dump, that it was he who dug up the two sets of gamblers—one headed by Abe Attell, ex-boxer, dandy and double-crosser deluxe, the other by the notorious Arnold Rothstein—and he who arranged the unfair split of the booty. After Gandil took out his big piece, the split went this way:

To Swede Risberg, the shortstop and the man closest to Gandil in the fix machinations, 15,000 dollars.

To Ed Cicotte, the pitcher who lost two games, 10,000 dollars, because he insisted upon it in advance.

To Happy Felsch the outfielder, 5,000 dollars. He at least had the sense to bet the money against the Sox and win 10,000 dollars (maybe more). There is no record of any other of the fixers having done this, although one would suspect that Gandil might have.

To Claude Williams, the pitcher who lost three of the five games, 5,000 dollars, although he had been promised more.

To Fred McMullin, 5,000 dollars and not bad pay because he appeared in the Series only twice as a pinch hitter.

To Shoeless Joe Jackson, 5,000 dollars, although he had been promised 20,000 dollars and tried to blow the whistle when he didn't get it.

To Buck Weaver, the third baseman, nothing, for while he was in on the original fix conference, he did not go along with the dump. It did not seem to occur to him, however, to dump the dumpers.

A baseball game, which often hinges on small acts performed with split-second precision, is ridiculously easy to lose purposely and, when it is, none can say that the pitching mistake, the fielding error, the strike out or the ground ball to the shortstop was deliberate. Heaven knows, a ball player playing his heart out will do all of those things. Hugh Fullerton, then of the Chicago *Herald and Examiner,* was a knowledgeable sportswriter who had been told even before the Series that it was fixed. During the games he circled plays on his scorecard which he found suspicious. Yet after the Series he wrote: "The fact is this Series was lost in the first game, and lost through overconfidence. Forget the suspicious and evil-minded yarns that may be circulated." Despite what he had been told, despite what he suspected he saw on the field, Fullerton could not bring himself to believe the truth. The game does that to people.

Cicotte told the grand jury how easy it all was.

Just a slight hesitation on the players' part will let a man get to base or make a run," Cicotte said. "In the first game in Cincinnati I was knocked out of the box. I wasn't putting a thing on the ball. You could have read the trademark on it when I lobbed the ball up to the plate. A baby could have hit 'em. Schalk [Ray

Schalk, the catcher] was wise the moment I started pitching. Then, in one of the games, the first, I think, there was a man on first and the Red's batter hit a slow grounder to me. I could have made a double play out of it. But I was slow—slow enough to prevent the double play. It did not necessarily look crooked on my part. It is hard to tell when a game is on the square and when it is not. A player can make a crooked error that will look on the square as easy as he can make a square one. Sometimes the square ones look crooked.

In the fourth game, played at Chicago, which I also lost, I deliberately intercepted a throw from the out-field to the plate which might have cut off a run. I muffed the ball on purpose.

At another time in the game I purposely made a wild throw to first base. All the runs scored against me were due to my own deliberate errors. I did not try to win.

Possibly the most amusing confession of all (and one that backed Cicotte on accidental errors) was made by Happy Felsch. Said the scrupulous Felsch:

I'm not saying that I double-crossed the gamblers, but I had nothing to do with the loss of the World Series. The breaks just came so that I was not given a chance to throw the game. The records show that I played a pretty good Series. I know I missed one terrible fly ball [in the fifth game, won by the Reds, 5-0], but you can believe me or not, I was trying to catch that ball. I lost it in the sun and made a long run for it, and looked foolish when it fell quite a bit away from where it ought to be. The other men in the know thought that I had lost the ball deliberately and that I was putting on a clown exhibition. They warned me after the game to be more careful about the way I muffed flies.

The execution of this big fix ran into more complications than a Laurel and Hardy movie. Asinoff did a good job of sorting them out, but it's interesting to note, for example, that in *Eight Men Out* he insists the third game was not fixed, that the players, upset about not getting the money promised to them, went to "Comiskey Park without any clear idea as to what was expected of them or what they expected of each other. The truth was, *nobody* knew how the third game would go." And yet there was this testimony before the grand jury by Shoeless Joe Jackson:

. . . And I'm going to give you a tip. A lot of these sporting writers that have been roasting me have been talking about the third game of the World Series being square. Let me tell you something. The eight of us did our best to kick it, and little Richie Kerr won the game by his pitching. And because he won it these gamblers double-crossed us for double-crossing them.

There remains the delicious possibility that poor Shoeless Joe had no idea what was really going on. For the most part, once they had agreed to dump, the players involved barely spoke to each other, except to ask for money. When Jackson talks of eight players, he obviously didn't know that Weaver had decided not to be involved. Imagine the scene, Jackson doing everything he can in his lumbering way to lose the game while the others were trying just as hard to win.

From the game itself it could be deduced that the only team trying to lose was the Cincinnati Reds. They lost it in the second inning, in much the same way Cicotte lost one of his. Jackson led off with a single. (He might have wanted to lose, but what's a little old leadoff hit?) Felsch was ordered to sacrifice and laid down a bunt. It couldn't have been a good one because Ray Fischer, the Cincinnati pitcher, decided he could go to second with it and beat the sacrifice. So he dashed in, picked up the ball and fired it into center field. That put runners on second and third, and then Chick Gandil, of all people, knocked them both in with a single through the middle. That was enough for the Sox to win, which they did, 3-0, on Kerr's three-hitter.

Add the bad Fischer throw to the strange things that

happened in the sixth game and you have the essence of a bizarre theory people who were there discussed freely at the time.

"Today's crowd paid 101,000 dollars to see the game," the New York *Times* story of that game read, "but you could see lots of better-played games on a bush league park for two bits." The game was played in Chicago and the Reds, leading four games to one, needed only one more to win the Series. There was every expectation they would get it, and it looked as if the White Sox wanted them to; by the time the fifth inning was over, the White Sox had committed three errors that had helped the Reds to a 4-0 lead. In the stands Cincinnati fans were giggling. But a funny thing happened in the sixth. Leading off, Weaver did what a lot of White Sox had been doing against Dutch Ruether, the Red pitcher—he popped up. It was high, short and to left field, and either Larry Kopf or Pat Duncan should have caught it easily. Instead, they both sort of watched it in admiration until it fell between them for a double. There followed a single by Jackson that was good for one run, a long double by Felsch that scored Jackson all the way from first and finally a hit by Schalk which tied the game at 4-4. The Sox won it in the tenth when Chick Gandil, our hero, singled to drive in Weaver, who had doubled.

That made the game score 4-2 and when Cicotte, of all people, pitched a masterful seventh game to win it 4-1, Jackson and Felsch contributing timely singles, the theory was this: *Both teams are dumping*.

"In Cincinnati on Wednesday," Dan Daniel wrote after the Series, "thousands of fans declared that Duncan had been fixed by a certain big gambler not to do his best in Tuesday's game and that he and Kopf stood by and let that famous pop fly drop for a two-bagger because they had been given a certain consideration to lengthen the series."

Given the temper and practice of the time, this is not especially far-fetched. There is little reason to think the Reds could not have been bribed to lose certain games. But as Lee Magee and Hal Chase could have testified, you

207

can't lose them all. Looking at it from this distance, it seems entirely possible that the only difference between the Sox and Reds in 1919 was that the Sox got caught.

Almost nothing can be told from the games. Jackson, who told the grand jury that throughout the Series he either struck out or else hit easy balls when hits would have meant runs, wound up hitting .375 for the series. The Sox, who lost on deliberate errors, made 12 in the Series. *So did the Reds*. Gandil, the gamblers' little helper, won two games with his bat. Felsch swears he wanted to dump, but never got the chance.

It is eerie to read accounts of the Series in the newspaper. There was so much talk about fix that all reporters had to have heard it. Yet they steadfastly refused—probably with a certain logic—to take into account something they could not prove, and could not, besides, bring themselves to believe was happening. If there was any genuine tragedy to the Black Sox affair, it must have involved these sportswriters reading their clippings in later years. Sometimes, they appeared to be edging close to the truth, other times they were either totally deluded or completely under their own hypnotic spells. There was even an invented story to explain the falling odds.

The report to the effect that Eddie Cicotte had a sore arm . . . had a material effect on the world series betting. Whereas the White Sox had ruled favorites at 7 to 10 last week, the quotation suddenly shifted and last night the best price to be had was 5-6. The sudden appearance of thousands of dollars of Cincinnati money was no doubt occasioned by the rumored indisposition of Kid Gleason's star pitcher. . . . In some instances even money wagers were recorded."

New York *Times*, October 1, 1919

Cicotte explained later how he lost that first game. He was slow trying for a double play. He got hit. So did the two pitchers who followed him. It was 4-0 when he left; the Reds won 9-1.

Cicotte was annoyed at his inability to do anything with the ball, and his efforts to conceal his chagrin made his fretfulness all the more obvious.

New York *Sun,* October 2, 1919

But Cicotte while beaten is not down. His head is still up. He didn't want to pitch today. He is superstitious, and his superstition extended to not playing in the first game of the series.

New York *World,* October 2, 1919

"It is hard to explain," Cicotte said, "but I was in no condition to pitch the game I expected. I felt perfectly confident before the game started and appeared to have "everything" when I was warming up, but when I hit Rath [*the first hitter, a signal, it is said, that the fix was on*] it seemed to have a strange effect on me. I felt so badly about it that I trotted with him along the first base line to see if the ball hurt him. When Rath assured me he was all right I went back to the pitching mound, but I did not seem to be right."

New York *Sun,* October 3, 1919

And so it went. Each time the Sox blew a ball game the poor sportswriters had to go to their typewriters and ignore the suspicions most of them had. After the fourth game, which Cicotte lost 2-0, the runs scoring on his deliberate mistakes, we have this gem:

There is no alibi for Cicotte. He pitched a great game, a determined game, and one that would have won nine out of ten times, but he brought the defeat crashing down upon his own head by trying to do all the defensive work.

New York *World,* October 5, 1919

When it became apparent that the Reds might very well win, there was a rush to hedge.

One can now see how the Reds were terribly under-rated during the National League season. The ability with which they won from the Giants in crucial series and the fact they won their championship with the highest percentage in ten years should have opened the eyes of the experts.

New York *Sun,* October 7, 1919

It was a best-five-of-nine Series and the Reds won it five games to three, although not before it began to look as though the Sox were going to come back to a 4-4 tie. Eliot Asinoff has a theory about the eighth game. It is his contention that the game was not in the bag, that there was still a lot of dispute about bribe money. Arnold Rothstein, though, seeking to protect the huge wagers he had made, called in one of his henchmen who was handling the fix for him and told him to *make sure* (a bit of teeth grinding here, maestro) the White Sox lost—early. Rothstein didn't want to worry about his money anymore. The man, Joseph "Sport" Sullivan, Asinoff writes, called a strong-arm hood in Chicago, who got the word to Claude Williams, the pitcher of the day. Whatever the truth of this theory, Williams was bombed out in the first inning. He left the game trailing 3-0 and the Reds won 10-5. "I wish," commented Kid Gleason, the White Sox manager, "no one had ever bet a dollar on the team."

But by this time the ink-stained wretches had begun thinking that perhaps the White Sox had the better team after all. They had visions of them tying things up and going on to win the Series 5-4. So when the end came it was abrupt and rather sad.

The end was discouraging. Yesterday the dopesters all agreed that the Reds were on the run. The Cincinnati fans who had been canonizing a lot of mediocre athletes, turned upon them and declared they were dogs, yellow curs and German quitters. Today the same Reds swarmed upon the cocky White Sox and battered them into the most humiliating defeat of any world series.

New York *World,* October 10, 1919

210

It is difficult to estimate how many honest baseball games were played during the 1920 season. The gamblers had their hooks into the Black Sox (who would not be exposed for a year) as well as men like Hal Chase (John McGraw told the grand jury he fired Heinie Zimmerman that year for offering Benny Kauff, a Giant outfielder, 500 dollars to help throw a ball game), and apparently could make them dance at the end of a string. None of the Sox was ever prosecuted for anything that went on during the 1920 season and to a man they denied dumping anything more than a little old World Series. But it was funny how they managed that year to lose just enough games to keep the pennant race going down to the wire even though they had by far the strongest team in the league. They might even have won another pennant and thus had another crack at a Series if the grand jury hadn't extracted confessions three days before the end of the season.

We can also assume that, since so many other players on other teams were familiar with what happened in the Series—many of them bet on the Reds—they counted their small salaries and were tempted. Every grifter in the country had to be waving big bills under the nose of every player he could find. Larceny was the baseball way of life. It was so pervasive it finally reached all the way into the office of the Illinois state's attorney. If it were a movie, critics would deride it as unbelievable.

On October 22, 1920, the grand jury handed down its indictments. It named the eight White Sox players, Abe Attell, Sport Sullivan and his sidekick, Sleepy Bill Burns, a former baseball player, a gambler named Rachael Brown and Hal Chase. Later five more indictments came down, against gamblers David Zelser of Des Moines, and Carl Zork, Benjamin Franklin and Ben and Lou Levi, all of St. Louis.

*Yet, not one of them was ever convicted of anything.*

One reason there was no conviction—besides the perfectly lovely fact that no one was sure exactly what kind of crime had been committed—if any—was that signed confessions of Cicotte, Jackson and Williams, along with

211

their waivers of immunity, had been stolen from the state's attorney. Just like that.

Of course, there had been a small change in administration between the grand-jury hearings and the trial, but charges that Maclay Hoyne, the state's attorney, and his assistant, Henry Berger, stole them were never proved. When they finally showed up, in 1923, they were in the briefcase of Comiskey's lawyer and they were being used to defend against Shoeless Joe Jackson's suit for back pay. In those days they didn't fool around about their larceny. In certain city halls you were advised to check your gold bridgework as you entered. This is not to say there is less larceny nowadays, only that it's more refined.

As the case was prepared for trial, it became apparent that somebody up there liked the defendants. Three of the best-known lawyers in Chicago were representing the players, who were asked to pay only a token fee. (Who paid? Comiskey? Baseball, which would certainly have liked to get off the hook? Possibly both.) Attell, represented by William J. Fallon, the Great Mouthpiece, who was also Rothstein's lawyer, beat an extradition rap in New York. Hal Chase did the same in California. McMullin was never found. Franklin was too ill to be tried. Brown and Sullivan were never arrested. The charges against the Levi brothers were dismissed before the case was sent to the jury. Sleepy Bill Burns was on hand, but as a prosecution witness.

Actually Burns was a damaging witness. He told exactly how the fix had been arranged with Gandil. The whole thing was made quite clear to the jury. But then the judge, aptly named Friend, Hugo Friend, told the jury that "the State must prove that it was the intent of the ballplayers and gamblers charged with conspiracy through the throwing of the World Series to defraud the public and others, not merely to throw ball games." This was the first the State knew about it. On that basis the jury could hardly convict. Not that it seemed so inclined anyway. It was out only two hours and 47 minutes before returning its verdict: not guilty. The courtroom became bedlam. Jurors picked up ball players and carried them around on their shoulders.

212

Cries of "Hooray for the Clean Sox!" rang out. Then everybody, players, gamblers and jurors, retired to an Italian restaurant where they ate pasta and drank chianti until well into the morning hours. A good time was had by all.

A further popular misconception has it that, with the end of the Black Sox scandal and the coming of Judge Kenesaw Mountain Landis as baseball commissioner, baseball became pure and sweet as a baby's breath forever and a day. Not so. The people who played the game were too deeply involved with the traditions of gambling. New cases were always being dumped, pardon the expression, in Landis' lap. Some involved games played years before. Others were new and shiny as today's bribe. Often Landis was as harsh and swift in meting out punishment as his reputation insists, yet he was not there to preside over the death of baseball at a salary of 50,000 dollars a year and he knew it. When he thought it politic, Judge Kenesaw Mountain Landis played ball.

It was not difficult for him to take a Eugene Paulette and ban him forever to a Siberian salt mine. Or a Shufflin' Phil Douglas. Their cases were open and shut and they were, besides, minor figures. Paulette, who was traded by the Cards to the Phillies in 1919, got the ax in 1921 for something he did two years before—at least that's what he was caught at. He was accused of accepting gifts and loans from two gamblers, Elmer Farrar and Carl Zork. Zork was, of course, one of the men tried and freed in the Black Sox scandal. Naturally Paulette got these goodies only because he was such a likable fellow. But Landis, the spoilsport, when he finally got around to it, said that Paulette had "offered to betray his team, and had put himself in the vicious power of the alleged gamblers." Goodbye, Eugene Paulette.

The case of Shufflin' Phil is sadder. Shufflin' Phil Douglas was a genuine baseball character, a spitball pitcher from Alabama, and an unquenchable, eternal alcohol flame burned brightly within him. He played for John McGraw's Giants and, in an effort to keep his flame down to a flicker, McGraw used to assign him keepers. But Shufflin' Phil was nothing if not slick, and regularly he would lose his keepers and a weekend or so. On one Western trip in August of 1922 he lost a good part of the middle of the week, too, and this upset McGraw no end. So in the presence of the assembled hired hands McGraw administered one of his famous tongue lashings to Shufflin' Phil. It had an effect McGraw could not have dreamed—it hurt Shufflin' Phil's feelings.

Casting about for a way to get back at McGraw, Shufflin' Phil hit on a great plan. The Giants were fighting the St. Louis Cards for the pennant so he sat down and wrote a letter to Leslie Mann, a Cardinal outfielder and his old buddy when they were both with the Cubs in 1918. The letter:

Dear Les: I want to leave here. I don't want to see this guy [McGraw] win the pennant. You know that I can pitch and I am afraid that if I stay I will win the pennant for them. Talk this over with the boys, and if it is all right, send the goods to my house at night and I will go to the fishing camp. Let me know if you will want to do this and I will go home on the next train.

                                        PHIL DOUGLAS

Shufflin' Phil went home on the next train all right, but only because Mann turned him in. On August 16, Landis pointed a trembling, bony finger at him and told him never to darken baseball's door again. So with Shufflin' Phil safely at the fishing camp, the Giants won the pennant anyway. The Cards tied for third.

Other cases were not that easy for Landis. Ever since the Black Sox scandal the pulse of baseball had been fluttering. Although Doctor Babe Ruth was administering adrenalin with his home runs, the patient was far from out of danger. Another major scandal and Landis might have found himself in the position of the successful surgeon with the dead patient. Actually there could have been two scandals, except that Landis joined with the people who owned the baseball clubs in enthusiastically sweeping them under the rug.

214

The first came in 1924. For the previous three seasons the Giants and the Yankees had wound up playing in the World Series. This was greeted in the hinterlands with profound annoyance and there was a great awakening of interest when it became clear that this was the year the Washington Senators were going to beat out the damn Yankees. Now if only the Giants . . . Sure enough there was a dogfight in the National League, too. It looked as if the Brooklyn Dodgers might knock off the mighty men of McGraw. They attracted a lot of rooters. In the last days of the season, however, things did not look good for the Dodgers. They were a game and a half out. Even if they won their two remaining games with Boston, the Giants would have to lose two out of three to the Phillies just to drop into a tie. Nevertheless, the Giant players must have been worried, for before the game of September 27 Jimmy O'Connell of the Giants had the following conversation with Heine Sand, the Philadephia shortstop.

O'CONNELL: How do you feel about the game?

SAND: We don't feel. We're going to beat you.

O'CONNELL: It will be worth 500 dollars to you if you don't bear down too hard against us.

SAND: Get away from me. You must be crazy.

O'Connell was, relatively, still only a rookie outfielder, presumably unsteeped in the dumping traditions of baseball. But before he had been purchased for the then astronomical sum of 75,000 dollars, he had played in San Francisco of the Pacific Coast League, a league which had undergone investigations of player gambling activities in 1919 and earlier that same year of 1924. O'Connell could not exactly have been a neophyte.

Still, this was the big league. So Sand blabbed to Art Fletcher, his manager, and was asked to repeat the conversation to John Heydler, the league president. Heydler passed it on to Landis. The Commissioner called in O'Connell and quickly got the story he didn't want to hear. Gee whiz, O'Connell said, he was only delivering a message. It was Alvin "Cozy" Dolan, the coach, who had asked him to do it. O'Connell said he assumed the whole Giant team knew about it, but he was certain that George Kelly, first

215

baseman, Ross Youngs, right fielder, and Frank Frisch, the famous Fordham Flash, second baseman, also were in on the scheme to buy some pennant insurance. He was picked to deliver the message, O'Connell said, because he was known to have been friendly with Sand in the minor leagues.

Dolan had a peculiar role with the Giants. He was a coach. He was also a sort of bodyguard and companion to McGraw and thus very close to him. If Dolan knew about the offer, could McGraw have been ignorant? No one will ever know, because when he was questioned by Landis, Cozy Dolan was stricken with a sudden case of amnesia. To every question Dolan answered, "I don't remember."

The other answer that deserves preservation was Frisch's. "Aw," said Frisch, "there is always a lot of kidding going on on every bench."

Shortly after the hearings, an anonymous letter was published in a New York newspaper. It said that a group had bet 100,000 dollars that the Giants would win the pennant by two games and that 5,000 dollars had been paid to an unnamed Giant player to be used in bribe offers to other teams. All of this came to naught. For one thing, the Dodgers lost their first game to the Boston club and the Giants beat the Phillies. The pennant race was over. And the Giants won it by only one and a half games.

But what of Landis? He could have hired investigators. He could have called in the district attorney. He could have dug and dug, put pressure on gamblers, had private detectives check out the underworld. And he might have gotten the goods on the Giants players. The conclusion is inescapable, though, that he did not want to. All he wanted was to get the whole thing over with. So he barred O'Connell for making the bribe offer and Cozy Dolan for having a bad memory. Then he banged his gavel and closed the case. He did nothing to Frank Frisch for being such a great kidder.

The next one was even worse.

At the end of the 1926 season the baseball world was shocked by the sudden resignations of two famous player-managers—Ty Cobb of the Detroit Tigers and Tris

Speaker of the Cleveland Indians. Both were legends in their time. From 1907 to 1919 no one else had been able to lead the American League in hitting. Cobb won in every one of those years except 1916. That year Speaker did it with a .386 batting average.

Speaker, called the Gray Eagle, was considered the best outfielder who ever lived. Between 1909 and 1924 he had only once batted below .300. His lifetime batting average was .344 and at the age of thirty-eight he was still going strong. Speaker said he had resigned to go into private business.

Ty Cobb, the Georgia Peach, was considered by many, Cobb included, to have been the best baseball player who ever lived. For 23 years he was a terror to the game. He stole 892 bases. His lifetime average was .367. From 1910 to 1913 he hit .385, .420, .410, and .390. He was forty years old, but he could still hit. He said he left the Tigers because he hoped to become associated with a team that had a chance to win the pennant.

On December 21, 1926, Landis dropped a bombshell. Deadpan, he assembled the press to release a report he had made to the leagues regarding a charge by former pitcher Hubert "Dutch" Leonard that in 1919, a big year for the game, Leonard, Speaker, Cobb and Smoky Joe Wood, Cleveland pitcher, had conspired to bet on and then rig a baseball game so as to win the bet.

It all started, Leonard said, when the four happened to meet under the stands after the first game of a series in Detroit on September 24, 1919. Cleveland had already clinched second place. Detroit was in a dogfight for third. There was a fair piece of World Series change involved. One thing led to another and it was agreed that the Cleveland team, since it had nothing to lose, would let the Tigers win. Leonard quoted Speaker: "Don't worry about tomorrow's game. We have got second place clinched and you will win tomorrow." The good friends congratulated each other on this clever strategy and then it suddenly dawned on them. If they knew who was going to win they might just as well make some money out of it. Fancy no one thinking of it before.

"Cobb," Leonard said, "said he would send West [Fred C. West, a private cop at the park who knew how to get a bet down] down to us. I was to put up 1,500 dollars and, as I remember it, Cobb 2,000 dollars, and Wood and Speaker 1,000 dollars each. I had pitched for that day and was through for the season, so I gave my check for 1,500 dollars to Wood at the ball park and left that night for Independence, Missouri." Leonard felt secure that all would be well with his bet cause he had Speaker's word that "he would go in and pitch himself if necessary."

Things seemed to go off without a hitch. Detroit jumped away to a 4-0 lead in two innings and won easily, 9-5. But Leonard didn't make much on the deal. His 1,500 dollars grew to only 1,630 dollars because, he was told, it was impossible to get a big bet down on the game.

Now this was as unlikely a set of circumstances as anyone in the golden twenties could imagine. Cobb and "Spoke" were heroic figures. That they would stoop to such a scheme and that the implication should remain that they were no strangers to this kind of action was beyond credibility. Except for one thing. Leonard had thoughtfully saved two letters, one written to him by Wood, the other by the great Cobb himself, letters which clearly proved the essential facts of Leonard's charge. The letters:

Cleveland, O., Friday

Enclosed please find certified check for sixteen hundred and thirty dollars ($1,630).
Dear Friend "Dutch":
The only bet West could get up was $600 against $420 (10 to 7). Cobb did not get up a cent. He told us that and I believe him. Could have put some at 5 to 2 on Detroit, but did not, as that would make us put up $1,000 to win $400.
We won the $420. I gave West $30, leaving $390, or $130 for each of us. Would not have cashed your check at all, but West thought he could get it up to 10-7, and I was going to put it all up at those odds. We would have won $1,750 for the $2,500 if we could have placed it.

218

If we ever have another chance like this we will know enough to try to get down early.

Let me hear from you, "Dutch."

With all good wishes to yourself and Mrs. Leonard, I am, always.

JOE WOOD

Augusta, Ga., Oct. 23, '19

Dear Dutch:

Well, old boy, guess you are out in California by this time and enjoying life.

I arrived home and found Mrs. Cobb only fair, but the baby girl was fine, and at this time Mrs. Cobb is very well, but I have been very busy getting acquainted with my family and have not tried to do any correspondence, hence my delay.

Wood and myself are considerably disappointed in our business proposition, as we had $2,000 to put into it and the other side quoted us $1,400, and when we finally secured that much money it was about 2 o'clock and they refused to deal with us, as they had men in Chicago to take the matter up with and they had no time, so we completely fell down and of course we felt badly over it.

Everything was open to Wood and he can tell you about it when we get together. It was quite a responsibility and I don't care for it again, I assure you.

Well, I hope you found everything in fine shape at home and all your troubles will be little ones. I made a this year's winner's share of World's Series on cotton since I came home, and expect to make more.

I thought the White Sox should have won, but am satisfied they were too confident. Well, old scout, drop me a line when you can.

We have had fine weather here, in fact, quite warm, and have had some dandy fishing since I arrived home.

With kindest regards to Mrs. Leonard, I remain sincerely

TY

It was not difficult for Landis to confirm the authenticity of the letters. Wood, for one, was quite willing to elaborate:

> I told him [Leonard] I did not care to put up as much money as the 2,500 dollars he suggested, but a friend of mine, from Cleveland, said he was willing to take a third of it. The day before the game he told me West would be at the hotel. West came up the next morning and said the best he could get was 10 to 7. Detroit was the favorite. We decided to lay the money. In a little while West came back to the hotel and said all he could get was 600 dollars against 420 dollars, but that he could get more at 5 to 3. We talked that over and decided not to bet at these odds.

If that isn't a conservative bettor there never was one.

Although this is pretty convincing stuff, Cobb and Speaker turned the air Day-Glo purple with denials. "I told Judge Landis, and I say now," Speaker said, "that I never bet a dime on a game and that I never had anything to do with a game being thrown or knew of a game being thrown." As proof he offered the fact that he had made three hits in the game and scored three runs. This sounds convincing, except that the testimony of the Black Sox shows just how complicated baseball fix can be. It is, of course, entirely possible that Cleveland lost without trying to. Happens all the time.

Cobb charged that the whole thing was a case of blackmail on Leonard's part:

> I'll stake my record on the diamond and off of it against that of any ball player, manager, club president or even Judge Landis. I'm clean and have always been so. . . . I've told everything I know. I rest my case with the fans of the country. The only blame that can be attached to me is that I knew there was betting going on.

That's the point. Cobb knew and he told nobody. If Shufflin' Phil Douglas could be banned for life for offering to leave a team, what should have happened to Cobb for being aware of betting? There is little question what Landis' instincts were. He wanted all four men out of the game. But he knew he had to tread softly. Coming so soon after the Black Sox scandal, a ban on two of the best-known players in the game could have been a disaster.

The very development of the case shows how frightened baseball was. In his report Landis said:

> This investigation was instituted by the Detroit club of the American League. They had been dealing with Leonard over his claims for money and it was in these conversations that Leonard made the charges against Cobb, Speaker and Wood. The Detroit club pursued the investigation informing the Executive Committee of the American League of what they had been told.
>
> This was early last summer. On September 6 last the American League turned over to me the two letters which Leonard claimed to have received.

It took so long to bring Landis in because the American League didn't want him. It didn't want any noise. Just as Comiskey didn't want the Black Sox convicted, so the American League didn't want to mar the reputations of Cobb and Speaker. The letters were strong stuff, however, and there was no keeping Landis out. The problem now was to minimize the noise.

Landis' solution was to allow Cobb and Speaker to resign their jobs. Since Wood, now a baseball coach at Yale, and Leonard were already out of the game, that would solve the problem in the quietest way. Indeed, when he made his statement to the press, Landis said that since all four were out of baseball, there was no need for him to take any action.

That was counting without Cobb's arrogant personality. If he was going down he would take baseball with him. He threatened a suit. He threatened to reveal other crookedness. "If crookedness was the subject," he was to write years later, in his book *My Life in Baseball—The True Record,* "I could say a few things about fake turnstile counts and juggled ticket counting practices by major league owners. I had certain proof that World Series tickets had been scalped through agents of club owners."

Cobb had Landis over a barrel. Baseball was frightened of the courts. It was a monopoly and knew it. Its reserve clause was always open to to legal challenge. Landis' evidence against the players was good, but might not stand up in court. There wasn't much he could do. On January 27, 1927, Landis capitulated and announced:

These players have not been, nor are they now, found guilty of fixing a ball game. By no decent system could such finding be made. Therefore, they were not placed on the ineligible list.

As they desire to rescind their withdrawal from baseball, the releases which the Detroit and Cleveland clubs granted at their requests . . . are cancelled and the players' names are restored to the reserve lists of those clubs.

In his book, Cobb wrote: "I'll reveal something here never before told. That famous Landis 'verdict' was dictated to him by attorneys representing Speaker and myself."

Landis died in1944 at the age of seventy-eight. Somehow he never got around to writing a book, the true record. Too bad. It would have been interesting to see what he had to say about Ty Cobb.

At any rate Cobb was now able to come back the next year to play baseball with the Philadelphia Athletics. Connie Mack paid him 70,000 dollars' hush money. Speaker went with the Washington Senators. Cobb played two years and was joined by Speaker in Philadelphia in 1928. Cobb hit .357 and .323 those last two years. Speaker finished with .327 and .267. No matter what is said about Cobb and Speaker, no one will ever say they couldn't hit.

Baseball authorities like to say that was the last gambling case baseball ever had to deal with. Of course, it's not true. There was the problem, for one example, that Landis had with the great Rogers Hornsby. The Rajah was a horse player; not a two-dollar bettor, a plunger. In 1927 Frank L. Moore, described as a horseracing commissioner of Newport, Kentucky, sued Hornsby for 70,075 dollars. He said Hornsby had lost that amount betting on horses through him over a three-month period and would not pay up.

Landis was acutely aware of the compromising position a man puts himself into when he loses that kind of money betting the ponies. He tried suggesting to Hornsby that he take up checkers or parchesi as a hobby instead. But Hornsby was a hard man. "Racing is legal," he said. "I don't do anything illegal."

Maybe not, but word got around he was borrowing money from his players when he was managing the Cubs in 1932 and for some strange reason he was fired. It was the third job as manager he had blown and he always insisted that it was all Landis' fault, and he could have been right. Still Landis was gone when young Bill Veeck fired Hornsby as manager of the St. Louis Browns. The horses had nothing to do with it. Hornsby was fired because he had been so crudely tough on his players they were about to go on strike.

Then we have the case of Leo Durocher, who was, in 1947, invited by Commissioner A. B. "Happy" Chandler to sit out a year of baseball. Durocher, manager of the Brooklyn Dodgers at the time, was probably picked on unfairly. Nevertheless his choice of friends—among them George Raft, Bugsy Siegel and Memphis Engelberg—was not exactly judicious. This can't be called a gambling case, but Leo's friends were not involved in tiddlywinks. In fact, one of the big raps on Leo was that Raft had used his Manhattan apartment for a crap game in which one sheep had been sheared of 12,000 dollars. After that Leo Durocher got a new set of friends, one of them Frank Sinatra, who only slugs photographers. Baseball doesn't frown on that.

It was also in the year of 1947 that the announcement came from Judge William G. Bramham, president of the National Association of Professional Baseball Leagues, otherwise known as the minors, that he had suspended five players from two teams in the Class D Evangeline league for not reporting having been approached by gamblers to dump baseball games. The "alleged irregularities"

223

had occurred the previous season. The players were Manager Paul Fugit, Alvin W. Kaiser, Leonard Pecou and W. C. Thomas of the Houma club and Don Vettorel of the Abbeville team. When told of the suspensions L. E. Lapeyrouse, president of the Houma club, said, "Is that all? How about the rest of the Abbeville boys?"

M. Lapeyrouse knew what he was talking about. Before the investigation was over, both teams emerged as combination horse rooms and bookie hangouts where the players did everything but run a hand book during baseball games. Indeed, a lot of the players *were* bookmakers who had beat it out of New Orleans because the heat was on there. Fugit, who once had played baseball in the Pacific Coast League and the Southern Association, both triple-A leagues, admitted that four players on his team had always worked in bookmaking places in New Orleans. "If the mayor hadn't closed up those places," Fugit said, "they would not have played ball, as they could have made more money working as bookies."

The boys were really active. One thing they did was past-post a local and unsophisticated bookmaker by turning his clock back a half hour. (They thus were able to bet on horses they knew had won.) Kaiser admitted making 185 dollars on this scheme and Pecou said he didn't mind tampering with the clock because "bookies are crooked."

Another thing the lads did was fix games during the season and at least one post-season playoff game was put into the bag so sloppily the people in the stands guessed it. Nor was anybody very contrite about it all. Pecou said he denied the right of anybody to tell him how to behave off the field and that he understood that gambling and betting were indulged in "by players throughout baseball and among the club owners and stockholders."

Vettorel denied allegations that he had flashed a fat roll of bills in a barroom and bragged that he had won the money by rigging baseball games. He said that "the league is lousy with gambling and even the stockholders of the clubs are connected with gambling houses."

Thomas, after noting that Kaiser was an Abbeville bookmaker, admitted being an avid gambler and said, "I don't know if there are many players who aren't."

Nobody went to jail. "Being called upon to find as a fact that a game of baseball had been thrown in the absence of a confession," Judge Bramham said, "is a precarious assignment." He said he had found enough evidence, however, to bar the men from the game. This he did. That there was no legal prosecution shows how difficult it is to prove fix if the players are tough enough to admit nothing.

Does that mean there have been a lot of undetected dumpings in baseball? That's impossible to say. A most respected New York bookmaker says flatly, "Baseball is one hundred percent honest." Yet there are angles, and when there are angles, there are people who will use them. This is the Second General Theory of Sports.

One widely circulated report had it that a major-league manager was working with gamblers on his pitching rotation. This supposedly was the scheme. His gambler friends would pick a day when the manager's team was playing at night and he had one of his best pitchers going, Sam Swifty. So the gamblers would bet a parlay, picking a team that played in the daytime and then their manager's team, specifying "if Swifty."

That means that if Swifty didn't pitch, all bets were off, including the first game of the parlay. This is not an unusual bet. The gimmick was that if the gambler's day pick won, if the first half of the parlay came through, they did nothing. Swifty pitched. If he won, as he was likely to, the gamblers won their parlay. If he lost, the gamblers lost. (You have to take *some* chances.) But if their daytime pick lost, the manager would be notified and he would bypass Swifty for one day on some excuse or another and *all bets would be off*. This gave the gamblers an edge. And that's all a gambler wants.

The bookmaker who insists that baseball is honest gave this as an illustration of the edge. One day he was deluged with bets against the San Francisco Warriors, the professional basketball team. He tried, but couldn't find out why.

When the game began, he knew, Rick Barry, the star player, was injured and out of action. "The smart money knew about it," he said. "I didn't. The smart money kills you."

It happened, though, that the Warriors won without Barry and by enough points so that the smart money bet against them was lost. Every nickel of it. "So what?" said the bookmaker. "I'll take that kind of edge every day and take my chances."

## 9  The Big Boat Race

OCTOBER 16, 1879, THE DAY OF THE GREAT ROWING scandal, dawned fair and unusually warm. A good thing it was, too, for the few rooms available in little Mayville, New York, on the shores of Chautauqua Lake, were crammed to overflowing and at outrageous rates running as high as ten dollars a day without meals. As a result, many of the 30,000 rowing fans, gamblers, pickpockets and New York and Philadelphia sports who had been pouring into town for a week, had, after the night's festivities wrapped themselves in blankets and slept alfresco.

The race was to be rowed over a five-mile course laid out on the lake in this most westerly county of New York State for an unprecedented purse of 6,000 dollars, which had been put up by the Hop Bitters Company of Rochester. The participants, who had been in training for this epochal event for more than a month, were Edward Hanlan, Canadian-born, twenty-four years old, fair-skinned, mustached, curly-haired and with eyes the color of a summer sky; and Charles E. Courtney, American, swarthy-skinned, tall and lean and six years older than his opponent.

Cynical opinion had it that the race would not be held that day at all. "There are too many people here," wrote the correspondent for the New York *Evening Post,* "and too much money to be made from them to have the race rowed on the day fixed."

His choice of words was unfortunate. It was true enough that the natives were profiteering and that, after a few feeble protests, the local constabulary proved amenable to protecting the wide-open roulette wheels and other gaming devices which filled the town. It was equally true that match sculling races of the time, wildly popular, were often postponed, and for a variety of reasons, ranging from high winds to low dudgeons.

But the word "fix" in *any* context about a Hanlan-Courtney match was less than politic. That's because these two men, as famous in their day as heavyweight-champion boxers are today, had been involved in a highly controversial race the year before, a race Courtney had been openly accused of "hippodroming," what we call "dumping" these days. It had taken almost a year of negotiation to put these two high-strung men in action against each other again, a year of charge and countercharge, of intense press speculation and a lot of private wagering.

Such large interest in, of all things, professional rowing seems far-fetched from the vantage of modern sports spectaculars. But in 1879 rowing was, outside of horse racing, the major American sport. "The pursuits of the savage," Thoreau was just through saying, "are the sports of the civilized." Rowing, an old Indian pursuit, dated back to 1833 as a college competition and is acknowledged as the first organized American sport. Rowing regattas for large cash prizes were counted as the most exciting of events and crowds of 30,000 would come out to watch them.

With professionals and amateurs rowing against each other, the gentlemen rowers were soon feeling left out of things. So in 1872 the Schuykill Navy, a Philadelphia club, decided that its regattas would be open only to amateurs. Not only were those who had won cash prizes prohibited from competing, but even those who had only made bets on themselves. This meant that more than half the entrants were ineligible (and a lot of others were lying). In the uproar which resulted, the National Association of Amateur Oarsmen was born. (The Amateur

Athletic Union, which started up in 1888, also traces its origins to this noisy affair.) The amateur rowing organization was a fine thing in that it enabled the amateurs to row in privacy, possibly with some of their wives looking on. Professional rowers seized the opportunity to take over the sport.

Very soon professional rowing, especially single sculls competition, got to be what boxing was in the so-called golden age of sports. Rowing matches were arranged like prizefights. Challenges were issued, ignored for a long time, there was a lot of breast-beating, and charges of chicken and chicanery flowed in the press. Finally, with reporters and photographers on hand, matches were signed for. The participants then went into training and for a month the newspapers reported their weight, breathing rate, lung condition and state of mind. Tension, the sports reporters would note, mounted. Rowers, writes Robert F. Kelley in his *History of American Rowing*, "became as famous and well-publicized—and spoiled—as any well-known athlete of today."

So the atmosphere of the first encounter between Hanlan and Courtney at Lachine, Canada, on October 3, 1878, was one of carnival. The New York *Times* reported:

> Train after train crowded with passengers was running into Lachine over the single track of Montreal Lachine Railroad, the nine miles of wagon road was packed with carriages, all hurrying in one direction, and the canal was alive with steamers, gay with British and American flags. By five o'clock 10,000 persons were in the grandstand, and as many more were on steamers, small boats and along the river bank.

But there was disquiet, too. The large amount of betting was leading to nasty rumors. "One misfortune of the delay [caused by rain]," one observer wrote, "is that it gives time for circulation of a renewed report that Courtney has sold out the race to Hanlan." (Libel laws must have been quite different then. At most, newspapers today would refer to "rumors of a betting coup.")

Hanlan opened as the favorite and, as race time approached, the odds on him soared. This despite the fact that Courtney was undefeated both as an amateur and as a professional. "Non-betting men who are acquainted with the oarsmen," wrote the *Evening Post* correspondent, "express surprise that so great and long-continued odds should be offered on the Canadian."

The start of the race was delayed until late afternoon, just as the wind began to freshen. Conditions were difficult, but the race confounded the odds by remaining close all the way. The *Times* ran its account of it on the right-hand side of the front page, a place usually reserved for announcing wars. The race, the *Times* said, was "stubbornly contested."

Hanlan, in his familiar red cap and blue shirt, started with a stroke of 31 and Courtney pulled 38 to the minute; both used long, smooth strokes with quick recovery. For the first four miles the lead changed hands several times, the shells "fairly hissing through the water." The first mile was clocked in seven minutes, the fourth in only six.

As they entered the last mile [the *Times* account said], Hanlan went slowly but surely to the front and at the half was leading by three lengths. . . . Here Courtney made a last terrible struggle and putting all his tremendous reserve power into his terrible telling strokes, crept up inch by inch and foot by foot in a way that would have given him the race had he kept it up to the end. But the strain was too great. He ran his bow to within a length and a half of Hanlan's stern part, but could get no nearer and Hanlan swept over the line the winner of the greatest scull race ever seen in this country.

Hanlan's time was 36:22, his margin of victory, a length and a quarter. And if the *Times* account had been altogether accurate, that would have been the end of it. But something had happened that the gentleman from the *Times* must have missed. Near the end of the race it appeared that both Hanlan and Courtney were headed for a group of barges that had wandered inside the racing lane. Hanlan slacked for a moment, then shot around them and over the finish line. Courtney, though, stopped rowing for a longer time, long enough to lose his last hope of catching Hanlan. Professional rowing began to die in the vortex created by this pause.

Wrote Edward B. Rankin of the Boston *Herald,* who acted as judge for Courtney and watched the race closely:

I venture the judgment now that Courtney is the better and more enduring sculler of the two, that despite the roughness of the water he succeeded, whenever he made the effort, in closing with Hanlan, and that at the finish he outraced the Toronto man, and only lost the race by ceasing to pull at a critical moment when nearing the goal.

The controversy raged for a year and at last, in this tiny town of Mayville, all was to be settled. Reporters were on hand from many sections of the country. Telegraphers were poised at their keys to flash the word through the nation, indeed, around the world, Mayville, woozy from the revels of the night before, awoke slowly. The sun was well into the sky when Courtney's handlers went to the boathouse to check his equipment. What they found was to stir an even greater brouhaha than the disputed first race.

The boat in which Courtney was to row had been sabotaged.

It was damaged beyond repair. It had been neatly sawed three quarters of the way through ten feet from the bow. Courtney's reserve boat had been treated even more roughly. It was sawed completely in two eight feet from the stern. There was no way the race could now be rowed.

Each side had its own version of what had happened, of course. In his biography of Courtney, C.V.P. Young quotes Charles S. Francis, editor of the Troy (N.Y.) *Times,* and later ambassador to Austria under President Taft, as to what happened. According to Francis, Hanlan was a bit of a playboy. The night before the race he had been out and "listened to the voice of the charmer." His friends were afraid that this would cause him to lose the race and them their money. They went to Courtney and offered him the 6,000-dollar prize money if he would see to it that the race finished in a draw. And Courtney's answer was: "Gentlemen, the race will be raced tomorrow, and whoever wins it will have to row for it." So Hanlan's backers sneaked out to Courtney's boathouse and destroyed his boats.

On the other side of this Rashomon-like tale, we have a man named William E. Harding, commissioned by Richard K. Fox, publisher of the *Police Gazette,* to write the story of Hanlan's life. And Harding wrote: "This much is pretty certain: Courtney was funking and did not want to start unless the race would be fixed for him to win." In order to get the race on the water, Harding wrote, Hanlan's friends agreed that he would dump. However, Harding insists, they had no intention of living up to this dastardly promise. In fact, they bet heavily on their man. The plan might have worked except that on the day before the race one of Hanlan's closest friends bet 1,000 dollars to 700 dollars against Courtney. He was careful to make the bet with a stranger, but here, Harding says, fate intervened. The stranger was actually betting only 200 dollars of his own money. He was getting down 500 dollars for a Courtney backer named J. H. Brister. When Brister learned whom the bet had been made against, he knew there was a double cross in the works. That's when Courtney's boats were ruined.

Which is the true story? It hardly matters. Chances are there was skulduggery on both sides. With enormous sums of money being bet, the First General Theory of Sports was in full operation.

Oddly enough, neither man was disgraced. A year later they tried the race again, this time on the Potomac, but Courtney came up ill and quit after two miles. Soon after, he stopped rowing professionally to become a rowing coach at Cornell. Hanlan was hired to coach rowing at Columbia. Both lived to respectable old ages. If any reget was ever expressed, it was by Courtney. He said he was sorry he ever became a professional rower. "I was a fool to do it," he said.

And in his most kind biography, *Courtney and Cornell Rowing,* Young wrote:

231

The probable explanation for some of the activities of which he was guilty during this period was that he not only became intoxicated with success, as he himself intimated, but was early seized up by professional gamblers, who took advantage of his inexperience and callowness and used him for their own ends.

# 10 The Sweetest Science

MR. BONOMI: Where did you fight Billy Fox?

MR. LAMOTTA: Madison Square Garden, New York City.

MR. BONOMI: And did that match take place on November 14 of 1947?

MR. LAMOTTA: I believe so.

MR. BONOMI: In the record book, Mr. LaMotta, that bout is listed as a knockout of you by Billy Fox in four rounds. In fact, the fight was fixed so that you would lose; isn't that correct?

MR. LAMOTTA: Yes, sir.

—from the *Record of the Hearings Before the Senate Subcommittee on Antitrust and Monopoly*, June 14, 1960.

What sport was once dominated by Frankie Carbo, the racketeer? What sport was run by an organization—The International Boxing Club—which was judged a monopoly and disbanded by the U.S. government? What sport has had as recent champions an army deserter (Rocky Graziano), a convicted mugger (Joe Giardello,) a panderer (Jake LaMotta), a professional union buster and cop beater (Sonny Liston) and as a top challenger a felony murderer (Ruben Carter)?

Boxing. Of course.

And yet this is also the sport which in the course of its long and dishonorable history has had only one documented fix—the LaMotta-Fox fight. This is not to say there have not been others or that boxing has any right to preen itself on its honesty. It is more a comment on the interest and performance of boxing commissions and law-enforcement agencies in this country. It also indicates how well-disciplined the practitioners of the sweet science must be in matters requiring the rigors of silence.

There are, actually, two other instances of fighters' having admitted dumping. In both cases, however, there is reason for disbelieving the confessions. This is an additional distinction of boxing. No other sport can boast of this sort of reverse duplicity.

On April 5, 1915, Jack Johnson, the man who touched off the search for a "white hope," was deprived of his senses and his heavyweight title by Jess Willard in the twenty-sixth round of their scheduled 45-round fight in Havana. Years later, Johnson sold a story of his life in which he said he had lost to Willard deliberately. As proof, he offered a splendid photograph of himself taken at the point of the knockout. Note, he pointed out, that while lying on the canvas he was carefully shielding his eyes from the brilliant tropical sun. Note also, he said, that his knees were raised off the canvas to save his legs from being broiled on the oven-hot canvas. This was proof, he said, that he was taking a nap, not being knocked out.

The reasonableness of this was accepted for many years, although Willard always pointed out that if Johnson was dumping he took a long time doing it, considering the searing temperature. Yet there could be no reasoned dispute because there was, at the time, a law against transporting films of fights over state lines. So there were no films of the fight in this country. Recent examination of the films, however, show that at the point of the knockout, Johnson wasn't shielding his eyes at all. He was merely doing what a lot of fighters have done before and since—falling down. It was sheer accident that the still photographer happened to catch Johnson's arm as it passed over his head. Moreover, his knees did not long remain in the air. The canvas may have been hot. Even so, Johnson was stretched out flat as frying eggs. The film also shows that, while Johnson was well ahead on points up to that moment, Willard landed a tremendous right hand that slammed Johnson against the ropes. He was falling down as he bounced off them, the ropes acting like a slingshot to add impetus to his fall. Nobody has ever been more thoroughly knocked out.

Then there was Joe Gans, the Old Master, a lightweight who fought from 1891 until 1909 (he died of TB in 1910). Gans swore that he had dumped his fight to Terry McGovern on December 13, 1900. It was only a two-round fight and, from watching the film at least, if Gans was dumping, he deserves a method-acting prize. McGovern hit him with everything but the ring posts. The last punch, a right hand, lifted Gans clear off his feet.

In those days it was not necessary to go to a neutral corner when you knocked a man down. (Much of Jack Dempsey's inflated reputation for ferocity in the ring stems from this fact.) So you waited for your opponent to get on his wobbly feet and, bam, you knocked him down again. Gans was knocked down seven times in the second round and after a while he was cringing. He tried to maneuver on his knees to keep McGovern in front of him. McGovern, in the meantime, moved around so that he could get *behind* Gans the better to knock him down again when he got up.

It was a bloody ballet and it is most difficult to believe that a fix was in. It probably wasn't. There are certain men, Johnson evidently among them, who would rather be caught cheating than losing Gans, who fought 156 bouts, lost only eight of them. He had a lot of reason to be proud.

Still, Gans was believed because the history of corruption in boxing runs deep. As long ago as 1834 journalists had turned their attention to the evils of prizefighting. In something called the *New Monthly Magazine and Literary Journal* the following little polemic appeared under the heading of "The Crimes of Prize-Fighters."

Our readers may recollect that we exposed the fact that what are pretended to be brutal exhibitions of savage and sanguinary combats between hired ruffians, are, in reality, nothing more nor less, in almost every instance, than mock fights, got up by black legs [gamblers], flash-house [gathering place of thieves] keepers, and the swell mob, for the sake of plunder; and that the fighters in general are comprised of felons and criminals of every description, who . . . terminate their career by keeping brothels, or houses for the resort of thieves—the highest point of a fighter's ambition.

Other people have left hilarious accounts of crooked boxing matches that took place before the turn of the century. A man who billed himself as "Geo. Siler, The World Famous Referee," wrote a book in 1907 called *Inside Facts on Pugilism*. In it he tells about a fight held in "about 1892" between Bob Harper and Wiley Evans in Chicago. Evans was favored, but the referee, a well-known ward heeler, was betting on Harper. In the third, Harper was put away by a right hand that must have been thrown from somewhere around Manitoba. He went down in one piece, like a tree, and looked as if he had about as much chance of getting up.

The referee started counting over him—slowly. "It took him," Siler wrote, "15 seconds to count to three." Then he went to the edge of the ring and made a small speech. "Gentlemen, you will have to keep quiet. Harper can't hear the count. [Harper couldn't hear *anything*.] There are a number of policemen in the hall, and if you continue hollering they will stop the fight." Then he went back to the body and counted, "Four." The count, Siler estimated, lasted ten minutes. That's how long it took Harper to come around. Then the fight resumed.

In the ninth round the somewhat discouraged Evans slipped to the canvas after taking a grazing left to the head. "The referee," Siler wrote, "counted him out in two seconds."

This sort of thing was not uncommon. Siler wrote that in a fight between a couple of chaps named Abel Cestac and John Thomas, the referee, Lou Magnolia by name, voted 7-3 for Cestac. Two judges both had it 9-1 for Thomas. When apprised of the vote, Magnolia blushed and reversed his tally. He said he had confused the identities of the fighters in his mind. Cestac was white, Thomas a Negro.

During the time of World War I the lightweight champion, Freddie Welsh, a Welshman, carried around his own referee wherever he went. The ref's name was Billy Roche. He was asked once what he would do if one of his opponents happened to render Welsh somewhat unconscious. "I'd count up to six," Roche said, "and then collapse on top of him with a heart attack."

Then we have the strange case involving Fred Fulton and the distinguished Jack Dempsey. According to Fulton, he agreed to box against Dempsey in 1918 only because he had been assured that Dempsey would go easy. Expecting that he would not be hit in anger, Fulton instead got knocked out in the first round. The story of Fulton's anguish was printed in the New York *World* of February 2, 1919:

San Francisco, Feb. 1—Fred Fulton authorized the statement here to-day that his fight with Jack Dempsey at Harrison Park, N.J. on July 27, 1918 was prearranged to the extent that he and Dempsey were to box an eight-round "EXHIBITION," and that Dempsey won in the first round by "DOUBLE-CROSSING" him.

Fulton said he wanted a chance to fight the winner of the proposed Willard-Dempsey match and added:

"I was IN on the Thing- ON THE FAKE, if you wish to call it that—because I went ahead and did what my manager told me."

There is no way at this distance to measure Fulton's veracity. But Dempsey's manager was the crafty Doc Kearns and, if anybody knew how to build up a record, it was he.

It is also noteworthy that, before his death, Kearns wrote a book in which he said that one of the reasons Dempsey was able to beat Willard for the title was that he had soaked Dempsey's hand bandages in plaster of Paris. Dempsey, always super-conscious of his image, denies this vehemently and will sue you if you take Kearns' word over his.

There are several reasons for arranging the result of a fight and not all of them have to do with cashing of bets. Return-bout contracts are an open invitation to skulduggery. The building up of a fighter's record so that he may get a big-money fight with the champion is another obvious temptation. But here, it is not necessary to fix the fights. The easiest way for a manager to insure the result of a fight is to put his tiger in with what is called an "opponent," meaning a poor fighter or one who is so old and battered he can no longer do well in the ring. This is done a great deal with potentially valuable fight properties. It is done to build up both a record and a fighter's confidence. One only has to leaf through a copy of *The Ring Record Book* to find lists of such opponents. Even Joe Louis has long lists of bums on his record. Floyd Patterson, it might be said, never fought *anybody* until he won the title in his fight with Archie Moore. These fights need not have been fixed, except in the very broad sense that the people involved knew who was going to win.

It is only in the case of the occasional turkey, like Primo Carnera, who burst upon the scene with all the impact of a dish of mashed potatoes, that it was necessary to make arrangements. Carnera, it is conceded, needed help even against "opponents." There are some who insist that eventually "Da Preem" actually learned to fight, but the way he was beaten to a quivering pulp by Max Baer and Joe Louis and later on by almost everyone else makes one doubt this proposition. John Lardner wrote in *White Hopes and Other Tigers:*

> I saw him one night in his dressing room in Brooklyn in 1936. He had just been knocked out by a fat rival tiger named Leroy Haynes. Attendants had led him floundering from the ring, one leg paralyzed. In the dressing room, a couple of doctors took turns sticking needles into his legs to see if he felt anything. He didn't.

Carnera was mobster-controlled. He was built up with

237

a series of easy matches he could not lose and was then thrown to the wolves. The only thing he showed against good fighters was courage. The mob made almost as much money betting against him on the way down as it had while he was on the way up. It is doubtful that Carnera ever understood how he was used. The pathos of this situation was dramatized by Budd Schulberg in *The Harder They Fall* and has since become a cliché of the boxing business.

There were not many Carneras in boxing, but the manufactured tiger is not so rare as some think. Billy Fox, by the way, was in the stable of Blinky Palermo, the well-known Philadelphia sportsman and convict, and boxing historian Nat Fleischer says: "Fox had no ability. He was built up by Palermo." It was quite a buildup. Fox won his first 43 professional fights by knockouts. And when he wanted to beat Jake LaMotta, he did that, too. Sin is its own reward, however. Fox wound up broke and muddled in the Kings Park State Mental Hospital.

LaMotta made a lot of excuses for his defection. He was such a good fighter that he could never get a shot at the middleweight champion, he said, and it made him bitter and eager to make a deal if necessary. At one point in his testimony before the Kefauver Committee (short for the Subcommittee on Antitrust etc.), LaMotta, in response to a question by John Bonomi, chief counsel, said:

> When I signed for the Fox fight, after a couple of weeks I received an offer of $100,000 to lose to Billy Fox, which I refused. I said I was only interested in the championship fight It was said it could be arranged, a championship fight might be arranged.
>
> That is all I heard for about a couple of weeks, and while in training I hurt myself and I went to a doctor and the doctor examined me and took X-rays and found out I had a ruptured spleen.
>
> He said I couldn't possibly fight, but I thought I could, and I started training again, and I instructed my sparring partners to concentrate their punches on my face, which they did.

But as the fight kept getting closer, I found out—I realized that I had no strength in my arms. So, therefore, when I was told again, if I would lose the Fox fight, I kept stalling them off because I still felt I could win. But as the fight kept getting closer, I realized that it was going to be kind of difficult.

But toward the end, when I realized that I couldn't possibly win, I said I would lose to Billy Fox if I was guaranteed a championship fight.

LaMotta was willing to be beaten, but he was not willing to go down for the first time in his career. "So I just stood there helpless while he threw a number of punches at me, and the referee stopped the fight."

Under tough cross-examination by Bonomi, however, LaMotta had to admit that his spleen was never hurt that much and that at no time during the fight was he ever really hurt. The point Bonomi was making was that LaMotta *could* have won were it not for other considerations. In the end LaMotta did not get a shot at the title for two years and then had to pay off 20,000 dollars in advance to somebody connected with the champion, Marcel Cerdan. He didn't know exactly who.

LaMotta also revealed that he had been involved in a series of what can only be called "semi-dumps." He says that, in order not to look too good, in order not to discourage the champion, he would not go all out to win most of his fights. The result was that against a certain Cecil Hudson he lost a decision in a fight he wanted to win. LaMotta: "I fought enough to win, and if you check the records, the records will show that it was a very close fight, and I am sure one judge gave me the fight, but the other two bums didn't."

If no other fix in boxing can be documented, it is still impossible to wade through its history without encountering numerous strange or inexplicable events. They remain so through the years because when they are investigated—sometimes even with Senate subpoenas—shoulders are shrugged elaborately and mouths clang shut like jailhouse doors. Yet it is worth recording here some of the more famous professional boxing encounters which contributed their full measure to the reputation of the sport.

## Daniel Mendoza vs. John Jackson
APRIL 15, 1795. HORNCHURCH, ESSEX

(While no attempt has been made to make this an *international* history of boxing skulduggery, I deemed this bout to be of special interest. It was something of a trend-setter.)

Mendoza was not only British champion, he laid claim to being champion of the world, and this in the home of the Marquis of Queensbury. He was also Jewish.

Mendoza was a 2-1 favorite in this fight but it quickly became apparent that he was in a spot of trouble with Jackson. In short order he was knocked down eight times. The ninth time he did not get up.

Those who had bet on him immediately charged what they called a "cross" in those days. But Mendoza explained that he simply could not cope with Jackson's strange style. This consisted of Jackson's grabbing a fistful of Mendoza's hair in his right hand (no gloves in those days, of course) and pounding him in the face with his left. When Mendoza remonstrated to the referee, he was told there was no rule against holding one's opponent by the hair and it was a darn shame, wasn't it?

## Primo Carnera vs. Ernie Schaaf
FEBRUARY 10, 1933. NEW YORK

There were many odd things about this fight even before it was fought. For one thing, although the price was close, ranging from even money to 7-5 for Carnera, Madison Square Garden already had signed contracts for Jack Sharkey to defend his title against Carnera the following June. Besides, Sharkey owned half of Shaaf's contract and was a second in his corner.

The fight was not spectacular. Although he was large— 6' 6", 260 lbs.—the shuffling, awkward Carnera was far from a deadly puncher. The experienced Shaaf made a good fight of it and, going into the thirteenth round, Carnera was only slightly ahead. Early in the round Carnera, who used his left tentatively, like a cat putting its paw into water, landed one on the top of Schaaf's head. The punch hit with all the force of a falling autumn leaf and as much anger. Schaaf dropped to his knees. Then he pitched forward, his head striking the canvas. Ten seconds later, he was still unconscious. An hour later he was in the hospital and, doctors said, still unconscious, but doing well.

The newspapers the next day, especially the New York *Journal-American,* went wild. "Fans Cry 'Fake'" read the headline on the lead story. "Even before the men entered the ring—yes, as early as a week or more ago— there were reports afloat that there was something reminiscent of Denmark in what was to come off."

Bill Corum wrote:

Nothing that Carnera did to him . . . could possibly have accounted for the desperate condition in which he appeared to be as he was carried away on a stretcher. . . . It just doesn't seem natural to me that a powerful 6-foot 200-pound man should have to be dragged away to the hospital as the result of a weak left-hand jab that *positively* didn't have enough steam to break a very old and weak-minded egg.

W. S. Farnsworth, the sports editor, put it even more delicately. "It was," he wrote, "the worst fake knockout I have ever witnessed."

Except a funny thing happened. The fight had been fought on Friday night. Tuesday morning at 4 A.M. Schaaf was still unconscious. Then he died.

Now Carnera was a killer. Now his attractiveness increased immeasurably. Now the public was *demanding* that he be allowed to fight Sharkey for the title. The demand was cheerfully met.

But there was still grumbling in the press. What happened to Schaaf? Can you die from a flea bite? There was, of course, an official investigation.

"Schaaf's death," testified Dr. S. Phillip Goodhart, "was undoubtedly caused by an injury to the brain caused in a fight previous to the Carnera fight."

Schaaf had taken a terrible beating from Max Baer six months before. He had since lost to a fellow referred to in the record book as Unknown Winston in October, turned around and beat Mr. Unknown in December and knocked out Stanley Poreda in January. Before the Carnera fight he had been in the hospital for treatment of what was said to be flu. If he had been carrying around an incipient brain hemorrhage, he carried it around for a long time. But at least there was an explanation to salve the wounded press. It was accepted with a minimum of grumbling. Boxing people have gotten away with worse.

### Primo Carnera vs. Jack Sharkey
### JUNE 29, 1933. NEW YORK

Old-timers like to recall the second Carnera-Sharkey fight (Sharkey won the first, two years previously, by a decision) the way they do the first Louis-Conn fight. Conn, it is said, had Louis beaten but became overconfident at the end, waded in and got knocked out in the thirteenth for his trouble. Sharkey, it is believed, did the same kind of foolish thing. And a study of the newspapers of the time seems to bear this out.

Hype Igoe, a famous boxing writer, wrote in the New York *Journal-American*:

Sharkey's actions in the sixth and fatal round were hard to understand. He had won all five of the first five rounds [syntax was not Igoe's strong point] on sheer boxing and clean hitting. As he left his corner for the 6th Al Lacey [his manager] called after him:
"As before. Your own way. Make him miss."
Instead Sharkey went into Carnera slugging, as if bent on ending it then and there.

The implication was clear, since it did end then and there. Carnera caught Sharkey with a right-hand uppercut and it was all over. The ungainly giant from little Sequals, a suburb of Venice, had climbed his highest mountain. He was heavyweight champion of the world. It was all downhill after that. He defended his title with successful 15-round decisions over Tommy Loughran and Paolino Uscudin. Then he lost his title to Baer, got beat up by Louis, became a wrestler and settled down with a liquor store in Los Angeles. In 1967, he returned to his homeland to die of a liver disorder.

It is possible, of course, that Sharkey, at thirty-one, was over the hill. Because his next fight was with Kingfish Levinsky, who was always regarded as something of a joke. It is said patrons could hear his knees clacking like castanets as far back as 20 rows when he was virtually carried into the ring to face the young Joe Louis. And Kingfish beat Sharkey. It is also possible, considering Carnera's history as a fighter, that Sharkey, willingly or not, sold his title. (It was considered good business for a champion to sell his title to a young comer for a share of his future earnings.)

What is a matter of objective knowledge, however, is that Sharkey did not change his style in the sixth round. He fought the same way that he had in the early rounds. So did Billy Conn against Joe Louis. The films show that clearly.

When you think about it, though, it wasn't necessary for Sharkey to change his style to get nailed by a right uppercut. Even against the lumbering Carnera almost anybody could have done it.

### Rocky Graziano vs. Cowboy Shank
### 1947. NEW YORK

This is an example of an interesting fight that was never fought. In 1947 Graziano was flying high, engaging in a bloody war with Tony Zale once a year for an enormous amount of money. The Cowboy Shank fight was supposed to be a warm-up against an "opponent." Suddenly Graziano announced that the fight would have to be called off, that he had wrenched his back and couldn't fight. That would have been the end of it, except that New York DA Frank Hogan had heard some nasty rumors. He asked Mr. Graziano to drop by his office for a cup of tea.

Later Hogan told newspapers this story. One day while Graziano was training at Stillman's Gym on Eighth Avenue, a man Graziano swore he did not know sidled up to him and told him there was 100,000 dollars in it for him if he would lose to Shank. (Once a fighter makes up his mind to take a bribe, he can, of course, arrange to increase his reward by betting on his opponent.) Instead of whistling up a policeman, the gutter-trained Graziano said, "See ya later."

According to Hogan, Graziano mulled the offer over for some time. He saw the stranger once more before deciding that he would not accept the offer. But by then, Hogan said, Graziano knew he was in trouble. If he beat Shank, he would be double-crossing people who had already made their bets on "See ya later." Graziano knew the kind of people he was dealing with and that they were rough customers. (No wonder, Hogan said, Graziano failed to recognize the man who made the bribe offer.) Graziano, deciding on discretion over valor, Hogan said, elected to come up with a sore back.

Graziano denied all to the newspapers and was still defending himself years later in his book *Somebody Up There Likes Me*.

"As far as bribes in fighting are concerned," Graziano's ghost wrote, " 'payola' offers for throwing a fight come your way all the time. All I ever done, all most boxers ever done, was laugh them off."

Since there was also some discussion in the DA's office about the relationship between Eddie Coco, Graziano's manager, and the ubiquitous Frankie Carbo, Graziano added: "So maybe there's mob money behind some fighters. So there's also mob money invested in American Telephone and Telegraph and General Motors."

Graziano's license to fight in New York was suspended for a while, although he always insisted he never did "nuttin'." And he didn't. Not even report a bribe offer.

The popularity of boxing in this country moves up and down with the remorselessness and inevitability of hemlines. But never again will it reach the height of the postwar years when television was still a wonder and observing a fistfight in one's living room every Friday proved so satisfying that television quickly came up with the rapacious idea of providing one *every* night. Of course, it could not. As a result, boxing suffered more than television.

During the time it was swallowing boxers whole, television thought it needed a boxer with a less squalid past than most of the active and successful fighters had. When television has a thought, the heavens start creating. (Like once somebody thought it would be wonderful to have a pretty lady who was an expert in sports for the *$64,000 Question* and Dr. Joyce Brothers was born, having sprung full blown as a boxing whiz out of the mind of a Madison Avenue executive.) So it was that Chuck Davey rocketed across the fistic sky in the year 1952.

Davey, a welterweight, was everything that television wanted. Davey was white. (The search for white hopes in boxing is never-ending and increasingly less selective; it was said that when he fought Muhammad Ali, Floyd Patterson was a white hope.) Davey was clean-cut. Davey was quick, intelligent and, for a romantic fillip left-handed. Davey was a Michigan State graduate. Davey was cute. The ladies loved him so much they were willing to stay home and watch him fight. This is very important to deodorant hucksters.

In less than a year Davey fought six times on national television, winning every time. This was enough to make people who did not trust his left-handed fighting style, who wondered about his punching power, begin to doubt their own judgment. He *must* be good, they began to think. All sports experts have this tendency to trot after a winner. That's why the boxing crowd was almost unanimous

245

in picking the first two Patterson-Johansson yo-yos the wrong way. The champion lost each time.

There *were* a couple of fights that looked rather odd, though. Ike Williams, once lightweight champion, was only twenty-nine years old when he fought Davey, but he didn't even look like a shadow of his former self getting knocked out in five. And after Graziano lost a ten-round decision to Davey, he retired to go into a different branch of television. He never fought again. "After that fight," he told friends, "I *knew* I was an actor." He never explained what he meant by that.

In quite short order Davey was deemed ready for a title fight. The welterweight championship was owned by Kid Gavilan, one of the greats of the division. The fight, which attracted great interest throughout the nation, was carried on a network of 63 television stations. In addition, it grossed 274,451 dollars at the gate.

Possibly because of a communications breakdown—Gavilan spoke Spanish—the Kid never found out how good Davey was. So he went out and demolished him. "Demolish" may be too mild a word. Gavilan humiliated him, destroyed him. He proved quickly, easily, graphically that Chuck Davey was no fighter. White, yes. Educated, yes. Cute, yes. But a fighter, no.

Gavilan put Davey down for a nine count in the third. Thereafter he was contemptuous. In the ninth Gavilan came out in a southpaw stance, mimicking the baffled Davey. Fighting left-handed, Gavilan knocked him down three times. Once a right sent Davey through the ropes and onto the apron. He retired ignominiously on his stool in the tenth.

After the fight Gavilan said: "He's very game. But no punch."

How come nobody noticed before?

## The Quaint Decisions

Yes, Virginia, it is possible to bribe a ring official. Oddly enough, none has ever been convicted of taking such a bribe, but there have been so many suspiciously insane decisions that one must assume there was more to them than common stupidity. We should not, however, sell stupidity short against cupidity in American boxing. At a guess, there is a greater supply of stupidity in the business than anything else, especially around politically riddled state boxing commissions.

However, people who are accustomed to engaging in sharp practices always suspect others of the worst. So it is that boxing officials are less well-regarded inside the business than out. There are constant references to "that *goniff*" and to commissioners and ring officials being in the hip pocket of promotors. And when funny things happen to the odds and the bettor suspects the fighter, the fighter sometimes worries about the officials. In his autobiography Rocky Graziano recalls that when he fought Marty Servo the odds against him were astronomic. He figured even money would be more like it. "It looks like somebody bought off the officials, that's how I got it figured," Eddie Coco, Graziano's manager, said. So Graziano took a little of the action and knocked Servo out in the second. His admission that he made a wager on himself did not cause a ripple.

One of the reasons officials are looked at with such jaundiced eye are the number of decisions which, even in an ordinarily smelly business, give off a distinctly discernible odor of putrefying sea life. One famous example is the Kid Gavilan-Johnny Saxton welterweight title fight in Philadelphia, October 20, 1954. Why Gavilan agreed to put up his title against Saxton, a Blinky Palermo fighter, in Blinky's home town, is anybody's guess. He did, though, and the result was a mess.

Gavilan lost the decision. The officials voted against him 9-6-0, 7-6-2 and 8-6-1. The newspaper reporters at ringside disagreed by a substantive 20-2 (a typical score was 10-4-1 for Gavilan.)

Gavilan admittedly had not fought especially well and one reporter wrote: "It was a poor fight and a worse decision." Angel Lopez, Gavilan's manager, protested noisily to Frank Weiner, then the Pennsylvania State Boxing Commissioner. Weiner seemed to understand that the decision was somewhat malodorous. He girded his forces, however, and told Lopez: "Gavilan doesn't deserve a lot of sympathy. The decision wasn't any more terrible than your fighter was." This closed the case for Weiner. He did not even choose to investigate why the odds on Gavilan, which had opened at 3-1, dropped to 7-5, at fight time.

"Before the fight," Gavilan complained, "every taxi driver in Philly know Saxton, he can't lose if he go the limit." Weiner ignored that, too.

Gavilan had been involved in another funny-decision fight earlier in his career. This one was fought in New York, August 29, 1951. It was against Billy Graham. Gavilan was a 3-1 favorite, but Graham put up a good enough fight to impress a lot of ringsiders.

The vote of the officials was announced by the peerless Johnny Addie in his usual teasing fashion. Judge Artie Schwartz, Addie said, voted nine rounds for Gavilan, six rounds for Graham. There was a groan from the crowd. Judge Frank Forbes, Addie intoned, savoring the suspense, scored it seven rounds for Gavilan, seven rounds for Graham and one round even. On points, Addie added after pausing just long enough, Forbes scored ten points for Gavilan, eleven for Graham. There was a yip of delight from the crowd. And referee Mark Conn, Addie said with all the nasal sonority he could muster, scored seven rounds for Gavilan, seven rounds for Graham and one even. The fans were now holding their breath. And on points, Conn had it seven for Graham, *ten* for Gavilan. The winner Gavilan. By the breadth of a silk thread.

Graham was furious. And when he encountered Conn outside the dressing room, he shouted, "Dammit, Conn, you're a disgrace to the Irish."

Conn shrugged. His real name is Cohen.

One of the classically poor decisions was committed in Las Vegas on June 1, 1963. Willie Pastrano, an affable 5-1 underdog, beat the skillful Harold Johnson for his light-heavyweight championship in 15 rounds. The decision was split, the referee and one judge voting for Pa-

248

strano, the other judge for Johnson. In the minds of many people with no axe to grind, Johnson had won easily.

Joe Louis, who usually does have some kind of angle, having been brought to the fight, usually, to shill for one fighter or the other, said: "Johnson won that fight but he didn't get the decision. If they keep this up they'll run boxing right out of the state of Nevada." Shows how much Louis knows. Stupidity never drives out anything but intelligence; mendacity replaces honesty. Things don't get better, especially around boxing commissions. And Las Vegas still has all the fights it wants.

The fact is that Pastrano was almost knocked out three times—in the fifth, ninth and thirteenth rounds. His offense was a defense. He stayed away from Johnson as much as he could. "I never heard of a challenger running away and still winning," commented a sad and wise Johnson. "And I don't think he'll ever fight me again." The downtrodden have a clairvoyance about harsh truths. Pastrano never did. He defended his title twice, then lost it to Jose Torres on a body punch and retired to the non-violence he so loved.

Nothing startling in any of that. Only one question is unanswered. What happened in Las Vegas?

## The Strange Endings

The most unsatisfactory way for a boxing match to end is with one of the fighters sitting on his stool looking as healthy as a Russian weightlifter and announcing that he is unable to continue fighting because of a severe, hidden injury to his left pinky. It is not unsatisfactory because, as most editorialists insist, the boxing fan is a luster after ever more blood. It is unsatisfactory *artistically*. The warm glow derived from any sporting event comes from the knowledge that a conclusion will be reached. Someone wins, someone loses, the superior force is decided. Life itself is full of little hangups that are never altogether resolved. It is a pleasure to observe a conflict which will be. (Football and hockey ties are greatly despised, which is why there are sudden-death periods in important

249

games.) So a fistfight, an event so elemental that it quickly and easily engages the emotions, becomes particularly frustrating when it ends unresolved because of some mysterious injury or a blow which did not appear damaging (viz. Carnera-Schaaf).

Yet we have had many such endings and, alas, will have others. A classic of its kind was the Willie Pep-Sandy Saddler fight of September 8, 1950. Pep and Saddler fought four times. They were featherweights but they fought heavyweight wars. Their fights were always well-attended. Saddler won three of the four fights, but they were more separated by the four-year difference in their ages than by talent.

In this fight Pep, who had regained the title from Saddler with a 15-round decision the year before, was well ahead after seven rounds. The card of one judge and referee Ruby Goldstein had him leading 4-2-1. The other judge had him ahead 5-2. Unless he got himself knocked out, there didn't seem to be any way he could lose the fight. But before the eighth round could begin, Pep announced that he had a terrible pain in his left shoulder and could not go on.

His shoulder was X-rayed the next day. Doctors said there was no fracture and no chips in the shoulder. They also said the shoulder had been dislocated but was now back in place. Dislocated shoulders are diagnosed by asking the patient, "Where does it hurt?"

"Aw, they shoulda put it in a sling and let him finish the fight," said one disgusted fan. "The way he was going he needed only one hand anyway."

Still, the loss set up another title fight in New York a year later. This time Saddler knocked him out. They never fought again.

For one of the strangest endings of all time we go backward in time with Harold Johnson, the victim of one of the most peculiar decisions. This was in 1955, May 6, when Johnson had no title, but probably was at the height of his considerable boxing powers. The fight was against Julio Maderos in Philadelphia and on television. It ended after the second round, when Johnson, a 4-1 favorite, toppled off his stool unconscious. And he hadn't been hit with anything rougher than an angry glance.

Johnson was carried from the ring on a stretcher and an investigation was started which lasted for months. Johnson's story was that some stranger had walked up to him before the fight and handed him an orange. Johnson obligingly ate it, even though it had tasted "bitter." The orange, he said, must have been doped.

First reports were that Johnson showed no signs of being doped and that tests of his blood, spinal fluid and stomach were negative. Although these reports later proved to be somewhat inaccurate, indignation quickly rose to a height of several inches. (Indignation does not rise very high in Pennsylvania, home of Philadelphia and such leading lights as Willie Sutton, Blinky Palermo, Pep Barone and Sonny Liston, who, when he left, remarked, "I'd rather be a lamp post in Denver than the mayor of Philadelphia.") Boxing was banned in the state for a period of 90 days and State Deputy Attorney General Herbert S. Levin charged that Johnson, his three handlers and Pete Moran, the matchmaker, were guilty of covering up a "sham, fake or collusive boxing match."

On that happy note hearings were begun. First, Dr. Alfred Ayella and Dr. William Strickland, boxing commission doctors, testified that evidence of barbiturates *had* been found (at least there were "traces") and that Johnson was *not* faking or malingering. Then Johnson swore that he did not throw the fight and that he was innocent as a babe and matchmaker Moran said hell, he didn't know anything about anything and it wasn't true he owned a piece of Johnson.

Two months later a decision was handed down. It was that everybody was a little guilty. Johnson, it was decided, "had administered to him barbiturate drugs by a person or persons unknown." Because of that, his handlers were suspended for terms up to three months, his manager had his license lifted and Johnson himself was suspended for six months. He also had to forfeit his 4,113 dollar purse.

The decision was as strange as the fight. If Johnson was guilty, the penalty was much too light. If he was not,

251

there should have been no penalty at all. But that is the way of boxing commissions all over. They find it no trouble at all to pick themselves up by the collar and throw themselves down the steps.

And now we have the sight of Sonny Liston, big, savage, impregnable Sonny Liston sitting on his ample duff in his corner and crying that his little shoulder hurt him too much and that he couldn't fight any more. All this cost little Sonny was his world heavyweight title and his reputation.

This was in Miami, February 25, 1964 against the man who was still calling himself Cassius Clay, and it had been a strange fight. In the sixth round Clay was blinded, apparently by a salve which had been smeared on Liston. He refused to come out fighting, but Angelo Dundee, his trainer, shoved him into the ring anyway. He fought the round blinking and holding his left hand on top of Sonny Liston's head, both to keep him away and to know where he was. Liston's much shorter arms pumped away furiously. But all his punches were short. It was then, if ever, that Liston hurt his shoulder. It is as likely that it was a psychic ache, the result of a humiliating round in which he could not lay a glove on a blind man. He must have suspected that there was no way he could beat this man. In the next round he quit.

The next time these men fought, May 25, 1965, in Lewiston, Maine, an even stranger thing happened. In the first round the man who was then Muhammad Ali—it was about here that I took to calling him Ali Baby—danced around Liston for a while. Then he threw out a right hand, missed with it, drew it back a short way and hit Liston in the mouth. Liston went down like one of those penny-arcade toy pugilists with a covenient button in its jaw. Then he got halfway up, only to fall down again. Finally he lurched to his feet.

All the while poor Joe Walcott, the referee, was running around the ring trying to shout Ali Baby into a neutral corner, find out what the count was and discover the time of day. He never really succeeded in doing any of them and, if Nat Fleischer hadn't told Walcott that

Liston had risen promptly at the count of 14, they might be fighting yet. As it was, the men had resumed fighting and Ali Baby was tattooing a cringing Liston with a series of fluttering punches

Now it is possible, I am told, for a punch that travels only a short distance to land just right and knock a man out. But we live in a cynical world and what it really looked like was one of the quickest and most ungainly dives in the history of boxing.

One dive theory goes like this. Liston never gave up his underworld connections and his best friends told him not to take a chance on hitting the kid and maybe knocking him out. The money was socked in on Muhammad.

I can't buy that, largely because there wasn't enough money bet on the fight to make an impression, certainly not enough to stir the odds. Anyway, if Liston was indeed still underworld-owned, a lot more money could have been made out of Liston's keeping the title.

Must I believe then only that the kid found the right button and pressed it? I can't, because he has worn his hands out on men like Floyd Patterson, who has a tendency to fall down in a strong breeze, without knocking them out. No. What I had to do is work up a different theory and I present it here not so much as an answer as for perusal.

The theory was born, *ex post facto,* the night before the fight when Cus D'Amato, the Merlin of the fight business, was encountered in the genteelly decaying lobby of the Poland Spring Hotel. D'Amato was eager to reveal that he had been instructing Liston in the fine art of making a ring smaller. D'Amato has hard, obsidian, mesmerizing eyes and he soon had a group of normally hardheaded people believing that Liston now knew how to move his feet so that he could maneuver Ali Baby against the ropes and knock him down so thoroughly they'd need a blotter to pick him up. D'Amato illustrated the foot movements, his shoes kicking up little puffs of dust in the decaying carpet. Step to the right, clomp, to the left, clomp, to the right again, clomp, don't cross your feet, clomp, clomp. I don't doubt for a moment that D'Amato had Liston believing he could do it.

When Liston came out at the bell, he looked as though he were trying to remember a new dance step. One could almost hear his not especially quick brain commanding him, left foot here, now the right, now the left, a one, a two, a three. Except that Ali Baby wasn't having any. He danced so nimbly around Liston that D'Amato might just as well have never existed. "Oh darn," Liston probably said to himself. (Or maybe "Oh shucks.") And then the first time he was hit he was knocked out.

A man who was his friend says, "Liston has a heart as big as a pea." I believe it.

Although no event in American sports can match a heavyweight championship fight for color, excitement and interest, boxing by and large is no longer much of a factor in American sports. Yet there is still money to be made in boxing, and funny things continue to happen. As this is written a New York grand jury is apparently investigating a recent fight between Dick Tiger and Nino Benvenuti in Madison Square Garden.

Benvenuti, middleweight champion, was taking on Dick Tiger in a non-title, over-the-weight match. Benvenuti, with nothing at stake, was favored by almost 3-1 over Tiger. He lost. Tiger, with much more at stake than Benvenuti, fought a better, more aggressive fight and deserved the unanimous decision he got. After the fight Benvenuti said he had broken his right hand in the first round and couldn't fight thereafter. These things do happen, but it's sort of funny that the toughest punch of the fight was delivered by Benvenuti in the ninth round. It was a punch that staggered Tiger. It was a right hand.

There was no evidence of any betting coup, but on reflection, one wonders why the fight was ever made. A Benvenuti win would have accomplished little but give both fighters a pay night. A loss, however, set up a lucrative title match for both fighters. That is, they can now fight for the middleweight title and the odds will be a lot less than 3-1. Even a dullard will now note that it was to

Benvenuti's advantage to lose all the time. No doubt Madison Square Garden's brilliant boxing department foresaw this. But it put the fight on anway. Madison Square Garden's boxing department doesn't care about adding to the air pollution of boxing. It only cares about selling tickets.

Also under investigation by the New York grand jury is the possibility that one James Napoli, alias Jimmy Knapp, a gentleman with a record as bookmaker and gambler and a conviction for felonious assault, has been the undercover king of the boxing business. Napoli, it has been rumored, took over from Frankie Carbo when Carbo was deposited in a California can.

Madison Square Garden of course disclaims any knowledge of such machinations. The Garden says it didn't know anything about Frankie Carbo, either, although anybody else who had anything to do with boxing knew a lot. The point is that while professional football, for example, spends a lot of money on exterminators to keep lice out of its basement, the Garden, a huge enterprise which exists largely on sports, spends nothing. And everytime there is a scandal people in the Garden express shock and protest their innocence. Sorry, I don't think there's anything innocent about ignoring the fire hose when the fire's at the door.

## 11 Let's Hear It for the Roundball

THERE ARE MANY SOLEMN HISTORIANS IN THIS WORLD who insist that Americans have no ability to learn from history. This may be true in some areas—the Far East, say —but it is quite certain that we have learned at least one thing very well: how to fix a basketball game. We have learned so well that every ten years or so we have a full-scale scandal, complete with hard-faced fixers, remorseful players and pious college officials. The only thing Americans do not seem to have learned about basketball fixes is how to avoid getting caught. This, however, logic tells us, is not accurate. We just don't hear about the fixers who don't get caught. On the word of a knowledgeable law-enforcement official in New York there have been many.

That's because basketball lends itself to manipulation. There are two reasons. One is the way in which wagers on it are made. There is a point spread. One cannot merely wager that Shortsighted U. will beat Confused College. One must decide whether Shortsighted will win by a stated number of points, say seven. If Shortsighted then wins by six or fewer, its backers lose their bets. It is obvious, then, that a reasonably educated basketball player, even if he is willing to cavort before mixed audiences in what looks like his underwear, will come to the conclusion that it would not hurt Shortsighted to win by fewer than seven while he himself and certain select henchmen collect on a wager placed on Confused. Thus the temptation is overwhelming (or at least whelming). Nobody is hurt but the bookmakers, and nobody worries about bookmakers, not even other bookmakers.

The second reason for the prevalence of the basketball fix is that it is, if practiced with any sort of élan, undetectable, at least on the basketball court. Crowds at basketball games often hoot when a player's shot misses the backboard, or a foul shot hits the rim and bounces off. Yet this is not, except *in extremis,* the way games are fixed. "You simply play your hardest on offense," said one practiced architect of the dump, "score as many points as you can—then make simple mistakes on defense. . . . So you let a man you're supposed to guard get a half step on you. He breaks loose and scores, but who can say you didn't try to stop him?"

Said Forddy Anderson of Bradley, who had the distinction of having coached at least eight players who took money from fixers—Mike Chianakas, Charley Grover, Jim Kelly, Bill Mann, Gene Melchiorre, Aaron Preece, Fred Schlictman, and Paul Unruh. "I've studied the movies [of fixed games] at least 20 times and can't find a single

256

play which indicates the kids weren't giving their best efforts every second."

The primer of the fixer must take into consideration, in addition, the way to get a large amount of money bet on a single basketball game. (Many of the top figures have underworld money and know-how behind them, so this is not much of a problem. We are discussing here the independent entrepreneur, like Salvatore Sollazzo, who was the main if somewhat befuddled architect of most of the fixes which were uncovered in 1951. He was sentenced to 16 years. Walk up to a bookmaker and tell him you want to bet 50,000 dollars against old Siwash, your alma mater, and he'll say "So do I." This is known as taking a game off the boards. Bookmakers do this a lot, sometimes on suspicion, sometimes on good information, sometimes because they don't like the pattern of betting.

What the fixer must do is divert suspicion. He does this by calling a bookmaker and betting 10,000 dollars each on two or more games. Then he calls another bookmaker, bets all of the games the other way, except the Siwash game. He can do this any number of times. All it costs is the vigorish, the ten-percent fee the bookmaker charges to make the wager—one must bet 11,000 dollars to 10,000 dollars no matter on which side one wagers. Thus a man who gets down five 10,000-dollars bets against Siwash will be losing some vigorish money, but the price is well worth it if he has a sure thing in Siwash.

It has also been found that, historically, certain other conditions must be present in order for a successful basketball-fixing ring to operate. These involve a psychological softening up process for basketball players. It works about like this. First the player is recruited. In order for a college to recruit a good basketball player, it must first convince him that there are reasons why Dismal College is a better place than Rotten U. It so happens there are no reasons. Both institutions have reasonable amounts of ivy on the walls, both have suitable collections of miniskirted coeds, both have huge, comfortable field houses, far-roaming schedules which take the basketball teams around the country and away from the drudgery of classrooms, both

257

have low enough academic standards to accept the tall man with the low IQ.

What then separates them? Often nothing but the enthusiasm of the coach and the alumni. This enthusiasm may express itself in a 50,000 dollar house for the father and mother of the athlete, a Mercedes for the boy and promises of a future business career—after, of course, a long and lucrative career in professional sport.

All this does several things for the boy. It teaches him his own value (high; sort of so many thousands of dollars per inch), the value of deception (infinite; it *pays* to lie), and the intrinsic honesty of the institutions of learning and the people around them (none; these people do what they want and then find high-sounding reasons).

Once in college, the athlete is imbued with the grand American principle of winning at any cost. He is unburdened by the necessity of obtaining passing grades and he considers this eminently fair since students who must work harder are not required to play winning basketball. And he notes with great interest and a certain tightening of the sphincter that athletes who don't produce can have their scholarships removed.

This was, until January of 1969, against NCAA rules. But there were a lot of ways a coach could lift a scholarship. One was to make things so tough for the boy he voluntarily left. Another was to lift the blanket that seems to protect athletes at a lot of universities from academic expulsion, at least until they use up all eligibility. The latest NCAA ruling, however, is that any student who breaks university rules can have his scholarship taken away. This was designed, the NCAA says, to enable colleges to lift scholarships from student protestors and campus demonstrators. Aside from its obvious undemocratic implications, the rule points up some funny things. One is that white athletes are seldom, if ever, campus demonstrators. Indeed, athletes, white athletes, are a conservative force on campuses. It is only the black athlete who has shown any inclination toward campus rebellion. Not only that. Now the coach suddenly finds himself with the kind of power he hasn't had for a long time. I mean, can a mediocre linebacker who parks his car illegally on campus lose his scholarship?

The reality of the results of this kind of academic leadership are always shocking. In 1951, for example, 33 basketball players from seven institutions of higher learning admitted conspiring to rig the results of 90 games. (There is ample reason to believe that these figures—which come from a report prepared by Frank Hogan, District Attorney of New York—represent only a small portion of the fix apparatus. Says Assistant DA Peter D. Andreoli, in charge of investigations in New York: "We discovered the fixing by virtually stumbling upon it during the course of other investigations. There is no telling how much more of it there was that we never uncovered.") At the sentencing of the kingpin of the 1951 fixes—it should be remembered that the fixing had gone back at least as far as 1948 and probably farther—Salvatore Sollazo, and 14 players, Judge Saul S. Streit summed up some of the highlights of the evidence. Among them were these:

1. Ed Roman of CCNY had accepted from Cincinnati University scholarships for himself and for his brother, including tuition, board, a job, 50 dollars a month expense money and the use of a car. After two days the Romans told the coach they wanted to leave. So they were offered more money.

2. Sherman White of LIU had an IQ of 82. He spent six months at Villanova, where he received two Ds, two Cs and an F. Whereupon he left and was accepted at LIU. His grades were passing at LIU. Of course, he was taking such subjects as music seminar, oil painting, rhythm and dance, public speaking and physical education.

3. Ed Warner of CCNY had an IQ of 87 and, although his marks were too low for admittance to CCNY, he was entered in a special evening class where, surprise, he became a good student.

4. Alvin Roth of CCNY had an average of 70.43 at Erasmus Hall High School in Brooklyn. That was too low

for entrance to City College but this transcript showed it to be 75.5. An error, no doubt.

5. Connie Schaff of NYU graduated from Seward Park High School in New York at the age of nineteen, having had eight failures in the ten (instead of eight) terms it took him to graduate. It was arranged for him to attend Brooklyn Academy Prep, alumni of NYU picking up the tab. There he became a good enough student to enter NYU by a just-passing mark of 65 in three subjects and a failing in a fourth.

6. Dick Fuertado of LIU complained to Coach Clair Bee that some of the other players were receiving more money than he while his mother was in desperate need. Athletic officials at LIU humanely arranged to send his mother 20 dollars a week.

Another notable fact which didn't come to Judge Streit's attention was that the New York City Department of Investigation found that the faculty athletics manager at CCNY had been purchasing equipment from favored sporting-goods merchants at prices that were, to say the least, uncompetitive. Besides, an instructor and athletics coach was found to be himself a dealer in sports equipment. He left behind vouchers in which he had recommended that the equipment be purchased from his company.

There is, of course, little reason to believe that the people at CCNY, LIU and NYU were more inventive than their brethren at other colleges. Indeed, there is much evidence that the New York schools were pikers compared to some with wealthier alumni in other parts of the country.

The medal of honor for shortsightedness in this area should go to Adolph Rupp, the Kentucky coach who has, in the years since this scandal, become a grand old man of basketball. "Gamblers couldn't get at my boys with a ten-foot pole," Rupp said while the boys in New York were being arrested. "Our boys are under constant and absolute complete supervision while they are on the road, especially in New York." In a matter of days Ralph Beard,

Alex Groza and Dale Barnstable of the Kentucky team had admitted fixing basketball games.

Rupp learned a great deal from this. What these boys had done, he decided after much soul searching, was not so bad as it sounded. "The Black Sox threw games," he said, bare-faced, "but these kids only shaved points."

It is in this manner that the men at the universities began educating themselves. They listened to Rupp, and they heard him. Others they listened to less well.

There was Alex Groza. "Some day, when I'm gray, when this is done and I've lived it down, I'd like to tell the whole story about what it's been like—about recruiting I mean."

"Recruiting," echoed Ralph Beard. "That's the start of it. How they went out and got us to play. It got so big, we got so big. Too big. It was all too big."

Then there was Clair Bee of LIU, who had to be something of an expert because eight of his boys were involved in the scandal—Adolph Bigos, Dick Fuertado, Eddie Gard, Jackie Goldsmith, Lou Lipman, Nat Miller, LeRoy Smith and Sherman White. Bee knew what it was about and told all in *The Saturday Evening Post*. "I was so absorbed in the victory grail I lost sight of the educational purposes of athletics," he said. Then he listed the four general abuses which had to be stopped:

1. Athletic scholarships.
2. Cash subsidies.
3. Guaranteed passing grades.
4. Over-emphasizing the importance of sports with extended trips, long schedules, year-round practice, post-season games and regular appearances in off-campus arenas.

This advice was taken so to heart that in ten years there was another huge basketball scandal.

According to Andreoli, it would be safe to assume that between 1951 and 1961 the fixing of basketball games *never stopped*. In his brief against Jack Molinas, Columbia basketball player, attorney and the master fixer of the sixth decade of this century, Andreoli listed fixes as far back as 1957. "That's as far as I could go because of the

261

statute of limitations," the DA said. "I would suggest that fixing basketball games is still profitable and the concept that you don't have to lose, because of the point spread, is a great inducement."

District attorneys do not run college athletics programs, nor do they run arenas. Have his quote from Ned Irish, the man who ran basketball at Madison Square Garden, home of the basketball fix. (Since Irish ran it so well, with only two scandals in ten years, he was eventually promoted to president of MSG.) "Why," said old Ned in 1954, "a boy would have to be demented to become involved in a fix conspiracy today."

With that kind of watchfulness at the top, it is little wonder that there was another fixing roundup in 1961. This time there were 49 players involved at 25 schools and 67 *known* games. Shocking? Not to Howard Hobson, the basketball coach at Yale. "Don't forget," Hobson pointed out in a magazine article, "there have been 50,000 college games in the last five years. Less than 50 are known to have been fixed." Ignoring the inaccuracy of his numbers, that's still like saying it's all right to trust sharks because, of all the millions of them, only a few have actually eaten a man.

As a result, Hobson went on, it was necessary to stop "unwholesome" subsidizing and recruiting. At this the wise men of our universities nodded their heads and went back to business as usual, thus laying the groundwork for yet another scandal. If the schedule holds, it's due in 1971.

The infinite capacity of so-called educators to bury their heads in the sand is no better illustrated than with the experience of a basketball player named Charley North of Detroit University. In May of 1960 North received a letter from a Mike Siegal, who introduced himself as an old friend from the West Coast. Siegal was operating with one Charles Tucker, later indicted as a fixer. He said he was running a basketball team at a mountain resort and did North want to make some fast money?

North was one of the few players in all the ugly history

of the basketball fixes to do just the right thing. (Another was Junius Kellogg of Manhattan, who touched off the 1961 investigation in New York by reporting a bribe offer by two ex-Manhattan players, Henry Poppe and Jack Byrne. Also Dave Shapiro of George Washington University, who set up four fixers—Jack Levy, William Rivkind, Joseph Aronowitz and Phillip Klein—for New York detectives. This was in 1949, four years after the first recorded fix attempt of Brooklyn College players, but two years before the first big one, which illustrates the constancy of the fix efforts.) When North took the letter to his coach, Bob Callahan, it was passed along to the director of athletics, John Mulroy. A second letter, in November, was handled the same way. In neither case were the police called in. After all of that, North wound up taking 50 dollars in "softening-up" money, but he did not have time to participate in a fix before the jig was up. When these facts came to light, Mulroy said he did not want to bother the police because the letter was "ambiguous." An athletic director's ambiguity, we thus find out, may be a policeman's bribe offer.

It is easy, when you have a great deal to lose, to ignore even a fly on your nose. Coaching is a business, a livelihood, often a very lucrative one. The men in it like to surround themselves with the mystique of educators, but they are something less. They are, by and large, no different than professional coaches and managers, and proof is that so many of them make the transition from college to professional coaching with enormous ease. Why not? The job is always the same—building winners. They leave building character to mothers. If something is lost along the way, like decent values, well, tough. Coaches have to make a living.

It is not, however, altogether fashionable to blame the educators for showing their students the high wages of sin. After the 1951 scandal, Arthur Schlesinger, Jr., for one, wrote: "One of the worst sides of modern liberal thought is a sentimental belief that the individual is never to blame; social institutions are the source of all evil; change them and you can achieve utopia."

I do not argue about the responsibility of the individual in our society. Nor do I deny a surge of resentment against these players who were laughing at me while I considered the game they played important. But I feel qualified to question Schlesinger's premise here because enough time has elapsed now to enable us to check on the characters of the people involved.

Of the 87 players who were known to have taken money from fixers, only two—Ed Warner and Sherman White—served jail terms and only one—Ed Warner, on a narcotics charge—was ever in trouble with the law again. (This does not count men like Molinas, Eddie Gard, Jackie Goldsmith and Dave Budin, who went onward and upward to become fixers rather than just fixes.) Many of the other players turned to good and selfless occupations. Floyd Lane of City College, for example, ran community programs for the Board of Education of New York, Ed Roman became a teacher in New York City 600 schools, schools for difficult and disturbed students. LeRoy Smith, a Negro, chose to become a teacher in the South. Alex Groza so impressed people with his basic honesty that for a while, although he was barred from playing professional basketball, he was allowed to coach a small college team in Lexington, Kentucky. Almost without exception the others became decent citizens with productive jobs, families, houses and lawns.

As a result, I can't help but feel that the boys involved were victimized as much as the rest of us. Many of them didn't even know what to do with the money once they had shaved for it. Ed Warner, for example, led police to the basement of the home he lived in with his aunt and turned over 3,050 dollars in cash which he had accumulated in a shoe box.

Jack Egan of St. Joseph's, who probably shouldn't have been in college, was trying to support a wife and two children while he played basketball. He took from a fixer. "I really needed the money," he said.

Said Gene Melchiorre of Bradley: "None of us had any money. . . . We justified ourselves, I guess, by saying the colleges were making plenty out of it . . . and it wasn't too wrong because we weren't going to throw any games."

One of the more poignant statements of the human condition and basketball fixes was delivered by a simple man, Sherman White's father. "It would have been different," he said, "if he was raised in the streets, but he had to go to college to learn something he was never taught at home."

Still, there are certain hazy lines when one ponders guilt of institution vs. individual. There is the case, for example, of a lad named Fred Portnoy. He was not, as they say in social-workers circles, disadvantaged. He had a 90 academic average. And he played basketball for an Ivy League college which did not make many of the errors other colleges and universities did. Yet he was a dumper.

Consider this. After the 1951 scandals, LIU and CCNY had the good sense to deemphasize intercollegiate basketball to a level where nobody but the kids involved could care about the outcome of the games. Columbia, untouched in 1951—although one wonders what miracles Molinas was accomplishing there as a player—felt fairly smug. It played its games in its little campus gym. It followed stringent rules about recruiting. But Portnoy, obviously a fine young man, ruined a good piece of his life there. "You don't realize the seriousness of what you're doing," Portnoy complained after he was caught. "It seemed so simple."

So blame Portnoy. Blame the corruption of gambling money, which is the money of organized crime. Blame the special problems of our young people. But a single fact stands out. *None of this would have happened if it were not for the emphasis—even in Columbia—on intercollegiate athletics.*

This question is hardly ever asked, but why do we need intercollegiate athletics? What happened to Carnegie Tech when it dropped football? What happened to CCNY when it de-emphasized basketball? Did the many schools in the East—Fordham and NYU among them—suffer in any way when they dropped football? The answer is: Not at all. They became, if anything, even better institutions of learning. So why must our universities accept passively the role of farm teams for professional basketball and

265

football? Why must they hire high-priced coaches who have the welfare of nobody but themselves in mind? What the hell good does it do them?

Says DA Andreoli: "As long as the people who profit most, the organized-crime people behind the scenes, can make extra money out of this kind of activity [fixing games], as long as there are games for them to fix, as long as a lot of money is bet on those games and it is profitable to fix them, it can always happen again."

Is there an educated man in our universities who doubts that?

With college players having been so thoroughly grounded in the art of the dump, it is hardly credible that some who were not caught in college did not go on to bigger and better things as professionals. True, there has not been a single case of professional point shaving which has been discovered. But sometimes funny things happen.

Sometimes the odds do funny things.

Sometimes there is a sudden, unexplained "no line," meaning no bets will be taken, on certain games.

Sometimes there are rumors that the players are giving themselves an extra payday from time to time.

Sometimes you see things in professional basketball games that you just can't believe.

But nobody has been arrested. Nobody, so far as I know, has even been questioned by a DA.

Yet there is a strange little story that *Life* uncovered in 1967. It appears that when Gilbert Lee Beckley, the New Orleans bookmaker, was arrested by the FBI in January of 1966, he had a notebook with the names of other bookmakers in it. And next to the name of Francisco Scibelli, described as a member of the Genovese Family of the Cosa Nostra and the man who ran a gambling syndicate in Springfield, Massachusetts, there appeared the name of Bob Cousy.

Cousy can make some real claims to the title of Mr. Basketball. As a superstar with the great Boston Celtics for 13 years, Cousy had a lifetime average of 18.5 points per game. His ball-handling artistry thrilled millions. When he retired from pro basketball in 1963, he took a job as coach of Boston College.

Cousy admitted to *Life* that he did know Scibelli. He said one of his very best friends was Andrew Pradella, who was Scibelli's partner. He said he knew they both were gamblers and that they often talked to him about basketball, both pro and college. So *Life* asked him if it hadn't occurred to him that they might be using this information in some way, to establish a betting line, say.

Said Cousy: "I thought they figured the betting line with mathematics. But it doesn't surprise me. I'm pretty cynical. I think most people who approach me want to use me in some way."

In 1963 Cousy was warned by local police that he was spending time with some fairly gamy characters. This did not disturb him. "In this hypocritical world we live in," Cousy told *Life*, "I don't see why I should stop seeing my friends just because they are gamblers."

After the *Life* article appeared, however, Cousy called a tearful press conference in which he swore he was guilty of nothing more than "indiscretion." Wiping tears from his eyes, sobbing, Cousy said: "I did nothing wrong."

He was believed.

The Fixer was a solid citizen, a businessman, honored in his industry as a shrewd operator who never got the worst of a deal. At the same time he was considered to be a super salesman. And he was, largely because he found out at the very beginnig of his business life, indeed, at the knee of his father, that the best way to reach a buyer was to bribe him.

There were buyers who had to be paid off with a percentage of your profits and they were the difficult ones, the kind the Fixer would have been if he were a buyer instead of a seller. Then there were buyers who prided themselves on their incorruptibility and they could be bribed only with what is called "entertainment."

Entertainment is a Bureau of Internal Revenue euphemism for booze and broads. Sometimes it's dinner at a racetrack or theater tickets or a night on the town. What it

267

come down to always, though, is booze and broads and that's what the Fixer made himself an expert at.

The Fixer was not cynical about it. He liked booze and broads himself and he liked to be seen with important people and he was willing to pay money to do it. He took his customers around with him and he beamed when the headwaiter bowed and said, "Your table is ready, Mr. Fixer. How are you tonight, sir?"

"Fine," he would say, "just fine." And he would pay for being asked about his health with a ten-dollar bill. Five would have done the same thing but there was nothing cheap about the Fixer.

During World War II when there were shortages, the Fixer had a houseful of things like cigarets and canned salmon and gave them away to his friends. At a time when no one could get a telephone, he had three in his East Side pad and, if he liked you, he knew somebody in the telephone company who would get you one, too.

The Fixer always had a good-looking chick on his arm, although he was married and had two children. He had a house in Queens for his wife, who forgave him his peccadilloes because he always came back to sob on her breast and ask forgiveness. Often she had to borrow money from her father for the Fixer and at such times her marriage was beautiful and she felt desired and important. But soon the Fixer would make a killing in something or other and he would be gone again.

The Fixer could have made it well enough in business but it was not glamorous enough for him. In the nightclubs and bar hangouts the important men were always the bookies and the gamblers who spent wildly and soon the Fixer was making big bets on sporting events. He'd attend them with his friends, the gamblers and the chick of the moment (who did not come cheap either; not that she was a professional: she just had expensive tastes). Pretty soon the Fixer was seeking out the places where the ball players went after the game, and he'd send them over a couple of rounds of drinks and just nod when they looked over to thank him.

The Fixer didn't have to buy many drinks or introduce

many ball players to his chicks before they were remembering his name and telling other ball players to look him up if they wanted to buy anything wholesale. The Fixer knew everybody and got everything wholesale, except money. Often he did not bill the players for the goods they had bought and, if there is anything that gives an athlete a warm sense of good will, it's not getting a bill.

At first the Fixer cultivated ball players only for the sake of his ego, but he soon saw the advantages to be had from knowing the athletes. He would ask them to call if they knew anything special about the health of a star on their team or if there was going to be a sudden change in the lineup. He became extremely well informed about the inside politics and gossip of all the teams. All the while he was providing gifts and drinks and backslaps and friends of his current inamorata or the inamorata herself. The players found it a joy to be invited to his parties because there were sure to be several attractive, willing girls about. No one ever left a Fixer party altogether sober or at all sex-starved.

It is surprising that for a long time it did not occur to the Fixer actually to attempt to fix a game. He was content with his inside information, which gave him only a slim edge, but an edge nevertheless. When he finally decided to take the fix plunge, it was because he had run into a series of bad picks and was hurting for money.

"I hate to ask you this," the Fixer said, "but I'm jammed up. Besides, I'm not asking you to lose the game. All you have to do is . . ."

It seemed like easy money to the players. They were full of resentment against the people who made all that money from their work and sweat and returned so little. They told themselves that what they were doing was important to no one but some detestable gamblers and would, besides, be impossible to detect. They were right on both counts.

It is a sad thing that the Fixer never made any real money out of his corruption. A lot of things went wrong. Sometimes the fixed ball players didn't stay fixed. Sometimes, because the Fixer had a big mouth, word got out about the fix and he couldn't get enough money down to pay off the players and still make a profit. Sometimes he lost money on his fixed games because there was confusion about the odds. Often he would make large bets on games he thought *other* people had fixed, because he was a staunch believer in fix rumors, and he would lose because the rumors were false. Above all, the Fixer was a gambler and a perfect example of the psychological theory that a gambler wants to lose. Certainly one reason he might have wanted to lose was that it meant taking more money from his father-in-law, whom he detested.

Always modishly dressed, quick to pick up a check, surrounded by what society columnists like to call "beautiful people," the Fixer, even as a loser, was held in slack-jawed admiration by the young athletes he courted. When they were made privy to his methods, they were less shocked than envious. So it was that the Fixer was able to spawn a whole new generation of little fixers. Players who dumped for him went into business for themselves when they could no longer play. Many of them caught the gambling bug, too, however, and few held on to much money for very long. While the money lasted, though, it was an exhilarating life, the fear of being caught acting only as a fillip.

When the Fixer finally got caught—through wiretaps on bookmakers—he confessed meekly, naming names and places. He implicated scores of players and gamblers. He was not, he wanted the police to understand, a criminal, and the codes of criminals did not apply to him. He ratted cheerfully and fearlessly.

The Fixer drew ten to 20 and served 12 years. When he came out of prison, he was no longer a dapper figure. His wife had not waited for him; she had married a jewelry manufacturer who used to sell the Fixer wholesale. The Fixer got a job selling groceries to retailers and makes a decent living. However, he never has any money because he has become a horseplayer. But he knows a lot of jockeys.

THERE IS A WELL-KNOWN COACH OF A SOUTHERN UNI-
versity who bets on football games. He bets a lot of
money. Once he bet 20,000 dollars on a single game.
Nassau County District Attorney William Cahn knows
his name. New Orleans District Attorney Jim Garrison
knows his name. Richard Gerstein, Miami District Attorney, knows his name. I know his name. I can't print it
for the same reason he hasn't been arrested.

Under a certain kind of ethic, he hasn't done anything
wrong because he only bets on his team to win. That's how
Cahn found out about it. When a coach puts down big
money on his own team, funny things start happening to
the odds. They go up. Everybody who hears about it
wants to get a piece of the action. They figure the coach
is trying to win, and by the proper number of points. This
is a lovely edge. How many bettors have ground their
teeth down to the gums while a coach who doesn't bet
on his team instructs his players to eat up the clock with
a three-point lead while the odds require him to win by
four and a half?

The way Cahn tells it, he had a tap on a couple of telephones in Nassau County, which is on Long Island. The
telephones were being answered by two guys, named David
Budin and Robert Cohen. Budin was a college basketball
player and he had been arrested for trying to fix college
basketball games and a football game at the University
of Michigan. Cohen was a known gambler and had been
used, Cahn says, to lay money around New York for a
New Orleans bookmaker with a big play. Layoff money
is bet with bookmakers by other bookmakers who, for one
reason or another, don't want to handle certain wagers.
One reason might be that he has too much one-sided action

and wants to even up his bets, which is to say the majority of his clients are betting on the same team to win a given game and the bookmaker does not want to take the risk of the large loss involved if that team actually wins. Another reason might be that the bookmaker has become leery of the betting pattern and suspects somebody knows something he doesn't know. Still another is that the bookmaker *does* know something and is looking to take the other bookmakers.

In this particular case, the New Orleans bookmaker had taken the 20,000 dollar bet from the coach. For some reason, he figured the coach intended to win, and by the proper number of points. He'd be a sucker to handle that kind of action. So he reached for the telephone and started making calls. He laid the bet off with Gilbert Lee Beckley, a large gambling operator out of New York and Miami. In addition, he made a substantial wager himself. He had a lot of faith in the coach. At this stage, the points started to edge up.

Beckley was no one's fool. He immediately started calling around to lay off the New Orleans money. And to bet his own. He called Budin and Cohen and told them to bet as much money around as they could without letting the price go up more than three points. They got a lot of money down. It is possible, without an enormous amount of effort and without upsetting the point market too much, to get anywhere from a quarter to a half million dollars bet on a single college football game. If it's a popular-betting game—Army-Notre Dame or Army-Navy—a great deal more can be wagered. It is hypothesized that some 250,000 dollars' worth of smart money was bet on the coach's game. Of course, only 20,000 dollars of it was his.

Cahn's tape recorder faithfully enshrined the frantic placement of bets by Budin and Cohen, the word from Miami about why the bets should be made and the reactions of certain other bookmakers once they realized something was going on and refused to take any more bets.

Beckley was arrested. So were Budin and Cohen and

six others. The coach is still instilling the fine points of life and sportsmanship in American youth.

"I'm tied here to prosecuting only in my own jurisdiction," Cahn told newspapermen. "I cannot bring his [the coach's] name into any case. If I could turn over what I have to the FBI this guy would be in trouble immediately. I can't. Everything I have is on wiretaps. I just have to turn over information to other jurisdictions and hope they can use it."

Other people in football have bet on games. Paul Hornung, for one. Hornung, called the Golden Boy when he was a handsome curly-haired blond back at Notre Dame, became an extraordinarily good player for the Green Bay Packers. This made him one of the best of the best. He made a lot of money and developed some interesting attitudes toward it. In his autobiography, *Football and the Single Man,* there is this paragraph:

> Still, I think I'm a little hypocritical about money. I go out and have a few drinks and there'll be dinner for twelve and I'll pick up the check. And then again I'll *need a white cashmere coat—really need it—*and I won't buy it if I don't think it's worth what they're asking. [The italics are mine:]

Then one day Paul Hornung met a man named Barney Shapiro. This was a fine fellow. Shapiro encountered Hornung when the young football player was in his senior year and in San Francisco for the East-West game. Hornung, alone except for 30 or so teammates, must have been lonely and he was glad to be befriended.

Barney Shapiro was only 11 years older than Hornung and owned a successful "novelty" business, a coin-machine operation. He met Hornung in a restaurant and took him to San Mateo for dinner and like that. Later Shapiro moved to Las Vegas, where he owned various gambling machines and a small interest in a hotel.

Again from the autobiography:

We became friends. In the summer of 1957, just before I was to report to the college All-Star camp for the game against the NFL champions, I went out to Vegas as Barney's guest and I stayed there and lost $400 or $500 on the slot machine and dice and I had a showgirl friend there and it was a fine time.

Six years later, in 1963, Paul Hornung was suspended by the National Football League for betting on games. Also suspended at the time was Alex Karras, fierce Detroit Lion defensive lineman. Commissioner Pete Rozelle at the same time fined five other Lions 2,000 dollars each for betting on football and the Detroit management 4,000 dollars for lax supervision of its players.

Back to good old Barney Shapiro. Since Hornung was his friend, Barney would call him up during the football season and ask him how he was feeling and how the other guys on the club were and then he'd ask him if he thought the Packers were going to win—by eight points, say.

From there it wasn't long before the impetuous Hornung was asking his friend Barney Shapiro to bet a hundred dollars for him, too. That was 1959 and Paul Hornung had a pretty good year betting. From his autobiography:

I think there were two reasons I started to bet. One, just for pure kicks. Two, when it looked like I might make the Pro Bowl I wanted to have some walking-around money on the Coast. I liked to have a good time there.

According to Hornung, that was his last good year. From then on, he bet more, but enjoyed it less. He bet on his own team to win. He bet on other NFL games. He bet on college games. He bet anywhere from 100 dollars to 500 dollars, he says, and "I think I was just average as a picker." He lost as many games as he won.

Early in 1963 Paul Hornung was asked to come to Pete Rozelle's office. There he was asked if he ever bet on football. He said never. It was only when he was asked to submit to a lie-detector test that he thought it over and admitted he had indeed been a bettor.

Not that Hornung didn't know there was suspicion about him. In August 1962, Rozelle had asked him casually if he knew two men: one of them was named Abe Samuels, the other was Gil Beckley. He knew both of them, counted Samuels a friend (and knew he bet on sports events) and Beckley as an acquaintance with whom he had dinner from time to time during the year, although not during the football season. Since Rozelle never mentioned Shapiro's name, Hornung didn't either. Rozelle told him to be careful of whom he associated with. Hornung said he would.

Karras is a different story.

Alex Karras has been described as a Jonathan Winters in shoulder pads. He has a mobile face, an agile brain, and he's hostile enough to give opposition football players second thoughts when they see him coming. But he got himself caught on the blind side in this case.

During the time of the investigation of Hornung, Karras went on television and, when he was asked if he ever bet on football, he said sure, all the players do; you know, cigars, cigarets, things like that. When Norm Van Brocklin, the well-known coach, heard of Karras' remarks, he said, "He must have been playing without his helmet."

Maybe so, for it later came to light that Karras had made at least six bets of 50 dollars or 100 dollars in addition to the cigars and cigarets. But, Karras said, "I never bet with a bookie or talked with one. I don't know any bookie."

For all of that, Karras served the same supsension as Hornung, a year. And he named his son Pete after Pete Rozelle. Said Karras, "I wanted to remember what happened."

Betting on sporting events is so widespread that stories about betting going on inside the game are quickly forgotten. In 1947, for example, four players on the minor-league Hawaii Warriors were barred for life for betting on themselves to win and ten were suspended indefinitely.

The suspensions turned out to be for life, however, when the league folded shortly thereafter. Carroll Rosenbloom, owner of the Baltimore Colts, is often rumored to be making heavy wagers on his club. He denies betting on anything but golf and has a certificate of investigative health from Rozelle to prove it. Still, it could not have been easy for the commissioner to investigate one of his own bosses.

Betting is such a common thing that players jumped to the defense of Hornung and Karras when they were suspended. Said Kenny Washington: "When I played for the Los Angeles Rams we bet ourselves to win. This is common in pro football. I'm sure Paul Hornung and Alex Karras were not the only ones associated with the National Football League who bet. . . . No question about it, Pete Rozelle had information against others—players as well as owners—in the NFL who were guilty. He just made Hornung and Karras the scapegoats."

This is an interesting attitude for it suggests that, by betting on himself, a football player only affirms his honesty and assures that he will try his utmost. And if a coach bets on his team, what matter? Isn't the name of the game winning? This all sounds sweetly reasonable, but only until it is examined.

Take the coach first. Suppose he bets on his team and, in an effort to win by the points, he finds he must drive his players for another touchdown. Suppose in this effort he must take a chance on a pass which is intercepted and loses the game. Or suppose in this driving effort somebody gets hurt. Suppose it's a star and, as a result, a couple of the following games are lost. And just suppose what the underdog bettor will be thinking as he watches the coach whip his players to score points he doesn't—or at least shouldn't—need.

Suppose, also, that despite the coach's efforts to win by the points, he loses. Suppose he loses again the following week and then doubles up in an effort to recoup his losses. Suppose he then loses again. How far away is he now from betting on himself to lose—at the least win *under* the stated number of points? A loser becomes a gambler, a gambler becomes a plunger and a plunger becomes vulnerable to the fix.

The same holds true for players. A player who bets on his team and loses may be heading for a financial jam. If he's hurting for money, what better way to be certain to make it than by manipulating the score? Even if he were not interested in a fix, would he not be open to blackmail by the man he was losing to, the bookmaker he owes a lot of money to? Or suppose he was just betting with a "friend." If they were both losing heavily, how long would it be before the "friend" started thinking about a sure thing?

In the case of Hornung, he was, moreover, guilty of what is called "broken-pattern betting." As he says, he sometimes bet 100 dollars, sometimes 500 dollars. This alone indicates an opinion upon which a bookmaker can act. Whether he means to or not, he is giving information about his team to gamblers.

Even innocent pattern betting can have wide effects. A player might, for example, place a series of 250-dollar bets and then, because of sudden personal expenses let's say, not bet at all. His bookmaker, or whoever was handling his bets, would then be justified in thinking that something was the matter with the team—or the game. This would jiggle the odds severely. Perhaps the game would be taken off the boards, that is, bookmakers would refuse to take any more bets on it. Suspicions would be freely voiced. Rozelle, who is acutely conscious of shifts in odds and maintains a 200,000 dollar a year staff of investigators to check on them, would be sorely tried. Even if there were no monkey business, it would be bad business.

The game is easily shaken. Shortly after the Hornung-Karras scandal, there were large headlines in the newspapers because a man named Maurice I. Lewis was indicted for running a bookie joint in Memphis. Lewis was small fish. What made the news was the discovery that he owed money to Charley Conerly, the well-known New York Giant quarterback. It didn't look good for Conerly, except he was able to prove that it was merely a loan and that he had a terrible habit of lending a lot of people money. He was believed, but a lot of skeptics were mumbling into their beer. Those who are cynical about the honesty of professional football were, of course, delighted.

It is not impossible to be cynical about the game even though there has never been a proven instance of a fix in either a college or a professional football game. There have been many approaches made, however, and this can easily make one suspect that there were approaches we never heard about because they led onward and upward.

The most famous approach in professional football was made by a man named Alvin J. Paris. In 1947 Paris, a small, dapper man, was known around New York night sports as a minor-league check grabber and an escort of fancy-looking chicks. One of his best-looking items was a girl named Ida McGuire. Paris was considered a solid citizen and had been a florist and a salesman of novelty items. He wasn't so solid, however, that he didn't make a lot of phone calls to a man named Eddie Ginsburg, who was a big-time gambler. It happened that Ginsburg's phone was tapped by the district attorney. So almost by accident, the DA found out what Paris was up to.

It seemed innocent enough. He was the friend of a couple of New York Giants football players. One of them was Frank Filchock, who was a passing halfback for the New York Giants. The other was his teammate, fullback Merle Hapes.

It was a classic kind of seduction, or rather attempted seduction. Paris, Hapes and Filchock were seen together in New York nightclubs and in a suburban trap in Mt. Vernon called the Studio Club. That's where Ida McGuire comes in. Also a perfumed dream named in trial records only Emmy Lou, and then somebody called Betty Bigelow or Betty Barthalomew, or both. They were *all* together a lot. What is certain is that, while Filchock and Hapes were married, it was not to Ida, Betty or Emmy Lou. Somehow it did not take Alvin J. Paris very long to become good friends with the two star gridders, as the

278

newspapers called them. And once, Paris was to testify, he gave each of the players 500 dollars for having won a bet on themselves against the Washington Redskins.

Eventually the time came to pay the piper. Again according to trial record, the conversation went like this (and there was no testimony that Lewis Carroll had written the dialogue):

Q: Did you have any conversation with the defendant about football?

HAPES: Yes, he asked me if the Bears would win by ten points. [The game in question was the championship between the Chicago Bears and the Giants on December 15, 1946.]

Q: What did you say?

HAPES: I said, "What do you mean?" and Alvin said, "I want you to throw the football game." I said, "What do you mean?"

Hapes went on to testify that, when he finally found out what the devil Alvin meant, he told him, "No soap." Filchock used the exact same words in his testimony, "No soap." He also added, he swore, "Hot damn, Alvin, I just ain't going to do it. The boys got too much confidence in me. They all got families, and they got much more at stake than any dough I can make."

What was at stake for Filchock and Hapes was an offer which, by present-day standards, sounds penurious. In addition to all the whiskey and women, there would be 2,000 dollars cash, a 1,000-dollar bet on the game and an off-season job in the novelty business owned by Paris' father. This last must have been tempting, for when Filchock and Hapes were asked why they didn't report the bribe offer, they said well, they were hopeful they would get the off-season job anyway.

They must have a lot of faith in Paris' character, a faith that other people did not share. At Paris' trial, for example, Assistant DA George Monaghan (who was himself to be accused of some deficiencies of character when he was, years later, New York State Commissioner of

Harness Racing) described Paris as "a cur, a dirty crawling snake; a miserable swindler, a fancy pants with well-groomed hair and beautiful toggery; a dirty, crawling wretch." A man like that, who would buy a used car from him, much less take his word about a job? Well, Hapes and Filchock.

Whatever information the DA was getting on his tapped wire, it was far from complete. For when the crackdown came just two days before the Giant-Bear game, Filchock denied having been offered a bribe and was believed. Hapes somewhat belligerently admitted the bribe offer but demanded to know what all the fuss was since he had turned it down. Filchock actually played in the game and played well. As hard as he tried, though, the Giants lost, and by the required ten points besides. This is one of the ironies of the fix gone wrong. Filchock could have collected his girls, his bribe money and his job, tried anyway and lost the game. And Paris and his friend could have made just as much money and avoided a great deal of trouble if they had simply bet on the Bears and let it go at that.

Hapes and Filchock were barred for life from playing professional football. Paris, who testified for the state, spent a brief time in prison. Also convicted with Paris was a fellow named Harvey Stemmer, who was one of the fixers involved in the Brooklyn College scandal of 1945. Stemmer was a cool cat. While he was serving time for that caper, he managed to conduct his bookmaking business from the safety of his prison cell. He had friends all over.

There have been other convictions of attempted fixes of football games. In 1952, a twenty-one-year-old student named Louis Leonard Glickfield was arrested for offering money to University of Maryland players to hold their margin of victory over Louisiana to under 21 points. The offer was 1,000 dollars to center Tom Cosgrove, 400 dollars to guard Frank Navarro and 100 dollars to quarterback Jack Scarbath. (Glickfield didn't seem to understand the game of football very well.) The boys reported the offer to their coach, Glickfield was grabbed and Maryland went over the points, 34-6.

In 1960 there were two attempts at bribing college football players by well-known basketball betting entrepreneurs. Aaron Wagman and a student named Philip Silber offered Jon MacBeth of the University of Florida 1,500 dollars to shave points in a football game and Michael Bruce of the University of Oregon said he was offered 5,000 dollars by Budin and one Frank Norman Rosenthal to see to it that Oregon lost by eight points or more to Michigan. Bruce reported the bribe, played hard and Michigan won by 21 anyway.

In 1966 a fellow named Samuel Joseph Graziano, a Baton Rouge barber, was charged by the FBI with trying to bribe three LSU players. In this case, too, an interesting name came up. It was Joseph Nolan, who happened to be the brother of Eugene A. Nolan, the man who, according to the Nassau County DA, originally took the bet from the heavy-betting Southern coach. It is not difficult to suppose that, if the coach had lost his bet, Eugene Nolan might have said, "Hey, coach, I'd like you to meet my brother Joe."

It should be noted, too, I suppose, that after the Brooklyn College basketball scandal of 1945, Grantland Rice, the famous sports columnist, wrote: "I know of more than one college football game . . . under heavy suspicion. My informants are members of the FBI." Still, nothing ever of Rice's rumor and the number of bribe-offer reports do not add up to much, especially since they were all singularly ineffective. So one might be easily puzzled at the strangely stringent moves which have been taken in certain quarters. They amount to a sort of precautionary overkill.

LSU, it turns out, has a "security officer," a former FBI agent, who has been hired to "screen athletes from gamblers and other undesirable sources." Lamar Hunt, owner of the Dallas Texans, now the Kansas City Chiefs in the American Football League, hired something called Truth Verification Inc., to give his players lie-detector tests at the drop of a suspicion. This seems like a bit much, in view of the fact that Pete Rozelle, who is now commissioner of both the AFL and NFL, maintains his own investigative staff. This staff checks into rumors, tips abrupt changes in game odds games that are taken off the betting board and the kind of joints players hang around in Rozelle's bloodhounds sniffed out Paul Hornung but they did not get to him until his betting had become a habit This says something about the effectiveness of this kind of sleuthing, although I'm not sure what.

Then there was this little shop in Revere, Massachusetts called Arthur's Farm. It was well known as a sports betting parlor not so well known as a place where stolen property was sold or exchanged It was run by a man named Arthur Ventolo and frequented by bookmakers and Cosa Nostra men Also by Babe Parilli, the quarterback of the Boston Patriots.

When this information was made public by *Life,* Parilli said· "Half the team goes out there We stop on the way home from practice to buy toys, razor blades and things we get at wholesale prices."

The word from Rozelle is that players don't go there anymore.

The very hint of gambling or betting of any sort drives pro-football people up the wall Heaven knows why. It has been amply demonstrated in almost all sports that dumping or fixing does not hurt attendance. It merely makes bettors try to discover in advance which way the fix is going One only has to stand among the railbirds at a crowded racetrack after a race is over and listen to the invective shouted at the jockeys to understand that the people at the race track think *every* race is fixed and get angry only because they haven't bet on the horse that was supposed to win. Indeed the discussion of a possible fix often becomes a sort of Sunday evening post-football game cocktail-hour pastime There was to take an outstanding example, excited talk all over the country in 1958 after the Baltimore-New York championship game.

In the sudden-death overtime Baltimore was close enough to score a virtually automatic field goal and win by three points. Instead, the coach, Weeb Ewbank (now coach of the Jets in New York) elected to go for a touchdown. He made it and the Colts won by seven points. The betting price was four points. Three would not have won the bet. So the heated debate was about whether Carroll Rosenbloom had a large bet on his team to win by four. Did he order Ewbank to go for seven points? Denials by all hands. Still, rumors persisted that Rosenbloom was a heavy bettor and that was exactly what had happened. Five years later, in 1963, Rozelle took public cognizance of the rumor. He said it wasn't true.

For a while, too, *Sports Illustrated* was following what seemed to be the cases of some strange betting patterns. Reports had it that odd things were going on in the AFL, especially in Kansas City and Houston. Games there, it was said, were often "circled," meaning that no bet larger than 50 dollars would be accepted.

Have an example of what seems like manipulation. On September 25, 1966, Buffalo was playing Houston. The opening line on the game, usually issued on Monday, had Buffalo as a six-point favorite. Large money began to roll in on Buffalo, minus the points, most of it from the Midwest. Naturally this money forced the price up. Soon Buffalo was an eight-point favorite and there was a perceptible shift in the Midwest money. It was now betting on Houston, plus eight points. Buffalo won the game 27-20.

Here's what this meant to the bettors, if indeed there were such, who gave six points and took eight. They won all their bets. *All* of them. Since Buffalo won by seven, they won the bets they had made on Buffalo to win by six. Since Houston did not lose by eight, they won the money they had bet on that club, too. Bookmakers don't mind winning both ways. Customers who win both ways give them heart attacks. Rumor has it that a syndicate took the books for 225,000 dollars on that game alone. And the beauty of it, of course, was that the syndicate couldn't lose. For if the point differential was anything other than seven points, it would have lost only half its bets. The only cost would have been the vigorish—usually ten percent, but sometimes half of that on big bets.

The Boston-Oakland game of October 30, 1966 also appeared to have the earmarks of the same kind of killing. Boston opened a two-point favorite. When there was heavy betting on Boston, the price went up to three and a half, or four. Boston won 24-21. If gamblers were betting both ends on that one, they hit it on the head again.

Then there was the game with the surprise ending. It was the Kansas City-Oakland game. Kansas City was a 14-point favorite. There was a lot of Oakland money, however, and the points started to drop. They finally went down as low as 11. It hardly mattered. Underdog Oakland won 39-13. It was the upset of the year. To some bookmakers it looked as though somebody knew something they didn't know. That's called information.

Largely, though, no one believes a game can be controlled to within a point unless there is an impossible amount of cooperation. It is believed that the double killings were accidents, a case of professional gamblers willing to bet both ways and invest the vigorish with the slim hope of hitting the jackpot.

There is no general feeling among bookmakers that the professional game is dishonest. "But put it this way," says one highly polished member of this illegal fraternity. "Watch out for the quarterback who knows he's in his last year."

Finally we have the strange case of Wally Butts and Bear Bryant. It was in 1963 when a man named George Burnett went around to a lot of magazine offices and told editors that he had notes of a telephone conversation between Butts, then athletics director at the University of Georgia and Bear Bryant, the famous football coach of Alabama who received a nominating vote for President from a delegate to the 1968 Democratic Convention. (Frank Howard, Clemson football coach, once said this of Bryant: "The Bear's always been ahead of us humans. Even when we started the two-platoon system he was using three platoons: one on offense, one on defense and one to go to class.")

Burnett said he had been plugged into the conversation by chance and he had heard Butts giving Bryant information about the Georgia team that would enable heavily favored Alabama to win even more easily. (Alabama won, as expected, 35-0.) Most editors mistrusted the provable if not the actual authenticity of Burnett's notes. The editors at *The Saturday Evening Post* did not. They printed a story detailing what they called a "fix." Butts and Bryant denied all and sued for damages. They won their cases and a lot of money. Not long after, the *Post* folded. Perhaps that is the reason why fixes are more talked about than written about.

Few incidents in the little world of sports so stirred up the nation as the sudden "retirement" of Joe Namath just before the 1969 pro football training season began. The facts are familiar. Namath, who led the New York Jets to their enormous upset of the Baltimore Colts in the Super Bowl, had been ordered by Commissioner Pete Rozelle to divest himself of his interest in Bachelors III, a saloon on New York's fashionable East Side. Rozelle told Namath that there were unsavory characters—gamblers, bookmakers, Mafia types—hanging around his barroom and making and accepting wagers on its telephones. Rather than give up his interest in what he fondly called "my club," Namath tearfully announced his retirement from pro football. "I have done nothing wrong," Namath insisted.

Maybe not. But there is ample evidence that Joe Namath enjoyed the company of tough guys and black hats and that they cultivated him in turn. Perhaps nothing more than a sort of friendship was involved. The fact remains, however, that it is to the great interest of a gambler to be close to a quarterback. Namath claims not to understand that.

The magazines jumped in to name names of the characters who have been seen with Namath or in Bachelors III. *Life* listed "gang boss" Carmine Tramunti, "triggerman" Carmine Persico, "fugitive bank robber" Jojo Davidson, "gangster" Thomas Mancuso and "thief extraordinary" Harry Bernow. *Sports Illustrated* said that underworld figures were running and playing in crap games in Namath's East Side apartment.

Even uglier were the rumors which suddenly swirled around Rozelle.

One of them insisted that Rozelle had the goods on Namath, that he had actually been caught dumping a game but that Rozelle had given him a chance to retire with some grace while saving pro football from a public scandal.

Not at all, went another. Namath hadn't been dumping. But he had been caught telling a "friend" on the telephone to take the points on the Jets because he and several other players were under par physically.

Not exactly, said a third. That was no friend. That was Namath betting against the Jets to win by the points. And then he lost control of the game and lost it altogether.

None of these things were true, of course. In the end Namath caved in under the pressure, sold his interest in his barroom and went back to football after missing only a week of training.

But don't bet that the last has been heard on this subject. Namath has already claimed (to denials) that the FBI started tailing him after he had five passes intercepted in each of two losses to Buffalo and Denver during the 1968 season. Now every time a Namath pass is intercepted there are people who are certain to ask whether the FBI is interested. It will not do much for Namath— or pro football.

## 13 A Shadow on Our Land

THERE ARE SOME OTHER THINGS ABOUT AMERICAN SPORTS which I treasure. One of them is a paper written by Paul Governali, the football player. The paper reposes in the library of Columbia University's School of Education and it is titled "The Professional Football Player." I treasure it because it is the best answer to a question often asked of football players. The question: "What do you like most about playing football?" The answer usually is "Contact, body contact." Governali, who starred for Columbia and the New York Giants, was able to elaborate:

The highly successful professional football player must not only be without fear of physical contact, he must have a desire for it. . . . Professional football players enjoy an intimate relationship with one another. Their closeness is founded on special living and working conditions.

As an example of this closeness, Governali gave a lighthearted account of an hotel-room wrestling match between two large, masculine football players. "The challenger undressed to the nude while the first player waited, wet and soapy from the bath." The two players came at each other in great glee. They grappled, the soap slippery between them. They fell to the floor and rolled over and over. Governali: "After an hour they finally stopped by mutual accord and sat on the floor, both players gasping for breath." In the immortal word of Al Capp, sigh!

There is another, and it seems to me interlocking, sentence in Governali's paper that sticks with me. It quotes a football player's wife:

Between playing and coaching I never get to see my husband at all. . . . And when I do get to see him, he's so tired and beat that it's almost like he's not around at all.

I don't know if Governali intended it just that way, but I can't help but draw some delicious conclusions about why some men play football.

Which reminds me of why some men own professional sports franchises. Because they love sports, of course. Walter O'Malley loved baseball. He also loved Brooklyn because his roots were there. And at the very moment he

287

was promising that the Dodgers would never leave Brooklyn, he was negotiating to take them to Los Angeles. With him he took Horace Stoneham, owner of the Giants, who is usually depicted as a wide-eyed innocent, who went to San Francisco because O'Malley needed another team out there And maybe he was. Stoneham is one of those very few men who don't do anything but run a baseball club Oh, they might have a drink or two with friends. But I mean they run the club for a *living*. Yet after Stoneham had been in San Francisco a while. some funny facts came out about the building of Candlestick Park.

I have my own favorite story about that ballpark. It is built on a spit of land that juts out into San Francisco Bay some ten miles from downtown San Francisco. It is the coldest, windiest, most God-forsaken area of the city. It is, in addition, an architectural monstrosity and. when I took a look at it while it was still under construction, I was impressed particularly by a vast unadorned facade that gazed blankly out into the bay. I asked Gary Schumacher, the very New York man who holds Stoneham's hand a lot and does Giants public relations a little, what would be done to dress up the ugly expanse of concrete. "They're gonna make it nice," Schumacher said. "They're gonna fix it up."

I asked how.

Schumacher was annoyed. "How should I know?" he said. "Maybe they'll paint a fucking flower on it."

Somehow they never did.

I am indebted to Burton H. Wolfe of *The Bay Guardian* for information about some of the other funny things that happened at Candlestick. For one thing. a man who gets a lot of credit for being Stoneham's friend and helping to bring the Giants to San Francisco was a millionaire contractor named Charles Harney. Harney built Candlestick Park. He also, it turns out, bought 65 acres of land at Candlestick Point from the City of San Francisco for 2,100 dollars an acre. This was in 1953. In 1957 the city bought 41 of those acres back from Harney on which to construct the ball park. The city paid him 65.853 dollars an acre. That's a capital gain of a cool 2,613,873 dollars.

There were some lies told, too. The good people of San Francisco were told that the stadium, which the city was building for Stoneham, would cost them no more than five million. This figure was later revised to ten million. In fact, the stadium cost more than 20 million and, with the Giants paying only 225,000 dollars a year rent and income from other sources amounting to only another quarter of a million, the debt service costs the city a substantial sum every year.

In the meantime, Stoneham treated Candlestick Park the way he treated the Polo Grounds, with neglect. The upshot is that at this moment the ballpark is run down, concrete is cracked, paint is peeling and repairs estimated to cost ten million dollars are needed. Not only that, attendance is falling, both because people don't like to go to cold, windy Candlestick and because the rival Oakland A's began to compete for fans in the area. In addition, the ball club never brought the increased business to the city that had been promised. So what's the answer?

A group of responsible citizens is trying to convince the city that what it needs is a domed 40-million-dollar stadium in the downtown area. I wonder who owns the land.

Stoneham and O'Malley are not, of course, the only owners who ever moved a franchise. Taking a professional franchise to your heart is like falling in love with a traveling salesman. I do believe, though, that one of the greatest strokes of muscial-franchise statesmanship was pulled off by a relative unknown named Williams C. Bartholomay. This is the gentleman who, along with his sporting henchmen, bought the Milwaukee Braves for the express purpose of moving them. This wasn't some poor fellow who sat for years losing money finally getting the chance to move on and make some. And it's true enough that the Milwaukee Braves, who were born in Boston, were being squeezed by the new Minnesota Twins (born in Washington) to the north and the two Chicago clubs to the south. But it's also true that local interests were willing to buy the Braves and keep them in Milwaukee even if there was little or no money to be made. But in Atlanta there was a huge, wide-open television market. It wouldn't have mattered to Bartholomay if the Braves should suddenly start drawing two million a year. The club was going to be moved.

The citizens of Milwaukee tried to fight. They thought that, because they had built a stadium and supported the Braves with love and money, they were entitled to keep the team. They were able to delay its flight for a year. This so angered the men who run the game of baseball that, when it came time to give out new franchises (and Milwaukee came begging, hat in hand), they saw fit to award them to such deserving cities as San Diego, Seattle and Montreal. Milwaukee did not get one.

That's the way people who own sports franchises are. They love the game so much they want to keep it for themselves. So it was, for example, that the National Football League labored so mightily to bury the new American Football League. It wasn't that they wanted seven great American cities to do without football. It's just that they wanted to save the game from destruction and the New York Giants from competition. Just how correct they were, just how usefully spent were the millions poured out in an attempt to kill the new league, was shown in the Super Bowl in Miami in January of 1969. A sell-out crowd of more than 75,000 in the Orange Bowl and an estimated 60 million more on television watched the AFL New York Jets beat the unbeatable Baltimore Colts of the NFL. This led at least one old NFL man to remark, "We never should've merged."

Shecter's Third General Theory of Sports is that, when a sportsman tells you he's doing it for your good, he's doing it to make money. It was, naturally, for the public good that the late Jim Norris had major interests in three hockey teams at the same time—in New York, Detroit and Chicago. It was also in the public interest that he befriended a man like Frankie Carbo, for without Carbo there might, heaven forfend, have been no boxing business. It is also for the good of the public—the new public

290

in the virginal city—that franchises are shifted, that local games are most often blacked out on television, that players like Wilt Chamberlain take down 200,000 dollars a year while every schoolteacher who can read wonders what he would have to do to make even close, and that we know more about sports in this country than about how to live together.

There are shadows on our land, shadows of hate and war and poverty and despair. So we get caught up in games. There must be better ways to spend our time. For when we spend it, we are returned falsity. We cannot even be sure our games are honest. The quick buck, the carpetbagging, cheating owner, the bet, the fix and the dump are always there, lurking just beneath the surface and at the edges of our minds. And I tell you, you have not heard the last of them.

# INDEX